The Practical Guide to Joint Ventures and Corporate Alliances

How to Form, How to Organize, How to Operate

ROBERT PORTER LYNCH

JOHN WILEY & SONS

New York • Chichester • Brisbane • Toronto • Singapore

Library of Congress Cataloging in Publication Data:
Lynch, Robert Porter
   The practical guide to joint ventures and corporate alliances:
How to form, how to organize, how to operate

      p.   cm.
   Includes index.
   ISBN 0- 471-62456-X

Printed in the United States of America

10 9 8 7 6 5 4 3 2

To Paulette
for the most exciting joint venture of all

and
To James F. Vaughn, Jr.
for inspiration and support

Foreword

In the closing decades of the 20th century we are seeing capitalism stronger than ever in the global marketplace, and emerging in new forms—more entrepreneurial, more daring, and more competitive. These factors, no doubt, are driving forces behind the re-emergence of the co-operative business alliance as a vital business form. Cooperative business alliances are springing up in many forms—as traditional joint ventures, as R&D consortia, as private-public partnerships, and as manufacturing networks. It will be imperative for future managers to understand these unifications, because more than likely in the decades to come managers will be either part of an alliance or competing with one. And with this cooperation comes the need for new management styles to adapt to the complexities of running an alliance controlled by neither partner. In this book, specific guidance is provided to enable business leaders to manage these new cooperative organizations effectively.

Even the small entrepreneur who is more concerned with local competitors than with the global economy will gain an important perspective on how to ally with other regional firms to secure his or her share of the marketplace. And for those younger companies that have found venture capital a scarce commodity, they may find the joint venture or other forms of strategic alliance a more fruitful alternative.

Joint ventures are inherently designed to address risky businesses, and therefore are more prone to failure than traditional business structures. For this reason, a guide such as this is essential to manage risks effectively. I can only speculate how many alliances would have been saved from financial hardship, frustration, and even failure had their founders had access to the information in these chapters.

Up until now, most written material about joint ventures has been the domain of lawyers and accountants. This book is written from the point of view of the manager on the firing line—the one who is ultimately responsible for the decisions that lead to success or failure. It places a balanced perspective on the strategic, organizational, behavioral, and managerial aspects of a cooperative business alliance, providing a depth and richness that is so often lacking in the one-dimensional treatises produced by the legal and accounting professions.

This is more than just a "how to" book. In addition to the handy "rules of thumb" and the anecdotes, it is laden with case examples, analytic frameworks, realistic advice, diagnostic and prescriptive measures, and a sound conceptual structure for the formation and effective management of business alliances. Each chapter weaves practical experience and sound business principles into a system for understanding why joint ventures are successful in many industries, and why others have a far higher failure rate.

Ethics has received a lot of attention in recent years, and many questions have been asked whether capitalism itself is the perpetrator of poor ethical practices. CEOs who have had extensive experience in the world of the business alliance all assert that sound ethical decisions are not just a nice thing to do, ethics is the essence that builds and maintains trust in the venture. Good ethics is good business. Perhaps the proliferation of joint ventures will help establish a higher criterion for future business dealings.

Joint ventures are not new creations. It is interesting to observe the return to an older form of business structure, one that was a vital mechanism during the first half of the 1800's, sparking the development of then new industrial technologies and spurring economic growth in a risky environment. Now, a new era is emerging—the era of the global marketplace, and the joint venture and other similar forms of cooperative business alliances are becoming one of the major methods of retaining American competitive strengths and market share.

PAUL R. LAWRENCE
Wallace Brett Dunham Professor
of Organizational Behavior
Graduate School of
Business Administration
Harvard University

Preface

Recently, I was called upon to lead a team of business executives presenting a seminar on joint ventures to a group of leaders from high-technology companies. To augment our own practical experiences with alliances, we sent a research assistant to the library to find a few books on the subject. To our surprise and disappointment, we found little of practical use to the manager or entrepreneur.

How could so many joint ventures and strategic alliances be announced regularly in the *Wall Street Journal*, but so little written about the subject? A few phone calls to other businesses revealed the answer: These endeavors were all done "seat-of-the-pants" style: "Try this approach," "Talk to someone in strategic planning, maybe they know," "What does the lawyer say?" "Use your common sense," "We tried that before and it failed," "Let's give it our best shot and see what happens," and so forth.

These responses were the inspiration for a book providing good practical advice, based on sound management principles, and illustrated with the successes—and failures—of others. This book is written from an "in the trenches" perspective for the business manager or professional advisor who must guide, construct, structure, manage, or evaluate a joint venture or strategic alliance.

Day-to-day operations has long been a dark corner of the joint venture field. Experts all agree that most ventures fail because of operational deficiencies in management, not because of the strength of the legal agreements. Also lacking at the operational level has been a systematic management approach to diagnose problems and prescribe solutions before these problems become insurmountable. This book is intended to begin curing these deficiencies.

The book covers a broad variety of alliances. Each step in the process—from conception, to finding partners, to negotiations, and finally, to operations—is explored in detail. In this book you will find the core material, the essential elements that make all business alliances work, whether they are with small companies or giant corporations, in real estate development or high technology, manufacturing or marketing. For some small or short-term ventures, far more details may be presented here than are needed. But to leave out these details would eliminate the depth, richness, and spirit that make formation of business alliances so interesting.

At every turn, I have found creative business leaders developing unique methods for corporate alliances. Some of them have been exemplified on the following pages. But, I am sure, many new forms will emerge in the years to come. I encourage anyone with further information or interesting variations to pass these along.

ROBERT PORTER LYNCH
The Warren Company
Providence, RI

Acknowledgments

For almost two decades my career has been filled with the risks and rewards, the successes and failures, and the adventures and exhaustion of owning, managing, or consulting to joint ventures, business alliances, and private-public partnerships—experiences interwoven into the pattern of this book. To those unsung heroes who contributed so much, but never received the recognition they so truly deserved, I give my thanks, and ask that they continue to keep America strong by building cooperation in the business world.

Writing a book is a demanding task when wedged into the busy schedule of running several businesses. I especially thank my wife Paulette and our exceptional operations manager, William Lauer, for growing these enterprises while I was researching, writing, and editing. And thanks to my mother for the tender loving care during long nights in the office while we struggled over revisions to the manuscript.

Mentors are valuable in anyone's business career. James F. Vaughn, Jr., is one of those rare people who provided a unique level of inspiration, insight, and the opportunity to explore new dimensions in businesses. To him I am grateful, and hope I have made a worthy contribution to furthering his vision and desire to expand entrepreneurial horizons. A. A. T. "Pete" Wickersham, Roy Bonner, and my father have provided some of the best hard-nosed common sense imaginable. I was fortunate to have been exposed to Paul Lawrence's writings when I was a young naval officer; he and Jay Lorsch played a seminal role establishing a strong intellectual framework for understanding complex organizations.

I deeply appreciate Barrett Hazeltine, Professor of Organization and Management at Brown University for finding research students—Abbas Rahimtoola, Diana Herrera, Elizabeth Vaughn, Julia Ho, and especially Marcel Katz—who were enormously helpful with the arduous task of digging through obscure accounts and compiling data from many disparate sources. My thanks also to Eric Weiner, Jean Madden, Nicolas Retsinas, Tom Gilbane, and Ira Magaziner for their invaluable assistance.

The legal profession has been the primary codifier of joint ventures; I am continually amazed how attorneys have kept this field relatively free from entangled documentation. My thanks to Robert Edwards, Jeffery Stoler, Hans Lundsten, and David Sweeney for their assistance on legal and tax matters.

At John Wiley & Sons, senior editor Michael J. Hamilton has given excellent guidance and displayed remarkable patience while this book has evolved.

Contents

PART TWO—THE STRATEGIC PHASE

PART THREE—THE STRUCTURING PHASE

PART FOUR—THE OPERATIONS PHASE

PART SIX—INTERNATIONAL ALLIANCES

PART ONE

The Basics of Joint Venturing

This book is divided into five sections, each of which explains a vital component of the venturing process.

Part One—The Basics of Joint Venturing—is an overview of all the basic elements one should know about the subject, in order to give a broad understanding of the field before getting into finer detail. The areas covered in this section include:

* Should Your Company Consider a Joint Venture?
* Types of Joint Ventures and Strategic Alliances
* Is Your Company a Good Candidate for a Joint Venture?
* Finding the Right Partners

After this introductory section, the subsequent sections bring the reader through a step-by-step process to design and operate an alliance:

Part Two shows the reader how to develop an effective strategy.

Part Three describes how to negotiate and design an effective organizational and legal structure.

Part Four provides the essential principles to guide managers in successful operations and troubleshooting of problems when they arise.

Part Five outlines methods to effectively transform the joint venture if strategic conditions change.

1

Should Your Company Consider a Joint Venture?

There is no shortage of creativity or creative people in American business. The shortage is of innovators ... the ones who have the know-how, energy, daring, and staying power to implement ideas ...

—Theodore Levitt, Harvard

JOINT VENTURING IN AMERICA

In 1982, General Motors (GM) and Toyota entered into their historic joint venture agreement, making a major policy change for one of America's corporate giants. For the first time in GM's 60 years, they accepted something other than a position of control in a deal with another auto giant.

Why the change? What did GM see as benefits? Foremost, GM saw that one of its major competitors could become its industrial ally, and thereby help GM remain preeminent in the auto industry. Toyota, on the other hand, saw opportunities for a stronger return on its manufacturing and engineering skills, as well as new markets for its products, both here and in other countries where GM was well established.

This is not an isolated case. Since 1980, there has been almost a tenfold increase in the number of joint ventures that have been established. In the process, the joint ventures trend is redefining the very concept of competition. In a recent *Wall Street Journal* article, authorities have suggested that collaboration is increasingly replacing confrontation; a new language of cooperation is forming between former antagonists. Peter Drucker, perhaps the world's most renowned business authority, predicts that coop-

3

erative partnerships will become the dominant form of business in future decades. Large corporations are establishing joint ventures and strategic alliances with smaller companies in order to develop new products, and find potential acquisition candidates; hospitals are venturing with medical laboratories and universities; real estate developers are forming joint ventures with building contractors; and technology partnerships are formed to design, manufacture, and market new, innovative products.

Although joint venturing is one of the oldest forms of business collaboration, very little has been written to assist those who are considering a joint venture. Noel McDonald, the Manager of Planning and Development for the 4 Corner Pipe Line, a large joint venture formed by several major oil companies, expressed the concern of many managers currently involved in joint ventures when he said, "So little is written on the subject that it creates a real lack of structure, wasting precious time and resources—a 'by gosh and by god' seat-of-the-pants approach." So many joint ventures start this way, it is a wonder there are any successes.

This handbook is designed to assist businesses in understanding why joint ventures and strategic alliances are such an important growth strategy, and how to use the joint venture process to achieve business success. It is written to address a variety of complex issues that can arise in both large and small business ventures. The reader should bear in mind that for smaller, shorter term ventures, some of the strategic, structural, and operational guidelines described here may be more than initially necessary for that particular agreement. But, should the venture grow in size over a longer period of time, a more detailed understanding of the subtleties of joint venturing will probably be required, and many of those subtleties will be found in the following chapters.

Readers should also bear in mind that each strategic alliance and joint venture is inherently its own unique creation. According to James Needham, a Mergers and Acquisitions Specialist for Arthur Young, "tailoring of the joint venture is so crucial, because no two joint ventures are alike— these are creative entities."

EXAMPLES OF SUCCESSFUL JOINT VENTURES

Examples of successful joint ventures abound everywhere, and can be found in numerous industries.

The GM–Toyota joint venture was certainly not GM's first sojourn into a corporate partnership. As long ago as 1924, GM joined forces with Esso (now Exxon) in forming the Ethyl Corporation to make and sell tetraethyl catalysts to Esso's competitors who were unwilling to buy directly from Esso itself. Later, Ethyl formed a joint venture with Dow Chemical, which gave Ethyl access to a constant supply of bromine. Dow has been involved in numerous joint ventures, such as Dow–Corning, a highly successful venture that produced electrical insulating resins, greases, and silicones.

Moreover, Corning, no stranger to the joint venture process, has created joint ventures in genetic enzymes, fiber optics, hollow glass building blocks, and probably its best known joint venture: Owens–Corning, which virtually controls the fiberglass insulation market.

The petrochemical industry is another prime example, driven largely by the risks of oil exploration, and by the large capital expenses inherent in this activity.

TriStar Pictures, a joint venture in the entertainment industry, includes CBS, Columbia Pictures, and HBO. TriStar makes films that are distributed by the primary partners. Capitalized with $300 million, this very successful joint venture provides the partners with important strategic leverage:

- HBO obtained a constant source of feature films.
- CBS gained entry into the cable television services market and a source of films for its commercial broadcasting channels.
- Columbia Pictures received a new source of pictures and additional valuable studio space.

As an example of an alliance between a large corporation and a small firm, Gillette Safety Razor recently entered into a joint venture with Eye Tech. Eye Tech operates a chain of stores marketing eyeglasses, prescriptions, and so on. Gillette purchased a 20 percent equity position in the smaller Eye Tech, with the option to purchase a larger portion (make an acquisition) at a future date. Gillette provided financing for the building of 35 new stores, and Eye Tech provided the expertise.

- Eye Tech received needed capital, and leveraged its smaller resources to commence a dramatic expansion.
- Gillette gained rapid access to a large and emerging market.

With the breakup of AT&T from its Regional Bell Operating Companies, major realignments have occurred in the telecommunications field, resulting in a phenomenal number of new joint ventures linking partners in telecommunications, publishing, computers, and banking. AT&T, now devoid of its subsidiaries, has joined domestically with Wang, GTE, CBS, Knight Ridder, Coleco, and EDS, and internationally with Philips and Olivetti to preserve its market strength.

For many years, chemical companies, such as Dow, Hercules, Olin, and Arco, have used the joint venture to build new plants throughout the world. When shortages of raw materials threaten their future production, it has been common practice for these firms to form a joint venture to secure future sources of supply.

Competitors in the oil and mining industry have continuously, for over a century, joined forces to explore and mine ores. Most bauxite, the raw material for aluminum, comes from ores mined through joint ventures.

Changes in international valuations of currency often stimulate strategic realignments through joint ventures. When the value of the U.S. dollar began falling relative to the value of the Japanese yen in 1986, Japanese products became more expensive in the United States and, in the U.S. tire market, Japanese tires quickly lost their competitive edge. However, these changes also made it more affordable for the Japanese to purchase *both* U.S. goods *and* U.S. companies.

For example, Bridgestone Tire, a Japanese firm, lacking a source of retail distribution in the United States, approached its competitor, Firestone (which owned a worldwide manufacturing network as well as 3,500 independent tire dealers) with a joint venture that resembled both a merger and an acquisition. The first step in forming the venture required Firestone, whose business was divided—about two-thirds in the tire manufacturing business and one-third in diversified rubber products and retailing—to transfer its tire assets to a subsidiary corporation. This subsidiary soon became the joint venture corporation, owning and managing Firestone's worldwide tire business.

Firestone then sold 75 percent of its interests in the tire subsidiary to Bridgestone, making the subsidiary a joint venture. In return, Firestone received $1.25 billion in cash. Two-thirds of the cash ($750 million) came from Bridgestone, and the joint venture borrowed the balance ($500 million). Upon the conclusion of the deal, Firestone received an infusion of $1.25 billion, while retaining 100 percent of its Diversified Product Divisions and 25 percent of its Tire Division. Bridgestone acquired a 75 percent interest in a much-needed worldwide tire manufacturing and distribution system.

Joint ventures are also common in the real estate industry. Smaller developers with financial, management, and marketing skills often enter joint ventures with smaller contractors possessing building skills, to construct, market, and manage buildings. Gilbane Corporation, one of the top

10 construction companies in the United States, uses this kind of joint venture extensively.

Business alliances are created to satisfy a wide spectrum of corporate objectives. Some ventures tackle such specific projects as the building of a plant, while others are loosely woven to explore new possibilities for uses of advanced technology; some partnerships are simply stepping stones to a future merger or acquisition, and others are designed to last indefinitely or until future conditions call for a restructuring.

WHAT ARE JOINT VENTURES AND STRATEGIC ALLIANCES?

Joint ventures are not a new business strategy. They were used extensively in the early 1800s to establish U.S. world dominance in the shipping and whaling industries. In the 1880s railroad and mining joint ventures were frequent and highly visible. Today, joint ventures contribute to oil exploration, mining, chemicals, and high technology. They are a favorite method used by many real estate contractors and developers to design, build, market, and manage hundreds of offices and shopping centers.

Throughout this book, this working definition of joint venture will be used:

A joint venture is a cooperative business activity, formed by two or more separate organizations for strategic purposes, that creates an independent business entity and allocates ownership, operational responsibilities, and financial risks and rewards to each member, while preserving their separate identity/autonomy.

The technical difference between the joint venture and the strategic alliance is whether or not a *new, independent business entity* is formed.

Strategic alliances are close kin to the joint venture, but differ in a few significant ways, although in today's world of creative deal structuring, the distinction is often blurred. *Strategic alliances do not create a separate organization or legal business entity.* In most respects, the joint venture and the strategic alliance are alike, and the strategic and operational principles similar. The strategic alliance is often a preliminary step to creating an agreement that may, if all proceeds successfully, become a joint venture or an acquisition. When one corporation signs an agreement with another for the transfer of technology, research and development services, and marketing rights, or invests equity capital for a minority position in a smaller company, but a separate business entity is not formed, a strategic partnership is created. Therefore, the relationship between many small manufacturers and their dealer/distributor networks classifies as a strategic alliance aimed at using the manufacturer's engineering and production strengths and the dealer/distributor's marketing and sales strengths.

The strategic alliance itself may be as simple as a *handshake* or *written agreement* between two businesses, or may be formalized into a joint venture as a *partnership* or *corporation*. But it is the nature of the enterprise undertaken, and not the form of the agreement, that determines whether a joint venture exists.

Joint ventures and strategic alliances are not passive investment relationships, nor are they contractor–vendor or contractor–subcontractor arrangements. In a similar manner, a joint venture is not related to such internal strategies within large corporations as "internal venturing," "intrapreneurship," or "strategic business units."

Joint ventures and strategic alliances are often compared to "marriages" between businesses. This is sometimes a good analogy, but more often than not the analogy confuses the business relationships and creates unrealistic expectations of the partners and other observers. In reality, both joint ventures and strategic alliances are simply *basic and natural forms of business cooperation*. Some are short-term love affairs to create a new product, a new building, or a project, only to be intentionally dissolved once the objectives are achieved. Others are designed to take advantage of rapidly changing environments and then terminate, with the former partners reemerging in another alignment to take advantage of the next opportunity. Still others are long-term, permanent organizations that take on a life of their own.

For businesses, the joint venture and strategic alliance form a bridge to the future to gain important strategic advantage. Neither participant is permanently bound to what might otherwise be an unwieldy merger, an ill-conceived acquisition, or an overly risky incursion into uncharted territory.

FORCES CAUSING JOINT VENTURES TO BECOME POPULAR

Peter Drucker, considered perhaps the world's foremost authority on business, has said that in future decades, the business world will see a proliferation of autonomous corporate partners linked in a confederation rather than through common ownership. Businesses forming these confederations will need to deal person-to-person rather than level-to-level to compensate for the cultural differences between partners. These partnerships will be more highly specialized in a more narrow range of products, ensuring that the people involved talk a similar language, regardless of their corporate or national cultural backgrounds.

Drucker goes on to say that because no one company will be the owner or sole parent, no one will be in total control, producing a relationship of mutual dependence rather than domination or subordination.[1]

The recent phenomenal growth in joint ventures and strategic alliances is not a fluke. Several major competitive forces have caused this proliferation, and these forces will probably continue for many years to come.

"Hybridization" of Technologies

Many companies have specialized in one particular segment of technology, but often lack the breadth of knowledge to integrate other technologies to develop new products. For example, the integration of laser disk storage and computers requires two very disparate specialities, which can best be accomplished by two companies with individual expertise in their respective fields. Similarly, robots also need the integration of complex mechanical, computer, and sensor systems. Many industrial markets prefer to purchase an "integrated" system—hardware, software, sales, service, and technology—rather than purchase these components from separate vendors, thus bringing companies with excellent technology together with companies possessing superb marketing and sales skills. According to Frank Heffron, head of one of AT&T's joint ventures, "Technology is moving at a pace no one can understand, let alone control."[2]

The Need to Bring Products to Market Faster

The competitive world has shortened the time window for the introduction of products. Bring on a good product too late, and there is likely to be a major loss of potential market share.

Confederations are often formed between small entrepreneurial companies that do not have bureaucratic systems to slow their engineering production processes, and larger companies with massive marketing distribution channels. Corporate giants are also driven by these same forces. Olivetti, the Italian conglomerate, wanted quick access to the U.S. office equipment market, and formed a joint venture with AT&T. AT&T, in turn, purchased a 25 percent share of Olivetti, and received access to all of

Olivetti's ready-to-go computers and office equipment. AT&T is marketing telecommunications equipment in Europe through Olivetti. This "is not something you can do in the traditional multinational way. You can only do it by a network of alliances,"[3] says Olivetti chairman DeBenedetti.

Sharing Risks of Enormous Capital Expenses

The cost of new technology products can be extremely prohibitive. Once the technology is developed, there is still the chance that a competitor will have developed a better technology in the interim. Therefore, companies have combined their expertise to reduce the chance of expensive mistakes.

ITT, faced with a billion-dollar development cost to design and manufacture a new generation of telephone switching equipment, chose a partnership with their European counterpart rather than take the risk alone or lose the market. Philips, the European electronics giant, faced the same dilemma, and chose to team up with AT&T, who had the technology and eagerly sought access to overseas markets. AT&T now could market to European government customers who prefer to buy from European companies. Uniroyal built the world's largest aniline dye plant through a joint venture.

Studies have also shown that large corporations can utilize smaller, more entrepreneurial joint ventures as a means of developing new products and technologies, at a cost saving of up to 75%, compared to the cost of development in a larger, more bureaucratic company.

Problems of Insufficient Management

Companies frequently lack sufficient management skills and resources to tackle extremely large and complex tasks. Building contractors and real estate developers have recognized this reality for years, and have pooled their resources to construct, market, and manage buildings that neither partner could handle individually.

In the health care industry, when Dow Chemical's research division developed a new fiber for kidney dialysis, a joint venture was formed with Cordis, a small but highly respected producer of pacemakers. Dow preferred this arrangement for entering the medical market—a market in which they had little experience. In the initial stages, both companies contributed money and personnel equally, but as the joint venture began selling products at almost a feverish pace, it began outstripping Cordis' ability to contribute personnel, at which point Dow stepped up its infusion of personnel to help this successful venture continue.

In other words, alliances enable smaller players to join forces to compete in markets dominated by "heavy hitters."

Tightening of Venture Capital Markets

The problems created by the overzealous financing of many high-tech companies in the early 1980s has resulted in a shortage of funds for many early-stage companies seeking venture capital. Moreover, the subsequent dismissal of many entrepreneur-founders by venture capitalists has driven many small company presidents to seek other financing sources to help enlarge their companies.

Furthermore, few small companies have the growth potential demanded by most venture capitalists. Consequently, many are forced to use a corporate partnership approach as their only other means of rapid growth. Martin Pinson, a venture capitalist in Washington, D.C., suggests that larger corporations seeking to invest in smaller companies through a strategic partnership tend to place a higher value on the smaller company than would the venture capitalist. The smaller company will, therefore, often receive more money and give up less equity because the partnership approach actually lessens the risk of the investment, thereby increasing the small company's valuation.

Lack of Technical Resources

Japanese corporations pool immense R&D resources and disseminate the results among the partners. This practice has enabled the Japanese to make enormous technical strides in a brief span of time.

To combat this strategy, 15 U.S. corporate giants, including Boeing, Control Data, Honeywell, Digital Equipment, Kodak, Harris, Lockheed, Martin Marietta, 3M, Motorola, NCR, National Semiconductor, RCA, Rockwell, and Sperry, joined forces in 1983 to form MCC (Micro-electronics Computer Corporation) to share the costs of developing semiconductor, computer, and software technology that could not otherwise be made available to companies, even firms of this size. Similarly, in 1988, Sematech was founded as a research consortium between IBM, National Semiconductor, Advanced Micro Devices, and a host of others. The automotive industry is now following suit.

International Competitive Forces

A major realignment of business forces has been marshalling its strength during the last two decades as European and Asian companies seek to enter the U.S. marketplace, and U.S. companies seek to take advantage of burgeoning overseas markets. This phenomenon has been called the "globalization of markets," and for some companies it comes as a shock. According to Howard Perlmutter at the Wharton School of Business, "What we are seeing is truly an evolution in the world economy. It is not easy for American companies to adjust to planning global strategy with other companies that are planning their own global strategies."[4]

Many companies have excellent production capacities, but do not have strong marketing/distribution channels. This creates opportunities for joint ventures between U.S. companies and foreign counterparts. A major foreign competitor could turn out to be a good partner to fight domestic competition; similarly, a domestic competitor could become a partner against foreign competitors.

With the emergence of a strong European Economic Community, many European competitors are joining forces to strengthen their market share in the global economy. These realignments in Europe have forced American competitors to act quickly to establish a European beachhead using joint venture alliances, for fear of "being on the outside looking in." General Electric, for example, has established vital liaisons with European competitors in the fields of appliances, medical electronics, electrical components, and gas turbines.

Margins and Economies of Scale

Joint ventures often present opportunities to take advantage of economies of scale, making it prudent for companies to use combined capital, knowledge, and strategic resources.

GTE Sprint and United Telecom, long-distance telephone companies, had both been losing money for several years. Neither had a substantial portion of the market. They formed US Sprint, a joint venture that made them the largest continuous fiber optic telecommunications system in the country, lowered overhead costs, and resulted in a far greater competitive advantage against their rivals AT&T and MCI than they would have possessed separately.

Some companies create a "captive" joint venture that sells only to its owners in order to supply them with specialized products and materials. For example, chemical by-products that are otherwise of no use have found their niche as the source of raw material stock for some joint ventures.

Better Timing of Major Capital Expenses

Particularly during inflationary periods, major capital expenses in plant and equipment can become immensely more expensive when a decision to invest is postponed. Rather than deferring these expenses, a joint venture enables the investment to be made immediately, and inflation ultimately escalates the value of the investment.

The mining, chemical, construction, and computer industries are excellent examples. A mine or chemical plant can cost a billion dollars or more, so rapid construction can result in savings of millions of dollars. Thomas McGinty of the Cleveland Cliffs Mining Company, a frequent organizer of joint ventures, states, "In the U.S., . . . the rate of price increase in capital goods—machinery, equipment, and their installation—. . . has been double (the rate of inflation)."[5]

Disappointing Merger and Acquisition Results

Despite the spate of mergers and acquisitions during the last decade, many companies are quickly learning that acquisitions are extremely difficult to manage. Frederick Withington of the management consulting firm of Arthur D. Little says, "The vast majority of acquisitions of high-technology companies by large corporations have ended in disaster."[6] One study of acquisitions by General Electric's director of planning, who surveyed a number of acquisitions over the last decade, came to the conclusion that 95 percent of acquisitions displayed disappointing results. "Most have died of corporate culture shock," adds Withington. The entrepreneurial attitudes, the speed and flexibility of decision making—the very advantages the large corporation sought to exploit—are often quickly exterminated soon after acquisition.

Raytheon's acquisition of Lexitron exemplifies this frustration. The electronic giant's corporate bureaucracy crippled the wide-open entrepreneurial management style of the small company. Report writing and lethargic or slow decision making ruined Lexitron morale. One Lexitron engineer boasted a sign on his office wall that read THE RAYTHEONS ARE COMING.

Rather than devour a new company through an acquisition, more large corporations are forming joint ventures or creating strategic alliances with minority investments in the smaller companies. DuPont, after having problems similar to Raytheon's Lexitron acquisition, turned to joint ventures to expand their presence in the pharmaceutical field. Wang Laboratories, after making an unintentionally destructive acquisition of Graphic Systems, learned an important lesson and decided to acquire only a 20 percent interest in InteCom. Frederick Wang, then Executive Vice President of Corporate Planning, said, "InteCom's key asset was its talent, and we didn't want those engineers to fear that they would be swallowed up."[7]

"Ten years from now we'll see alliances turn into acquisitions,"[8] predicts W. James McNerney, Jr., of General Electric's Information Services Company. By then, the corporate cultures will have had a chance to work together, and, if harmonious, join together permanently.

KEY ADVANTAGES TO JOINT VENTURES AND STRATEGIC ALLIANCES

Why construct an alliance? What are its real advantages? Should my company consider teaming with another?

First, companies should enter into alliances in order to concurrently:

1. Improve market or strategic position,
2. Reduce risks while increasing rewards,
3. Leverage precious financial and human resources.

Alliances solely created for either convenience, operational efficiencies, or to buoy sinking finances will usually yield unsatisfactory results.

Second, alliances offer certain significant advantages that may not be available through other mechanisms, including:

· Synergies by combining strengths from diverse corporate resources
· Increased speed of operations, particularly when large corporations team up with smaller companies
· Risk sharing, enabling companies to tackle opportunities that might otherwise be too risky
· Transfer of technology between companies to maintain a competitive position in their separate marketplaces
· Increased sales by gaining access to larger markets resulting from new distribution channels and strengths in product planning

· Infusion of capital into smaller companies by a larger corporate partner who invests in either stock or in contracting research and development

· Protection of equity in each company, because the joint venture normally does not involve equity dilution investment

· More rapid adjustment to new technological changes as a result of better access to engineering and marketing information

· Increase of vertical or horizontal marketing domain

When managed skillfully, the partners gain a wider range of strategic flexibility than they would have on their own.

2

Types of Joint Ventures and Strategic Alliances

Champions of new inventions display persistence and courage of heroic quality.

—Edward Schon, MIT

HISTORICAL BACKGROUND

The joint venture is one of the oldest forms of business collaboration. The first joint ventures were used in ancient Egypt when merchants cooperated in their commercial activities. The considerable increase in the number of joint ventures since 1980 reflects that corporations, both large and small, are now less reluctant to use this strategy, realizing potential that had been demonstrated centuries before.

Joint ventures are not new in the United States. Unlike their Spanish counterparts, the English settled the American colonies not to conquer land, but as venture merchants, collaborating with merchant bankers, trading companies, and even the royal crown, to further their business interests.

Empress of China

This English tradition continued unabated in America after the Revolution. No sooner had the British troops departed for England in November 1783 than prominent Philadelphia, New York, and Boston shipping merchants, knowing that the lucrative British markets would be closed to the new nation, immediately planned a brilliant joint venture.

Recognizing that the British West Indies, once a preeminent market for colonial merchandise, were now inaccessible to American shipping, the ex–colonists took action. With their ship building industry decimated, and with overseas trade relations having fallen into such disuse that it would take years to recover, a swift and dramatic act was necessary.

In a bold stroke, the merchants authorized the construction of a ship named *Empress of China* to compete with the more powerful English. This swift new vessel, designed with the most advanced hull of its day, was built to make the voyage in record time. It was to be a daring voyage across poorly charted seas to a land halfway around the world, where no ship under the American flag had navigated before.

In the eyes of the Chinese, the only exportable commodity of any value from America was the ginseng root, a highly prized medicinal herb. An expedition by the promoters into hills of western Virginia and Pennsylvania quickly brought back a quality crop. The *Empress* was laden with this domestic cargo for trade in the Orient in exchange for silks, spices, teas, and porcelain.

Before the *Empress of China* was ready to set sail, its owners made sure that both the ship and its cargo were insured. However, there being few established insurance entities in the new country, the merchants turned to another joint venture consortium in France. It consisted of 41 individual underwriters, who insured the vessel for a premium (typically 7 percent to 8 percent of its value), with 97 percent coverage upon total loss, and no payment if losses were less than 5 percent. (Throughout the early decades of the next century, insurance companies frequently relied upon the joint venture format to underwrite insurance policies for U.S. shipping.) An agreement was written into the insurance document for appointment of an independent arbitrator in the event of contestation of payment for losses.

To reduce risk of loss on the voyage, insurance companies insisted the captain receive strict orders from the owners regarding which ports the ship could call upon; any deviation from those orders were grounds for canceling the insurance.

Aboard the ship were two attorneys (called supercargoes) who acted as the business managers and agents for the merchant owners during the entire voyage. They were assigned the responsibility of paying for any repairs needed to the vessel, to oversee the ship in any ports-of-call, and more significantly, to negotiate any trade deals with foreign merchants. While at sea, the captain commanded the ship; while in port, the captain answered to the authority of the supercargoes.

Commercial alliances in the days of early America were far more elab-

orate than we might believe today. An international web of interconnect-
ing relations was the norm. Merchants maintained close business and
financial relationships, not only among their fellow entrepreneurs on the
Atlantic seaboard, but also throughout France, Spain, Italy, Portugal, the
West Indies, and later, again with England.

As P. C. F. Smith says in his book about the *Empress of China* venture:

"Potential investors in an untried, precarious voyage such as that of
the *Empress of China* had to be men of substance, influence, or enormous self–confidence. No single merchant could have pulled it off on
his own; the daunting sums required to engineer such a gamble could
only be tapped by powerful men working in concert.

Once begun, there was no turning back for the principal actors. Too
much capital had been laid out to permit withdrawal. Too many interlocking lines of credit, some of them reaching across the Atlantic into
the banking houses of France, had been pledged to entertain retreat."[1]

The initial plan for the *Empress of China* called for one-third of the
financing to be provided by Robert Morris, a prominent Philadelphian
known as the "financier of the American Revolution," one-third from a
New York merchant company that had a history of joint business ventures; and another third from a consortium of Boston merchants. Just before the voyage was to embark, the Boston merchants retracted from the
venture, causing the organizers to trim back on more grandiose plans
rather than leave such a risky venture precariously undercapitalized.

Understandably, with the withdrawal of the Boston merchants, additional financing for the venture was necessary, resulting in a mortgage
(called bottomry) being taken out on the ship with a Parisian merchant
banking firm to leverage whatever finances were available without diluting existing shareholders. While the ship was on its voyage, mortgage
payments were due regularly. The race was on—the ship must sail for
China via the Cape of Good Hope, trade its cargo, and return safely—
before the mortgage payments depleted the preciously limited funds of
the American merchants.

But in a classic foreshadowing of a common modern business malady,
one of the joint venture partners ran into serious financial difficulty in
another venture while the ship was at sea, causing him to have severe
trouble keeping up with his portion of payments to the bank, and forcing
other partners to mortgage additional business interests in order to satisfy
the bank. Eventually, the solvent partners had to advance more than

double the stock stipulated in the Deed of Co-Partnership, as the joint venture agreement was then called.

Fortunately for American business interests, the voyage of the *Empress of China* was fantastically profitable. Further voyages to the Orient were organized from virtually every seaport in the new country, and the beginnings of American trade dominance at sea were established.

Several decades later, the American whaling industry, using the joint venture organizational framework, built a vast industry which, by the 1840s, dominated 75 percent of the world whaling market.

Venturing in the Old West

With the discovery of oil, the whaling era came to a close, but the whaling merchant owners invested wisely in oil wells and refineries. Using their highly successful method of spreading risks and rewards through the joint venture in the whaling industry, they organized oil explorations as joint ventures—an organizational structure that exists to this day in oil and gas exploration ventures.

As the Wild West was being tamed, the joint venture was used extensively by wealthy East Coast financiers to build railroads and to mine gold, silver, and copper in the Rocky Mountains. Today, joint ventures still dominate the aluminum mining industry and are still prevalent in other forms of mining.

Now, joint ventures are experiencing a resurgence. We see them as international consortia, technology alliances, spin-off ventures, research and development teams, unions between private and non-profit corporations, real estate development ventures, and interlocking "spider webs" of related partnerships. Each will be explored in the following pages.

INTERNATIONAL ALLIANCES

The international joint venture generally enables a company to establish a marketing or manufacturing presence in a foreign country by forming an operating alliance with a company in that country. Knowledge of government regulations, the ability to cut through red tape, and access to local markets permits the foreign corporation to combine its knowledge of the territory with the expertise and resources of its "partner" to produce a very successful joint venture.

Superior Graphite, a small firm with $6 million in revenues from the sale of a unique synthetic chemical product, formed a joint venture with a Swedish company whose sales force consisted of distributors located in Italy, France, England, and Germany. Superior gave up its own European force of uncommitted sales representatives in favor of the larger and stronger force of its Swedish partner in the joint venture.

Whenever the dollar is strong, U.S. companies are at a disadvantage in selling overseas because their prices are not competitive. Under these circumstances it is often more profitable for the U.S. company to send its raw materials to the processing plant of its European "partner," where it may be converted into a finished product and ultimately sold at a more competitive price. The U.S. company then receives an additional benefit of the joint venture because the product can be sold on the European market as a European-made product—a "plus" in a culture where business prefers to support its brethren! When the dollar is weak, the U.S. partner in the joint venture has competitive price advantage for its European sales force.

Political-economic development policy has also spurred the use of the international joint venture. In Japan, for many years, the joint venture was the only way the Japanese government would allow a U.S. corporate presence.

Many Latin American and Asian countries still operate under restrictive commercial policies of this type. Uniroyal, for instance, combined with a local Mexican firm to enter the Mexican petrochemical market. Mexican government regulations required that domestic firms control 60 percent of each company in the petrochemical industry, hardly surprising in a country whose economy depends very heavily upon oil. Uniroyal was still able to reap 40 percent of the profits while it developed critically important knowledge of the Mexican market through the joint venture arrangement.

The Uniroyal experience is clearly reflected in an observation of Alexander Giacco of Hercules Chemical: "With traditional domestic joint ventures, you banded together only if you were not large enough to do something that required huge outlays of capital, or if pooled technology led to lower costs. With an international venture, you're also looking for cultural savvy, for a partner that has knowledge of the local market and operating conditions."[2]

Hercules Chemical, a frequent participant in joint ventures, formed a partnership in Taiwan to build a polypropylene plant. Although begun a year after Hercules commenced building their own plant in Canada, the Taiwan plant was completed a year earlier. Giacco claims the joint venture was "profitable from day one" because the principals of the Taiwan investor group "knew how to make the venture's financing work in Taiwan.

And they understood the training that was needed and what had to be done to get the plant built on schedule."

In another international joint venture between Mitsui and AMAX, the two aluminum companies produced an offspring: Alumax. AMAX converted a division into a joint venture by selling 50 percent of its aluminum division to Mitsui, getting a massive cash influx to fuel its expansion plans, and Mitsui acquired a source of aluminum, essential in Japan, where shortages of aluminum were projected several years hence. Mitsui was then able to bring aluminum into Japan without purchasing it from a foreign producer. Both partners had previous experience together in an Australian iron ore project, both were innovative, and both were looking for long-term growth and small short-term dividends.

TECHNOLOGY/MANUFACTURING-MARKETING ALLIANCES

The technology-marketing alliance is an excellent way for a small technology company to enter a market, particularly when the "window of opportunity" is quite short and the market entrance costs are quite high. Typically, one partner has technology expertise—patents, know-how, manufacturing plants, a special service, or production skills—and the other partner, often much larger in size, has marketing abilities—sales force, service support, distribution channels, reputation, and credibility.

The technology-marketing alliance, however, is not just a one-way street for the betterment of the small technology companies. Large corporations have recognized that technology development can absorb huge amounts of cash to achieve the critical mass necessary to be successful on a global level. Smaller companies can generally develop technology at better than 50% of a large company's costs.

Studies have shown the cost of transforming a new technological idea into a workable new product is usually less than the cost of gearing up for production of that product and bringing it to market. The small technology company, on the other hand, seldom enjoys the brand name respectability of its larger partner and would, therefore, encounter severe difficulties in bringing its product to market without assistance.

For example, Energy Devices Corporation gained immediate acceptance for its microfilm system after 3M, a highly respected leader in the microfilm industry, signed an agreement enabling the Energy Device product to be sold through 3M's network of Business Product Centers.

Medical technology is a particularly fertile ground for the company-to-company alliance, with over 430 joint ventures and strategic alliances formed in health-related industries during 1986 alone. A great number have taken place between large pharmaceutical or hospital care companies and smaller technology firms, and have included marketing distribution, product development, and licensing arrangements.

For example, Electro–Nucleonics Inc. (ENI), a small instrumentation company, entered a venture with Pharmacia AB. Pharmacia, in return for an equity investment in ENI received access to ENI's instrumentation skills. In return, ENI gained access to Pharmacia's expertise in medical chemistry for future instrumentation development, as well as immediate profits from Pharmacia's business with doctors.

The electronics industry is also a prolific creator of partnerships. In the late 1970s, for instance, Siemens, a large European electronics conglomerate, bought 17 percent of Advanced Micro Devices (AMD). The two companies set up a separate joint venture company, of which Siemens held 60 percent and AMD held 40 percent. Siemens gained access to the U.S. market and to advanced technology, while AMD gained capital and important worldwide marketing channels, a superb way for a medium-sized company to thrive in the rapidly changing high-technology market where tremendous amounts of capital are needed for marketing and systems development.

The joint venture frequently represents a tactical business opportunity of major importance to both large and small companies. Properly developed and effectively managed, collaborations utilize the strengths of each company without imposing limitations of one upon the other:

- Small company managers and engineers are not engulfed in a barrage of the bureaucracy so frequently essential to the smooth operation of large corporations. Decisions can be made and actions can be taken in a rapid manner.

- The large corporation is able to absorb the new product line and insert it into its manufacturing or marketing program without encountering the problems imposed by the limited staff of the smaller company.

If a strategic alliance is managed skillfully, it can avoid problems similar to those Raytheon experienced in its full acquisition of the smaller, younger, and more entrepreneurial Lexitron, where the two corporate cultures simply clashed. Ideally, within the framework of the joint venture and strategic alliance, companies maintain their autonomy, and combine the strengths that independence brings them.

RESEARCH AND PRODUCT DEVELOPMENT ALLIANCES

Research and product development alliances help reduce the risk of developing a new technology or a new product. In the joint research venture, there may be a dozen or more members of the alliance, and the results of the research are disseminated among the partners. In the product development venture, it is customary for no more than two or three companies to team together and jointly share the rights to market the product.

The research and product development alliance often starts with a written agreement forming a strategic alliance as a forerunner of the technology-marketing joint venture. Should the quest be successful, the technology developer may choose to continue to make refinements to the technology, and the other partner may decide to focus on the marketing functions within the joint venture.

Highly capital-intensive industries use joint ventures to reduce both costs and risks. Mammoth companies such Uniroyal, IBM, and AT&T have entered ventures in order to cooperate on the development of technology.

Some research and development can cost so much that, even considering the disadvantages of sharing facilities and information, joint ventures remain an efficient strategy. In the oil industry, for example, drilling an oil well that has a meager 10 percent chance of producing oil may cost as much as $20 million dollars. Oil companies are almost forced to cooperate to manage the tremendous risks associated with drilling.

Technology companies also cooperate to develop products. MCC (Micro Computer-Technology Corporation) was established as a consortium of 20 partners representing such major American corporations as Digital Equipment, Honeywell, and Rockwell International (minus IBM for anti-trust reasons). It was the purpose of MCC to pool the partners' technological expertise in order to effectively compete against "Japan Inc." Using engineers, money, and technology from the partners, MCC develops new computer software technologies and makes this knowledge available to any of the partners.

Four years later, another similar consortium of 14 high-tech companies (this time including IBM) formed another partnership called Sematech (Semiconductor Manufacturing and Technology Institute) to develop high-speed computer chip technologies competitive with Japan's recent manufacturing advances. Sematech is funded by the founding companies and the federal government, and the shareholding companies have rights to the knowledge developed by Sematech. In the spirit of cooperation that

Charles Sporch, President of National Semiconductor Corporation and Chairman of Sematech, believes to typify most joint ventures, Sematech will coordinate its efforts closely with computer science research at MCC.

Research and development alliances thus illustrate classic reasons for cooperating: high risks and high costs. If those risks can be spread among several firms, then large, risky projects, impossible to manage individually, may be feasible. Smaller businesses, in particular, are using larger companies both to finance expensive R&D and to enter markets that might otherwise be too difficult to penetrate. For instance, Liposome Technologies, a small, early-stage developer of a proprietary method of delivering medication into the bloodstream, partnered its product development costs with the giant American Hospital Supply (AHS). Liposome received operating capital for product development and a royalty on future sales in return for giving AHS the rights to market the product and an option to purchase Liposome stock, should Liposome's future look promising.

Without AHS, Liposome was faced with exceedingly burdensome costs of financing both R&D costs and marketing costs. In the medical field, a new entrant is also at a disadvantage because of the need to establish credibility. AHS provided both marketing muscle and credibility to the cautious hospital buyer.

Other agreements call for the funding of research and the purchase of certain licenses, technologies, and quantities of product.

SPIN-OFF VENTURES

In our entrepreneurial business environment, many large corporations have watched experienced and creative engineering people leave their companies to form independent start-ups. Some corporations have offered bonuses, stock options, and performance-based incentives to retain talent.

Xerox and Control Data are two companies that have watched key personnel leave and decided to do something positive about it. They often invest in these spin-offs, preferring to link with promising, highly motivated young companies rather than face them later as fierce competitors. "If he's leaving the company, then let's get a piece of the action,"[3] proclaims Richard Hayes, Director of Corporate Business Development for Xerox.

Other companies see the spin-off as a mechanism to license technologies that are too small in scope for a large corporation but make sense as a foundation from which a spin-off can grow, while providing a return to the larger corporation in the form of royalties. As an added advantage, the problem of culture shock is greatly reduced because the spin-off managers come from the "mother culture."

PRIVATE–PUBLIC–NON-PROFIT PARTNERSHIPS

Private-public partnerships create jobs and stimulate the economy, both goals of the public sector; they provide access to labor, corporate growth, and subsidies to the private sector. This type of confederation tests all parties' abilities to cooperate. In business joint ventures there are a variety of partners from which to choose, but in private-public partnerships, marriage partners are usually limited to governmental boundaries, typically state or city in scope.

In private-public partnerships all those involved must learn to cooperate with people—even with those with whom they disagree. All confederations are an exercise in building trust; and private-public partnerships are a special illustration of that aspect of joint ventures. The most common forms of private-public partnerships involve public investments in manufacturing facilities, community development programs where the public sector revitalizes public infrastructure in return for the private sector's investment in building improvements, and science and technology partnerships where the public sector provides financing for risky commercial product development in return for royalties and the hope of new jobs.

Businesses, non-profit community institutions, and local governments often form alliances. In Lawrence, Massachussetts, for example, city officials and local business leaders agreed to cooperate in an attempt to solve the problems of a declining neighborhood where dozens of different ethnic groups lived amidst tremendous tension. The city agreed to provide low-interest business loans, homeowner grants, and increased police patrols. Businesses agreed to fix their stores, and reinvest in plant and equipment to improve the services and physical appearance of the neighborhood's main street. Residents, churches, and social agencies agreed to paint houses, clean yards, and participate in crime prevention programs. Representatives from the neighborhood, local business, and city officials signed a cooperative agreement to bind each other to certain principals and commitments.

A similar collaborative approach has been used by state governments, which have established programs to fund risky science and technological product development ventures for business in return for royalties and the prospect of new jobs.

Another relatively new mechanism is the corporate-university partnership, which transfers university-based research to the private sector in return for royalties and sponsorship of further research. Recently IBM entered into a $15 million agreement with Brown University for joint state-of-the-art computer research. Integrated Genetics, already a partner with AMOCO, has a joint research agreement with Tufts University for developing commercial quantities of drugs from genetically altered animals, and numerous universities, such as MIT, have signed similar agreements with industry.

Large corporations and hospitals are also entering the fold. Arthur Young, a major "Big Eight" accounting firm, entered a joint venture agreement with Scripps Hospital in California to sell and install physician's referral software to other hospitals throughout the country.

Distinctions between the private and non-profit sectors are becoming less precise in the health care field as "for-profit" health care companies, such as American Medical International, forge joint ventures with non-profit hospitals. In another recent joint venture, a Swiss medical firm linked with a non-profit hospital and the medical school of a major university to form a "for-profit" diagnostic center.

The French government and American aircraft manufacturer Mc-Donnell Douglas combined to produce a new European aircraft, a much-needed lift for the rather troubled McDonnell Douglas firm and a welcome supply of jobs from the point of view of the French government.

REAL ESTATE JOINT VENTURES

For decades real estate developers with expertise in marketing, finance, leasing, and building management have pooled their talents together with contractors and architects for their building, engineering, and construction subcontracting skills. The real estate joint venture has traditionally been used primarily by smaller real estate companies, but now it is also being embraced by some of the country's largest development firms to take strategic advantage of smaller, locally prominent partners who enjoy good working relationships with governmental agencies and have intimate knowledge of quality subcontractors.

Instead of extracting profits immediately, in a real estate joint venture the developer and contractor hold equity in their project, providing them with an investment and with collateral for future loans. In a more sophisticated version of the real estate joint venture, the architect, a bank, and even the "lead" tenant may become members of the venture, along with a developer and building contractor.

Most real estate joint ventures are structured legally as partnerships, with the principal partners providing management skills; and financing is generated by a combination of outside investors and bank loans.

Compared to most other forms of joint venture, talent, skills, and contacts are "of the essence" in the real estate joint ventures; they are as much a sharing of material resources as they are a combination of more intangible talents and contacts in local markets.

SPIDER-WEB JOINT ALLIANCES

"Spider-webbing" refers not to one single alliance, but an intricate array of interconnections between companies, often across international and industrial lines. These interrelations truly blur distinctions between competitors. In many respects, one can see the same two companies as competitors in one arena and as collaborators in another. In some ways, these interlocking alliances resemble the entangling alliances between countries that preceded the first world war.

It would be impossible to outline or diagram this phenomenon completely because so many alliances are being formed so frequently that any attempt would be futile. However, a small example of spider-webbing will demonstrate the principle: GM is allied with Toyota; Nissan with Alfa Romeo; Ford with Mazda; DuPont with Philips; Philips with Control Data; Control Data with Honeywell; Honeywell with NEC, NEC with 3M, IBM with Sears; AT&T with Olivetti; AT&T with Philips; AT&T with Chemical Bank, Time, & Bank of America; AT&T with EDS, a subsidiary of GM. AT&T with Wang, RCA with Citicorp; Citicorp to McGraw–Hill . . . and so on!

In another style of spider-webbing, a massive joint venture was assembled to bid against AT&T on the $4.5 billion contract with the U.S. government for the federal telecommunications system, a nationwide voice, data, and video network, which will become the largest single private telecommunications network in the world. The bidding alliance was led by Martin-Marietta, an aerospace and communications conglomerate seasoned in joint ventures. Martin-Marietta would be responsible for the venture, providing integration, management, and network control. Their teammates would be the Regional Bell Operating Companies (formerly subsidiaries of AT&T until the divestiture) providing local communications services and local access to national networks; US Sprint (itself a joint venture between GTE and United Telecom) providing long distance carrier service; and Northern Telecom, an American subsidiary of a Canadian firm, and its Canadian research arm, Bell Northern, providing network design, technical support, and software development.

OTHER VARIATIONS

Alliances are not limited to big corporations or to the fields of technology. Small businesses also use the joint venture extensively to gain a competitive advantage over larger companies in their present market, to expand into new markets where alone the smaller company is not capable of establishing dominance, and to leverage precious managerial, technical, and financial resources.

It is now far more common to see two smaller firms in different (or similar) fields paired together, each taking advantage of its strategic strengths, and using its entrepreneurial capabilities to the utmost.

Food Service

In a recent example, two restaurants, one specializing in seafood, the other in Italian cuisine, were not pleased with the price or quality of their pastries, desserts, and breads. However, it was simply not economical for either to have its own bakery on the premises because their individual sales volumes would justify neither the additional staffing nor the capital equipment costs.

The owners decided to form a joint venture, purchase a small building located across the street from the seafood restaurant, and establish a bakery. The seafood restaurant owner was designated the operating partner. While the partners split the equity contributions 50/50, the profits were split 60/40, with the 60 percent share going to the seafood owner in return for taking an operational role in the business.

The partners also agreed not to steal either of their "proprietary" baking recipes contributed to the venture; also, they agreed to purchase all their bakery requirements from the joint venture bakery, provided the bakery sold its products to the two owners at the lowest wholesale cost.

These two "guaranteed customers" enabled the bakery to break even, thus allowing the bank to justify a loan. After filling the founder's orders on a priority basis, the bakery then sold goods to other wholesale and retail customers. With these additional wholesale and retail accounts, the venture became a highly successful example of "vertical integration" in a small business.

Legal Service

Five law firms representing large regional corporate centers throughout the country recently formed a strategic alliance to share expertise in specialized fields. Named UNILAW (United Law Network), this consortium is designed to replace the traditional "correspondent" relationships and the "old-boy" network of the past, installing in their place a sophisticated marketing and service operation. The ultimate objective of this innovative and strategic approach to the marketplace is an improvement in the firms' competitive stance.

Deming Sherman, a spokesman for Edwards and Angell, a member of the UNILAW consortium, suggests that this form of joint venture "will provide experience and resources far beyond that of any single member, and will enable each member firm to service clients with business interests in multiple geographic locations."[4] Edwards and Angell subsequently established cooperative agreements in China to handle Chinese-Western legal affairs.

Accounting

A regional accounting firm formed a joint venture with a software engineering firm to develop computer software. The accounting house absorbed the R&D costs of the engineering firm, and the two will share in the royalties resulting from marketing the software to other accounting houses in noncompetitive regions.

Often small local accounting firms form strategic alliances to combine expertise in order to gain access to larger clients. This confederation is then frequently a significant step taken in advance of a subsequent merger of the two firms.

Sales Representatives

One of the oldest and simplest forms of strategic alliances is between a manufacturer and an independent manufacturer's sales representative. Both parties sign an agreement outlining the principles, the commissions, supply schedules, support, and so on. The manufacturer spreads his risk by paying the rep a commission only when the product is sold, and the rep is rewarded handsomely by a sales commission, usually ranging from

6 to 10 percent. Rep agreements can generally be canceled on 30 days' notice, but many have remained in existence for over a generation as family-owned manufacturers have retained an ongoing relationship with the next generation of manufacturer's reps.

Publishing

Publishers and authors use another variant of the strategic alliance. A publisher agrees to publish a book if the author writes it. The author receives a royalty between 10 and 20 percent of the gross, and the publisher takes the remainder. Each has spread their risk, and divided their reward; each needs the other. The author, with technical and creative skills, designs (engineers) the product; the publisher edits, manufactures (prints), and markets the final product. These agreements are usually written to cover only one book, but successful alliances are often continued for as long as the author continues to write.

Entertainment

Concert promoters enter into shorter-term joint ventures with concert bands and entertainers. The promoter brings management and marketing skills to the venture; the band or entertainer brings creative musical skills. Depending upon the specific arrangements, each will risk something and share in the profits. Although these are usually committed to contractual form, in one instance, Frank J. Russo, a concert promoter, took Frank Sinatra on a national tour simply on a verbal understanding of the terms.

Information Services

Information transfer is a ripe field for joint ventures and strategic alliances, and the combinations of partners have become extremely imaginative. Recently, a natural gas pipeline joined forces with an investment banking house and a law firm to create a national pipeline grid similar to that of the electrical industry. The joint venture—the U.S. Natural Gas Clearing House—is intended to arrange spot purchase transactions between buyers and sellers.

Another small information transfer venture links a real estate title research firm with a newspaper publisher to sell detailed lists of property transfers to lawyers either via a computer link or in published form.

TRENDS IN CORPORATE ALLIANCES

Since the late 1970s the quantity of joint ventures and strategic partner-ships has increased dramatically—not only in numbers, but in scope. What was once a trend limited to a few industries has become increasingly common in virtually every segment of business. Corporate partnering is an important alternative to outright mergers and acquisitions, an alternative that may help entrepreneurs avoid many problems inherent in these two procedures.

More and more frequently, alliances are being used as a pre-acquisition move—to test the waters on a limited scale, to see if a future acquisition would be beneficial, and, if not, to come away winning nevertheless. And by taking an equity position in a partner, a corporation can position itself for a friendly takeover or, if judged ill-advised in the future, the corporation can simply sell the equity in return for cash.

As Russia and China transform their economic systems, the joint venture is the predominant form of foreign investment.

3

Is Your Company a Good Candidate for a Joint Venture?

The critical skill . . . will be that of coordinating units that cannot be commanded but which have to work together.

—Peter Drucker

WHEN TO UNDERTAKE A CORPORATE PARTNERSHIP

This chapter is a guide to discovering if your company's situation makes either a joint venture or a strategic alliance a wise alternative, or if better means exist to achieve your goals. Knowing the proper timing, conditions, and support requirements is essential for a successful venture.

Preconditions for Success

A cooperative venture is most advisable when conditions are right both within your company *and* within your target industry.

Company Conditions.   The most favorable circumstances exist when your company:

- Has something very valuable to *offer* to a prospective partner
- Has something valuable to *gain* from another company
- Has *insufficient resources*
- Has a *cooperative corporate culture*
- Has prominent but not debilitating *strategic weaknesses*

32

- Is ready to jump into a *leadership position* in the marketplace
- Knows that pursuit of a strategic objective is too *risky* to undertake independently
- Is very *doubtful* of its ability to independently complete an important project or to obtain customer acceptance of a new product

Industry Conditions.   In a similar manner, collaboration is advisable when certain conditions within your target industry are advantageous. These include:

- *High capital costs* result in the need to *share financial risks*
- *Rapid changes* occur in *technology* and *customer traits,* or there is a need for *product differentiation*
- *Decline or maturation of an industry* requires horizontal consolidation to protect market share
- *High entry costs or entry risks* (such as new products into new markets) make risk-sharing advisable
- *Major competitive realignments* (mergers, acquisitions, foreign entry into the market) occur or uncertainty exists about a response by major competitors
- The market is expected to respond positively to the *"best product,"* which can only be produced by a superb team combining excellent resources
- There is a need for *rapid market entry* and acceptance

Nicholas Retsinas, the head of a trading company that has arranged business partnerships between U.S. and European companies, warns: "This is not a short-cut for a diversification, and don't venture into areas you are not knowledgeable about; it takes time to know an industry."

Alliances are also particularly attractive to businesses seeking greater market penetration. George Cioe of Gilbane, a major building firm, states that the first reason for a joint venture in his company is "the effective and efficient delivery of a product that will satisfy an identifiable need in the marketplace." Alliances should improve your market or strategic position and reduce your risks while increasing your rewards.

The reward may be to reach an economy of scale, or it may be participation in a new market. Joint ventures and strategic alliances frequently reduce risks, for any losses are spread between the partners. In R&D joint ventures like MCC, companies acquire technology that would be too risky and too expensive to develop alone.

Conquering risky and unknown frontiers are highly motivating forces. Hercules, a major chemical company with a long history of alliances, entered into an alliance with Temple-Eastex, a paper manufacturer, and Peerless Machine & Tool, a machinery manufacturer, after Hercules had spent over $100 million in research and development of a new synthetic polymer fiber to replace paper for high-heat food packaging and food service applications. Spokesmen for the venture commented:

> "Bringing this new product to market, especially when it involved leading-edge technology, was initially analogous to solving a triple simultaneous equation with all unknowns. The first unknown was the optimum formulation for the new product. The second unknown was the type of converting machine it would take. . . . The third and most important unknown was the market demand."[1]

With so many uncertainties, neither company would have undertaken the project alone.

While there are many excellent reasons for companies to enter a joint venture, a significant word of caution is contained in a frequently repeated axiom: "Never seek a partner solely for money or convenience." All too often, managers of failed alliances have said a "financial" partner had very different goals than those of a "business" partner. Typically, a financial partner measures success by short-term return on investment (ROI), whereas business partners may be striving for market share, long-term strategic positioning, access to new markets, and competitive advantage. When these conditions exist, the goals of the strictly financial partner are not compatible with those of the business partner. As Nicholas Retsinas comments: "If your only weakness is money, then you don't need a partner, you should be a vendor."

Similarly, many businesses seek partners out of convenience. This is particularly true of smaller businesses that link together because of trust and friendship between owners. Unfortunately, much to the dismay of the owners, the friendly bond seldom carries with it sufficient motivation or strategic muscle to propel a venture to success.

SEVEN CHARACTERISTICS OF A
WELL-STRUCTURED ALLIANCE

Most well-conceived alliances begin with seven characteristics that comprise the motivating factors for entering the partnership. Elimination of any one or more of these factors will reduce the likelihood of a successful venture.

1. *Strategic Synergy.* Always look for complementary strengths—strategic synergy—in a potential partner. To be successful, the two partners should have more strength when combined than they would have independently. Mathematically stated: "$1 + 1 = 3$" must be the rule; if not, walk away.

2. *Positioning Opportunity.* You should gain an excellent opportunity to place your company in a leadership position—to sell a new product or service, to secure access to technology or raw material—and one of the partners should be uniquely positioned with the know-how and reputation to take advantage of that opportunity.

3. *Limited Resource Availability.* No company has unlimited human and financial resources, nor does any company possess strengths in every dimension. A potentially good partner will have strengths that complement your weaknesses, but if you have the necessary resources, an alliance is probably not the best approach—simply because you don't need a partner.

4. *Less Risk.* Lowering risk is an essential ingredient in forming an alliance. Product introduction costs can be exhorbitant. Manufacturing and development costs can sap the financial strength of even the largest corporation. However, with a partner, the likelihood of success is significantly higher.

   Even such corporate giants as Mobil found that a joint venture with tiny Tyco Laboratories was far less risky than attempting to develop a product for solar energy cells on its own. To an even greater extent, small companies reduce their risks by joining larger companies to perfect and market new products. A joint venture between Japan's Kirin Brewery and Plant Genetics Inc. enabled the smaller California company to complete development of a process to produce seeds from plant cells. Since it takes as long as five to seven years to develop and enter the market, teaming with the larger Japanese company substantially reduced the time element and, consequently, the risk.

5. *Cooperative Spirit.* Your company must have the managerial ability to cooperate efficiently with another company, and the other firm must have an equally cooperative spirit. David Beretta, former Chairman and CEO of Uniroyal and veteran of numerous joint ventures, frequently reiterates the importance of "chemistry" between cooperative partners. George Cioe of Gilbane points out that part-

ners often have to treat divisions of their partners' companies as if they were their own company. Without a cooperative environment, poor communications will ultimately result in a failed marriage.

6. *Clarity of Purpose.* One of the most frequently cited reasons for the success of a joint venture is the capability of the sponsors to be clear about their overall purpose. It is not enough to have high levels of trust, energy, vision, and communication. Ventures with specific, concrete objectives, timetables, lines of responsibility, and measurable results are best suited for potential success. Wise companies have learned to avoid alliances when the partners cannot clearly delineate results, milestones, methods, and resource commitments.

7. *Win–Win.* All members of the joint venture must see that the structure, operations, risks, and rewards are fairly apportioned among the members. Fair apportionment prevents internal dissent that can corrode and eventually destroy the venture.

IMPORTANT CONDITIONS TO ENSURE SUCCESS

In addition to these characteristics, several other important conditions give a strategic alliance a better chance of success. These will be touched upon here briefly, and expanded upon later in this book.

- *Style of Operations.* Companies with similar goals, rewards, methods of operations, and corporate cultures tend to make better partners.
- *Time Perspectives.* For IBM, the "long term" means 10 to 15 years; for a small business living hand to mouth, the long term may mean only one year. Major differences in time perspectives can result in divergent goals, missed deadlines, poor communications, and ultimately a divorce among the partners.
- *Financial Goals.* More often than not, the goal of the strategic alliance is to seek increased market share rather than quarterly earnings. Companies driven by shareholders who seek short-term financial rewards are generally not excellent candidates for partnerships, particularly when they attempt a courtship with companies seeking long-term strategic positions.
- *Collaborative versus Hierarchical Decision Making.* It's hard enough for companies to maintain good internal communications, but when decentralized/collaborative companies attempt to work with central-

ized/hierarchical companies, the chances of good communications between the companies are diminished.

- *Similar Strength Level.* Both companies should be considered "strong" to lessen the chance of feeling that one company is carrying the burden for another. This can be a problem especially between large and small companies, and should be addressed at an early stage of negotiations.

  If the members within the alliance are too different in relative strengths, an imbalance may arise that Dow Chemical's Robert Lundeen calls "the elephant and the flea" syndrome. An informal working relationship may be a better alternative.

- *Past Working Relationship.* A history of collaboration is very beneficial because top and middle management can build trust and communications on an already existing foundation. These past relationships can encompass a broad range, including supplier-customer associations, patent assignments, licensing arrangements, or distribution agreements.

  This factor is mentioned innumerable times by successful joint venturers. Paul Rizzo, IBM's vice chairman, says, "It's extremely difficult for two parties . . . to put together a venture . . . without having first worked together."[2] If no history of working relationships exists, and the partners have never entered a formal joint venture with another company, a less formalized strategic alliance may be the most prudent first step in the collaboration process.

- *Support at Top Echelons.* It is important to realize that an alliance is not a guarantee of success. There must be a corporate "meeting of the minds" to ensure that the top management fully supports the joint venture. This attitude filters to the lower managers. Success, to a larger degree, depends upon the continuing efforts of both CEOs to support the project. Companies tend to reflect the attitudes of their presidents. Without top-level support, middle managers may devote their energies to other things that will lead to a promotion.

  It must also be remembered that top-echelon managers in large corporations are more likely to move on to other jobs than those in the smaller companies. When the top person is no longer in the picture, a continuing structure of organizational support must remain in place.

- *No Threat of Unfriendly Takeover.* The slightest suggestion of an unfriendly takeover can sour a strategic alliance. A strong element of trust must be present, which precludes the use of antagonistic power as a control mechanism. This should not, however, prevent any discussion of a buy-out by one of the partners.

RULES OF THUMB FOR MEASURING THE RISKS AND REWARDS

Measuring risks and rewards in any business venture is probably as imprecise as predicting next week's weather. There are always unknown variables. For example it may be legally impossible to know what new technology a competitor is working on in a laboratory halfway around the world. Or will the supply of a vital raw material increase because of a new discovery, thereby driving its price downward, and destroying the market for a synthetic alternative?

These are typical risks that must be constantly evaluated by a business considering an alliance. There are no hard-and-fast rules for measuring risk and reward, but the following rules of thumb are used frequently:

1. *Best Alternative:* Create an alliance only when there is no better alternative and it would be foolish to go at it alone. If in doubt, but when other alternatives are not exciting, first test the waters with a smaller-scale, less risky strategic alliance. If it succeeds, consider a deeper plunge with a formal joint venture.

2. *Risk Assessment:* If the chance of failure is greater than 50 percent even with the alliance, don't proceed unless you are willing to lose all the marbles. If the chance of success is better than 70 percent, give it careful consideration.

3. *Market Share:* If the alliance won't enable you—at the very least—to hold existing market share, the strategy is probably wrong and the venture will not be to your advantage.

4. *Return on Investment:* The return on investment should be significant and generally should be measured over a three- to five-year period.

5. *Murphy's Law:* Remember Murphy's Law: "If something can go wrong, it will—and exactly at the wrong time!" Then remember "O'Brien's Law": "Murphy was an optimist."

6. *Future Options:* The future isn't what it used to be. Alliances, by definition, are designed to tackle risky ventures. If the future does not develop as you imagined, be prepared to buy out your partner or fold your tent.

7. *Ambiguity:* The higher the future ambiguity, the higher the probability of failure. Alliances are the stepchild of uncertain risks and opportunities. Uncertainty breeds ambiguity, and ambiguity is the seed of business failures.

8. *Product/Market Risk:* Beware of entering *new markets* with *new products.* The only endeavor with a higher risk is the development of a *new technology* in a new market for a new product. It is far safer to enter an existing, known marketplace with a new product, or to introduce a tried-and-true product into a new marketplace.

ASSESSING THE DRAWBACKS

As with any business strategy, the alliance has drawbacks that must be carefully weighed:

1. *Control:* Your company will seldom have complete control of any alliance, and may not even have majority control if there are more than two partners. You must be comfortable with the partners (who may change over a period of time), the rules for making decisions, and the method of buying out your interest should you desire to leave the venture.

2. *Competition:* Most alliance agreements stipulate that your firm may not compete directly with the alliance itself. While this may be prudent when the agreement is signed, your strategic position may change dramatically in the future. If you can foresee this repositioning, then recognize the alliance does not necessarily have to be a permanent structure, and proceed accordingly with escape hatches built into the agreement.

    Remember that an alliance is not always intended as a permanent structure. A partner today may be a competitor tomorrow. Technology derived from one alliance, unless properly protected, may subsequently be used by a partner for his own purposes or in another alliance with a major competitor. This occurred when Savin joined with Ricoh, and Canon with Bell and Howell. Some companies may keep their newest, most advanced technology out of production and out of a joint venture in order to stay one step ahead of a competitive move such as this.

3. *Insurmountable Risks:* While an alliance is designed to reduce the element of risk, some risks are insurmountable, regardless of the

care taken in formation of the agreement. Tackling insurmountable problems is one of the principal reasons for the failure of cooperative ventures. Explorations into new electronics technologies, development of new products for new markets, and introduction of unique, untested services are often insurmountable risks—unfortunately unrecognized until after the fact.

4. *Political Changes:* Many multinational joint ventures are constructed because political policies of some developing nations prohibit majority ownership of corporations by outsiders. However, once a particular industry is on solid ground, the political policy that fostered the industry may change dramatically, thereby undermining the principal condition that caused the creation of the joint venture in the first place.

5. *Strategic Changes:* Alliances are created when two companies recognize they have inherent weaknesses complemented by the other's strengths. After a period of time, one company's weakness may no longer exist, and the underpinnings of the alliances may be withdrawn, requiring dissolution or buyout.

6. *Operational Ineffectiveness:* Joint ventures and strategic alliances are not unlike any other business ventures: Once the right strategy is in place, success depends upon the effectiveness of operational managers. If the selection of managers is wrong, the venture will fail. In an alliance, it is easy to be lulled into the belief that the other partner will handle all the problems effectively, especially when you believe the problems to be within his or her specialized area of expertise.

CONSIDER THE ALTERNATIVES

The strategic alliance or joint venture should be carefully weighed and compared to other alternatives before an alliance is selected. For example, it has been Dow Chemical's philosophy to avoid the joint venture unless the project could not be completed more successfully in another way.

Merger or Acquisition Alternative

A merger might make more sense when two companies have a dominant share of the market and can take advantage of economies of scale by joining together as one.

Acquisitions can also be an effective tool if the strategic and operational "fit" is correct, and if the acquiring company has the ability to control the "after shock." Acquisitions may also be a preferable alternative when one company needs better locations for distributing its product or service, larger facilities for production, additional resources or sources of supply, greater opportunities for expansion, and the like. The determining factor is frequently the need of one company to completely control the resources of another.

When one company has the financial resources to acquire another company *and* make a bold strategic move for market leadership as well, the acquisition alternative may be worthwhile; but if its financial and human resources are limited, the joint venture may be more advisable. In the chemical industry, U.S. companies are twice as likely to form a joint venture with a foreign partner than they are to make an international acquisition. U.S. chemical companies are, however, more likely to select another U.S. company for total acquisition.

Large corporations, whose stock is selling well below book value and with highly leveraged debt, are often positioned out of the acquisition market. Under these circumstances, the joint venture or strategic alliance may become the preferred alternative.

When major strategic and operational overlaps make the two companies more similar than they are different, and if the corporate cultures can be assimilated, the acquisition makes great sense. But if a smaller company is freewheeling in style and driven by motives to double or triple sales in a relatively short period of time, and the acquiring company is bureaucratically regimented and substantially larger in sales, such energy and enthusiasm for growth may end in frustration for the small company and minimal impact on the bottom line for the larger corporate acquirer.

As many executives have learned to their regret, mergers may be more successful on paper than in reality. "Corporate Identity" means more than ego gratification to a CEO. Corporations are often wise to protect the highly successful culture that has made them profitable.

On the other hand, an alliance can often protect a winning corporation from diluting its effectiveness, a condition that often results from a merger. In other instances when a merger might trigger an antitrust case, the joint venture or strategic alliance may serve as an equally effective alternative.

Many CEOs have learned that the joint venture or strategic alliance is a good preliminary step prior to an acquisition. Rushed by the momentum of trying to consummate an acquisition before a competitor moves in, many acquisitions have been abject failures. According to David Jemison of Stanford Business School and Sim Sitkin of the University of Texas in their study of acquisitions, one CEO complained, "We made quite a few acquisitions quickly because we truly believed that if we didn't snap them up, someone else would. After several years, we had indigestion so badly . . . We didn't . . . consider the implications of what we were doing." General Electric's Director of Planning, after surveying acquisitions over the last decade, found that 95 percent yielded poor results.[3]

All too often an acquisition looks good on paper, only to fail to meet the financial performance standards established initially. In such cases, instead of an acquisition, an alliance with a future buy-out clause might have been a more desirable course of action. (This would be highly unrealistic in the case of a hostile takeover, however.)

Licensing

Licensing enables a company that owns proprietary technology or know-how to sell its knowledge to another company. Licensing is a cooperative venture, but differs from a joint venture in that there is no sharing of both risk and reward by the parties, and there may be no strategic relationship between the companies.

Generally, a licensing agreement stipulates what specific knowledge is being sold, in what locations this knowledge can be used (i.e., Europe only, California only, the automotive industry only, etc.), and for how long the knowledge is authorized for use. Typically, a licensing agreement will be purchased for an up-front fee paid by the acquirer, who will then pay royalty fees in the future based upon a percentage of future sales.

A great deal of technology and knowhow can be licensed very simply. Most companies will arrange for consulting and training assistance to be included in the licensing fee. For smaller companies with proprietary technology, a licensing deal with a large corporation can enable the smaller company to recoup its investment rather quickly, but the return on investment may be significantly higher in a joint venture. A strategic alliance may result in both a license and a product development contract, manufacturing rights, and even a substantial equity investment, all of which could greatly benefit the smaller company in the event of an initial public offering of stock. Many joint ventures have started with licensing agreements or OEM agreements (see below), and later advanced into strategic alliances as their next stage of cooperation.

OEM (Original Equipment Manufacturer)

The term "original equipment manufacturer" (OEM) was originally coined in the auto industry with suppliers of equipment to the auto giants. An OEM, such as Goodyear, would capitalize on this unique relationship as vendor to the car manufacturer by advertising this relationship in the auto after-market.

Many manufacturers looking to increase sales will serve on an OEM basis for a large marketeer. Under an OEM agreement, the manufacturer produces the product, and the marketeer uses their own brand name. Sears is one notable example. It purchases OEM products and labels appliances with the Kenmore brand name, tools with the Craftsman name, and batteries with the Diehard name.

An OEM is strictly a vendor or subcontractor relationship. However, after a period of close cooperation and coordination, the OEM relationship may experience just the right conditions for a joint venture. This happens quite often in the real estate development industry when a developer/marketer has subcontracted a number of new construction projects to a general contractor. After several successful projects together, a joint venture will often emerge with the developer and the contracter as partners in a relationship that shares both risk and reward.

If an alliance is the best choice, proceed, remembering that in the future, you may need to restructure the alliance to make it fit the conditions of the business world five years from now.

4

Finding the Right Partners

Is it better to pursue a relationship with a future competitor or wait for a consortium to attack you while you play singly in a doubles match?[1]

—Conrads & Mahini, McKinsey & Co.

Alliances begin with finding the right partner. The right partner must be interesting, maybe even exciting. Look for more than just strategic strength in a partner. Look beyond partners who can provide a "quick fix" to fill a gap in a product line or act as a "sugar daddy" with big bucks. The best partners provide depth of talent to give long-term continuity when business cycles and buying patterns change downstream.

COURTSHIP

Finding strategic allies is similar to finding a marriage partner. Styles, personalities, and perspectives on life must mesh. But do not be dismayed if, upon contacting a company to explore a possible alliance, the response is "no." It may mean you've approached the wrong person, or the timing is wrong, or you've selected the wrong division of the company.

Today many large corporations are looking for strategic allies. The job titles of those responsible for the selection process often include:

Director of Corporate Planning

Director of Strategic Development

Director of New Enterprise

Director of Business Development

Small- and medium-sized companies may not have someone with such a specialized position, but if the company has already been involved in strategic alliances, then someone is an alliance maker. They may be found in marketing or R&D departments, or in the office of the Executive Vice President. There is no quick and easy method of finding the right contact person, but good sleuthing and persistence will yield the best results.

Foreign corporations may also provide excellent opportunities. They often have agents who can provide a link to the right person overseas.

It may be presumptuous and imprudent, however, to request an immediate marriage. It is often best to have a "date" first. The date may take several forms: mutual work developing a new marketing channel, a contract to supply materials, joint engineering on a new product, or the like. Unless each partner has had considerable experience in formal joint ventures, the less formal strategic alliance is the best first step in the marriage process.

Your company may ask several prospective partners for "dates" and then find them to be a poor choice for the future. In today's dynamic business world, partners must have the ability to work compatibly in structured alliances where the rules may be continuously evolving to meet changes in the business environment, as well as the internal corporate changes demanded by organizational growth. Not every company will be able to handle such enormous changes.

Another critical objective will be to find the right person within the prospective partners company, who will spearhead the alliance and serve as a "champion" for the cause. Your own company will also need a champion fully committed to making the alliance work. According to A. A. T. Wickersham, a strategic consultant for the health care industry. "Who you do business with is just as important as having the right business strategy." William Norris, the architect of Control Data's numerous joint ventures, advises that, no matter how inspired the strategic alliance, it is the people who will make or break the deal.

FIVE LIKELY SOURCES FOR FINDING PARTNERS

There is no guaranteed method to finding the proper partner. However, certain methods have been very successful for many companies:

1. *Within Your Own Industry:* Right now, within your industry there is probably a company that would make a good joint venture partner. Generally, these companies are not direct competitors, but occupy a market niche compatible with yours.

   In some circumstances, "head-to-head" competitors may also be good potential partners, depending upon their operating style, their ultimate strategic goals, and the courtesy with which competitors have treated one another.

   Industry newspapers are excellent sources because they comb the field of corporate activity for details, mentioning names and rationale for decisions. These sources are paid to be "in the know."

2. *Vendors:* A company that supplies a product, service, or specialized technology may be another good possibility. You may already be doing business with this company, and an alliance may be a far more attractive alternative to the existing vendor relationship. A certain level of mutual respect will have grown, and each other's business practices may have already become understood and found acceptable.

   A vendor will often possess excellent manufacturing strengths, well-established distribution systems in other market areas, financial and management strength, or credibility associated with long-term success, which can help achieve rapid penetration into a new area.

3. *Associated Industries:* Partners are often found in "shoulder industries," industries related but not directly competitive to your own. Examples are a textile company and an apparel company; a computer software and a hardware company; an auto manufacturer and a tire company.

   Large, complex projects often call for an amalgamation of skills and resources. Prime contractors may be willing to join with smaller companies in order to utilize their expertise.

   Even unsuccessful bids can lead to future relationships on other projects. For example, requests for proposals for an overseas hospital resulted in two American companies submitting an unsuccessful bid. But they worked so well together while developing the proposal, a joint venture was formed for selected domestic markets.

4. *Networks:* Industry associations often provide convenient forums for informal exploration of joint business opportunities. Large corporations and small businesses use trade shows, conferences, business organizations, industry associations, and boards of directors as their networks. Some corporations use industry research institutes

to comb the world for new products, technologies, and potential partners. Start-up companies use chambers of commerce and personal contacts. Every industry has its own informal network. It is just a matter of finding the right linkage.

5. *Professional Advisors:* Brokers, consultants, venture capitalists, accountants, and attorneys all make excellent sources for leads. They are paid to know who is looking for opportunities because they are used as sounding-boards for future planning as well as for their professional services. Investment bankers who have been involved in mergers and acquisitions are often good "deal finders." A company that almost succeeded as a merger or acquisition candidate may make an excellent prospect for a joint venture or strategic alliance. Sharing ideas with these professionals may lead to introductions with companies eager to embark on similar ventures.

CREATING A WIN/WIN CONDITION

Successful alliances are built on the fundamental premise that *all the partners must be winners.* Without the presence of this condition, no strategic plan, no legal structure, no formal agreement, and no operational schedule will overcome such a fundamental deficiency. A partner who believes he is losing will not perform well, and may eventually undermine the alliance itself.

Creating the win/win condition results in synergy and teamwork that makes the whole alliance larger than the sum of its individual members. Successful joint venturers live by the premise "1 + 1 = 3."

The importance of the win/win condition is illustrated by a joint venture in the chemical industry between a large U.S. company and a Japanese partner which had excess production capacity in Japan. The agreement specified a 50/50 split in the cost of running the plant. Both companies were to receive products from the jointly owned plant at cost, with the Japanese company reaping all benefits from Japanese sales, and the American company selling solely to the export market.

All proceeded well for 20 years, until the bottom dropped out of the Japanese domestic market (while export sales continued to thrive). The Japanese, a proud and honorable people afraid of "losing face," never let on that they were on the verge of bankruptcy because of the burden of half the venture's cost. They never asked to renegotiate the agreement. Eventually, the American CEO learned of the condition of the Japanese partner, and a more equitable distribution of costs was proposed. The new agreement meant less profit for the Americans, but the joint venture resumed being profitable for both parties—a classic, and touching, win/win condition.

THE IMPORTANCE OF "CHEMISTRY"

Experienced joint venturers know the term well: *chemistry*. It is an intangible—but absolutely essential—ingredient to any alliance. Examine any successful joint venture, and it is apparent that its orchestrators know the meaning of chemistry as the glue that keeps the joint venture working.

"I know it sounds cornball, but the most important element for a successful partnership is chemistry,"[2] says Herbert Granath, president of a joint venture between the American Broadcasting Company and the Hearst Corporation.

But what exactly is chemistry? Chemistry is *not* quantifiable, tangible, or visible, nor can it be created, codified, legalized, or contracted. When asked to define the term, various people have defined it as:

"trust in the other partner"

"faith that your partner will do the right things—strategically and operationally"

"knowing that the other party will live up to the unwritten terms of the agreement"

"unfailing commitment to a win/win arrangement"

"cherishing a reputation as a hard but fair dealer"

"respecting integrity"

These descriptions may smack of "apple pie and motherhood," and, in some respects, they do. Successful cooperative ventures are built on some old-fashioned values; that is why the joint venture structure has endured for so many centuries.

David Beretta, former chairman of Uniroyal, states: "Chemistry is very important between the partners, because problems will always arise—you can guarantee it—and if there is not trust, the partnership will be on the rocks rather quickly. And if the trust is not genuine, there are innumerable ways you cannot even conceive of for your joint venture partner to siphon off funds." Beretta illustrates the value of trust with a story:

"Uniroyal was looking for a way to supply chemicals to our rubber divisions. Since we had no distribution system in Brazil, we looked for a company that had distribution to that market, and we found one who was selling zinc oxide, a critical ingredient in the curing of rubber. This company was important to us, yet the CEO did not know all of the other aspects of the business.

"In this man we found someone who needed us and had both strong capabilities and high integrity. No matter what problem came up, we both worked it out. Following this we built a chemical plant together. All went very well, we both prospered, and there were never any serious problems, whether they be financial, social, or political."

How then can one determine if the chemistry is there? Past experience may be the best answer; but in the event that a prospective partner is not well known to you, how can you tell?

Two Key Questions to Test "Chemistry"

Fairly early in the dating and courtship stages, at some informal moment, ask the top executive of your prospective partner at least two critical questions. These can yield great insight into the nature of an executive's underlying motives within his own organization. The answers to these two simple questions will tell you if there is the potential for chemistry:

Question 1. *"What single most important factor has contributed to your business success?"*
Answer: If the answer is: "I'm a pusher," "I work hard," "I am tough with my people," "I can squeeze a buck," "I watch the bottom line," or something in that vein, then more likely than not, there will not be enough chemistry to make the joint venture successful.

The answer most often given by successful joint venturers is: "The people that work on my team have made us successful." There are many variations of this answer, but they all lead to the same conclusion: *the executive valued people above all else*—one of the prime secrets of chemistry.

It is uncanny how many top CEOs involved in cooperative ventures give this reply without even thinking twice. Companies must understand the value of their personnel, and also know how to delegate authority, how to gain loyalty, how to keep commitments, how to be fair, and how to work together as a team—all critical to the success of an alliance.

Question 2. *"How important is your reputation?"*
Answer: Unless the answer runs along the theme of "It is the most important thing I have," then beware. Reputation is the accumulation of

of continued respect for integrity, successful accomplishment, management, and leadership. Those who do not value their reputation more than likely do not have the respect of their top managers, who, in turn, will probably not support their boss's decisions in the joint venture.

While conducting the search for a partner, carefully probe your prospective partner's reputation. William Norris, founder of Control Data and a pioneer in using cooperative strategic ventures, has a far more subtle method of judging if chemistry is present. He used this method when a joint venture was proposed with the Romanian government. Cynics told Norris the Romanians would bleed Control Data of its computer peripherals technology, and then dump the venture. To better understand his prospective partners, Norris decided to go on a fishing trip with them on the Danube. He "became convinced these people were straightforward and they meant what they said . . . We signed the agreement,"[3] which, according to Norris, was mutually profitable.

Gut intuition can also be a good judge of whether the "chemistry" exists. One joint venturer will not enter into any business partnership unless his wife meets the prospective partner. He says his spouse has better intuition about chemistry and she is right more often than he.

Two other factors are present in the chemistry formula—ego security and aggressiveness. People who are too insecure tend to need too much nurturing and attention to make good venture partners. Yet, on the other end of the spectrum, those who feel too secure tend to lack the aggressiveness and energy to break through barriers and overcome hurdles. Finding the right balance is very important.

A theater director involved in a joint venture in the entertainment industry says: "Chemistry is right when we spend time making things happen, rather than talking about it . . . The pressure to bring a new program on line in a very short period of time is too great to give insecure people the luxury of letting personal idiosyncracies interfere with our goal. That is why our energy is so high."

PARTNERS TO AVOID

Several patterns emerge that are warning signals to help you avoid a partnership that won't work:

- *Those Not into Partnering:* Some people just do not have the good chemistry, expertise, or desire to enter into partnerships of any sort.

Their experience and motivation require their sole control of the venture. No matter how well the deal is structured, their personalities simply do not lend themselves to a cooperative approach.

- *Dependent Companies That Need You to Survive.* If a company is on the decline and needs you and the alliance for survival, they will make an impossible partner. Companies that latch onto an alliance to stay afloat might be better off being acquired or merged.

   Small, growing companies are different, however. Although a strategic alliance may be a means of short-term survival, it should not be a form of long-term dependency. However, also remember that this dependency at an early stage of partnership will send off warning lights in the executive chambers of a large company. Fear is a far stronger emotion than the desire for gain in any large company, and many large corporate executives begin questioning any cooperative deal even when it would be beneficial to them if they fear a "straphanging" partner.

- *Over-Dominant Egos.* The ego make-up of corporate CEOs can be a critical factor to success. Every good CEO will have a strong ego. But the overdominant ego may not be able to generate cross-corporate teamwork, may create one-upmanship, or may not hear feedback that enables the alliance to make mid-course corrections.

   A good potential partner with a "strong" ego can be differentiated from a poor one with a "big" ego. One experienced manager understood this differentiation well when he said: "A strong-ego leader knows his strengths and weaknesses well and is willing to deal with them openly. The one with a big-ego has a 500-pound ego and a 600-pound insecurity complex."

- *Investors and Short-Term Profit Maximizers.* Marriages between investors seeking rapid financial returns and companies are really not strategic alliances because they lack the fundamental strategic focus. Conflicting objectives will inevitably cause frustration, and probable divorce.

   Future market share, long-term growth, and strategic positioning are normally of greater importance to alliances than quick profit returns. Within any industry, some producers are looking for long-term market share, and other producers are looking for short-term profit. Be inclined to chose the former, as long as they are realistic and have a history of success. Beware, however, of the long-term dreamers.

- *Family-Run and Owner-Dominated Businesses.* Joint ventures tend to be stronger and longer-term when the partners represent companies that are "professionally managed" rather than "owner or family dominated." Professionally managed companies are more likely to have a corporate culture that will endure for years, whereas the owner-dominated company tends to change if the owner leaves. Also, the professionally managed companies usually have deeper and more skilled personnel in the middle ranks of the organization who greatly assist in the communications and coordination of a joint venture.

Incremental Approach

If you are not sure a partner is the right match, many venture managers say you should trust your intuition. But if the signals are still mixed, then try the incremental approach. Become involved in a smaller venture first, maybe a licensing agreement, or sharing technical or marketing research. If a small venture succeeds, then consider a more involved alliance. If it fails, you will know if it was because of the partner, or because of other factors outside of the control of the cooperative agreement, such as a poor competitive strategy, market timing, or insurmountable technical, engineering, or legal obstacles.

A corporate alliance is an intricate agreement, susceptible to failure. Ignorance is no excuse for failure; it is the responsibility of those who establish the venture to ask the right questions before signing any agreement.

PART TWO

The Strategic Phase

If a business alliance appears to be the right method for growing your company, then the next step will be to ensure that the venture's business strategy is focused and effective, making your company a strong and financially sound competitor in the marketplace.

This section describes the *Strategic Phase* of venture formation, and delineates basic methods for:

* Analyzing the Strategic Issues
* Preparing the Financial Analysis

These are not easy procedures and should be done carefully before designing an organizational and legal structure—the subject of a later section.

The strategic phase does not end abruptly, but continues on until the negotiations have been finalized.

5

Analyzing the Strategic Issues

If you don't know where you're going, then any road will get you there.

—old Yankee saying

EVALUATING YOUR STRATEGIC POSITION

Constructing a corporate alliance begins with gaining a grasp on your own company's strategic position and then proceeds to a strategic plan that encompasses a partner. If your company does not have a sound strategic plan, then the venture will be built upon a weak foundation.

Realizing your company's strategic position can be a tedious, but a vital step in forming a strategic alliance. Companies have frequently found that by first analyzing their own corporate strategies, they discovered the proposed alliance was structured to cover weaknesses that could and should be firmed up *internally*—the alliance was unnecessary! If, on the other hand, internal weaknesses are too difficult to overcome alone, then look for a partner.

For example, as the auto market became more globalized, American Motors Corporation (AMC) knew it would need a European or Asian partner if it was to continue operations. Mounting losses were undermining the foundation of the corporation. The French car maker, Renault, also faced a similar predicament.

The joint venture between AMC and Renault helped both companies supplement weaknesses in marketing and technology. Renault needed, and acquired, the broad distribution network of AMC auto dealers. The

French company optimistically claimed at the outset of the venture that AMC was the ideal partner because its dealers were accustomed to selling smaller cars. AMC, on the other hand, needed new smaller cars to compete against the Big Three industry giants at a time when smaller cars seemed to be the trend. AMC also needed to meet U.S. government fuel economy regulations quickly—and did so through technology it gained from Renault.

As history has shown, the small-car trend did not continue when oil prices fell, but AMC stayed alive long enough to be an attractive acquisition for Chrysler, who wanted AMC's Jeep line, its new version of luxury Eagle cars, and its extensive dealer network.

Strategy Defined

What exactly is strategy? How then does one develop a good strategy?

The following definition can help focus a subject on which volumes have been written:

Strategy is a long-term, competitive, and systematic program of action that allocates precious resources to take advantage of specific emerging opportunities, resulting in positioning the company for future market strength, organizational security, and profitability.

Let's look at this definition more closely, and break it down into more digestible components:

· Strategy positions your company for long-term success.

· Strategy assumes the business world is constantly changing; these changes will bring conflicts, problems, and opportunities. A good strategy recognizes the coming changes and responds with the "best" answer for your company.

· Strategy is a comprehensive, systematic, and coordinated set of actions, based on a realistic plan.

· Strategy must result in improved long-term market, organizational, and financial strength.

· Strategy recognizes that competition will always be actively seeking creative means of gaining market share and financial rewards. Your company's strategic moves must also anticipate the competition's moves well in advance, just as in a chess match.

These issues should be discussed with top management, analyzed, and explored creatively and entrepreneurially to develop a strong strategic perspective and subsequent action plan.

ANALYZING OPPORTUNITIES

The first step is analyzing your current strategic position, and the next step is to identify and analyze future strategic opportunities. Opportunities will often exist to enter into a new market, a new field, or a new industry, or to bring a new technology or a new product into an existing industry, or to make a major capital investment that will enhance a company's ability to become dominant within their industry or region.

The highest risk exists when new products with new technologies are brought into new markets. To reduce risks to more acceptable levels, it is best if both (or at least one) partner knows the dynamics of the industry, the intricacies of the market, and their real potential to attain market share.

Change is present in every industry, and every change brings about a unique opportunity as well as new risks. Changes in technology, market preferences, and investment perspectives provide new potential for the right venture to achieve prominence.

Within each industry, however, certain companies will be better poised and more willing than others to enter strategic alliances. Typically, the company with the largest share of the market will not be an inspired candidate in that market, usually preferring instead to acquire smaller companies. There have been major exceptions to this rule, however, such as the recent ventures led by General Motors, AT&T, and IBM. The emerging trend may be for market leaders in certain global markets to secure and maintain their positions through such alliances.

The market leader might be a good prospect to venture into a new market. (Thriving companies in troubled industries are more likely to use a growth strategy based on acquisitions rather than alliances.) In the construction industry, Gilbane is the seventh largest construction firm in America; it has been using joint ventures extensively for over thirty years, often with competitors as partners. George Cioe comments:

"Very seldom do companies compete for a given project or development with the same perceived benefit. Many times after we have been successful in getting a contract, we sit down with our (local) competitors. A case in point may be the Watertown (shopping mall), which is a 500,000 square foot marketplace. We were designated to be the developer, and after we were awarded the contract, I think we shocked three or four of our competitors, because we invited them all to a meeting.

"We began by outlining Gilbane's strengths—construction management skills, track record, and large size. Of the other groups at the table, one had strength in leasing retail malls, another company was strong in management of malls, the other was our lead tenant, who, along with the others, became partners in the joint venture we proposed. The project has been very successful."

Gilbane, while quite large themselves, also realized how Gilbane's project was perceived in the local community, by the people themselves who would shop at the mall, as well as by local political boards. Having local partners therefore enhanced Gilbane's effectiveness as the lead developer.

One major real estate development company enters into joint ventures to bid on, build, and manage major construction projects. If the field of competitors is narrow, and they are strong in the field, they will refrain from alliances. If the converse is true—they are not strong and the field of competitors is wide—they will select a partner prior to bidding.

Within any given industry, two smaller companies with marginal market share may become allies in order to achieve better competitive position. When they join forces, it is usually to take on a new market segment within their industry, which neither is currently able to exploit.

For example, a marginal software company might profit from the managerial expertise of an established computer hardware company. Or an under-capitalized manufacturer of restaurant equipment may link with a fast-food restaurant franchiser eager to invest capital in a venture to ensure a constant source of quality equipment at the right price.

STRATEGIC SYNERGY: THE PROTOTYPICAL ALLIANCE

In addition to having good *chemistry*, a joint venture must have good *strategic synergy* to ensure that the weaknesses of one company are offset by complementary strengths of the other company. In other words, businesses should seek out strategically *dissimilar* partners whose combined resources *unify* within the alliance, making it a strong business entity.

"Joint ventures are formed because of weaknesses, not strengths. Real synergy requires that a company cannot achieve alone what the joint venture could achieve,"[1] according to Phillip Zwick, manager of American

Cyanamid's corporate planning department and orchestrator of one of their successful joint ventures. Overall, the venture as a whole should be stronger than the sum of its individual parts ("1 + 1 = 3").

Make a chart, and rate your company's strengths and weaknesses. Then, confidentially, have several other people in your company do the same. Let your top management team make an evaluation, and then let your board of directors or management consultants do it. The result will be a profile of your company. Then do the same for a potential partner. If there is a complementary match, an overture for courtship might begin.

The following chart outlines a generic listing of corporate assets and resources that will help identify dissimilar strengths:

Company A	Company B
Market access	Market access
Management	Management
Technology	Technology
Capital	Capital
Materials	Materials
Manufacturing	Manufacturing

The best partners will have what you don't have, and vice versa. Companies with identical strengths will have a high likelihood of disagreement over the value of their contributions to the venture, while joint venture partners with identical weaknesses will suffer from a critical lack of essential resources.

Be sure you do not neglect the converse of the strengths and weaknesses formula. Ideally, your partner should not be strong where you are strong, and weak where you are weak. Proper construction of the synergistic relationship will build mutual respect and trust, and prevent bickering, second-guessing, and devastating expectations at a later date.

Uniroyal's former chairman David Beretta comments on the joint venture between two rubber giants:

"Uniroyal and B.F. Goodrich formed a horizontal joint venture to achieve significant economies of scale. In the past, U.S. Antitrust laws would have prevented a joint venture between two tire giants with over a billion dollars of business each. The government feared a horizontal joint venture might control too much of the market. However, we are in a global market with global competitors. The government saw the major part of our business was original equipment to the car manufacturers, and Goodrich's was the after-market. They were strong in areas where we were not, and vice versa. We were able to combine our technologies to better compete with the other major world players."

EVALUATING YOUR PARTNER'S STRENGTHS AND WEAKNESSES

Before actually courting partners, a careful evaluation of their strengths and weaknesses is valuable. Be sure your prospective partner is sufficiently different to make an exciting match, but similar enough to permit a harmonious working relationship.

In the case of one European gourmet pasta company wanting to use a joint venture to enter the U.S. market, the attempt was not satisfactory. The pasta company could not enter the U.S. alone, for it did not have the distribution channels or knowledge of the U.S. market. Yet, its attempts to link with an American pasta company proved unsuccessful, mainly because the Italians were unable to prove their technology complemented that of the American company. The Americans saw a company with an interesting but not entirely unique product, one that might even compete with their own. The European company was not clearly offering a supplementary strength to the American company.

The Italians should have either looked for different partners with different strengths or considered another channel with which to enter the market. Such a close examination of strengths and weaknesses would have caused the pasta company to seek a wholesale distributor or grocery chain store with excellent geographic distribution as a joint venture partner rather than considering another manufacturer.

Compare the corporate alliance alternative to other alternatives, such as merger, acquisition, licensing, or subcontracting. Ask the cynical questions about what could go wrong at every stage and how you think a potential partner and you would deal with these problems. Trust your intuition—if everything looks right on paper but doesn't "feel" right in your stomach, trust the stomach.

CLARIFYING THE ALLIANCE'S STRATEGIC GOALS

Finding a partner with "strategic synergy" is not enough, however. The alliance itself must have a strong, well-defined strategy of its own. An alliance without good strategic foundations will be lost in the competitive marketplace, and no amount of chemistry will save it. Unless "strategically driven," most joint ventures will probably be unsound and eventually will unravel.

According to Roy F. Bonner, former Senior Executive at IBM, "Joint ventures established primarily for operational rather than strategic reasons will have a far greater likelihood for failure. Operational (tactical) issues are far more likely to change rapidly in the near term, and consequently place pressures on the joint venture that it was never conceived to endure."

Key Strategic Questions

It is imperative that a number of critical strategic questions be asked of both your own management team and that of your prospective venture partner and that both parties be in harmony with the answers. Remember, inherent differences between companies may be very beneficial resulting in one member playing "rhythm" while the other plays "melody," and the combination in harmony.

Some of the strategic questions you must consider include:

- What are the strategic objectives of the alliance?
- Is the strategic plan based upon marketing and product strategies or financial strategies?
- Does the plan have both a long- and short-term focus?
- Is the mission clear, direct, and realistically targeted to the marketplace?
- Can this plan be effectively communicated to my own staff as well as to the executives of a partner?
- What are my major strengths and weaknesses compared to those of my partner? the alliance itself? and the remaining competitors?
- Are we being honest and realistic in our assessment? Have outside experts played "devil's advocate"?
- What competitive profile must we have in order to be winning three to five years from now?
- Which major trends must we recognize as potential opportunities and which trends may represent potential threats?
- What key events or actions could critically damage the plan? What alternatives could we employ to counter or deter such an event?

· What information exists that enables us to take advantage of a desirable economy-of-scale?

At this stage, the critical issue for any corporate CEO is to honestly and candidly face the real strengths and weaknesses of the alliance. This is often a difficult task, for it is too easy to idealize the strengths, underestimate the weaknesses, and fantasize the readiness of a partner to enter an alliance.

Short- or Long-Term View

Some alliances are designed only for a short-term duration in order to bridge an interim condition until future circumstances force it to change direction or form. Others are open-ended, with a long-term view toward continuity.

It is reputed that some Japanese corporations have 100-year plans, broken down into 20-year increments. The Japanese have a particularly strong emphasis upon the value of market share, recognizing that, in the long run, market share will bring far greater profit than a short-sighted earnings statement.

IBM recognized that some of its products might require a decade or more before the firm would begin to see positive returns on investment, and IBM's current position in the top of the Fortune 500 bespeaks this long-term perspective. Most of Uniroyal's alliances have lasted over 20 years.

Corporations with heavy emphasis on quarterly earnings statements will not be sympathetic to the long-term strategy of many alliances.

Competitiveness

All good business strategies are also built upon a good competitive strategy. A number of alliances have been formed because they created a barrier to entry for other competitors by creating efficiencies of scale that made market entrance costs excessive. Other joint ventures have created a new corporation to operate at arm's length from its sponsors, thereby enabling competitors who would not buy from the sponsor to buy from the joint venture offspring. Some ventures make competitors into allies, enabling smaller competitors to have leverage in markets dominated by larger firms.

Focus

Beware of the "fuzzy" strategic plan. Note that the definition of strategy emphasizes a "systematic, competitive program of action." It is essential that any program of action be crisp, precise, and timely. Compare these two strategic mission statements:

Statement #1. "Alfa and Beta Companies establish this joint venture to use Alfa's patented laser technology and Beta's proprietary instrumentation and process control systems to manufacture and market laser welding systems for the precision tool industry with the intention of capturing 25 percent of the marketplace by 1995 at a 15 percent pre-tax profit margin."

Statement #2. "Fuzzy and Wuzzy Companies intend to create a joint venture to work together to explore the potential of applying concepts of laser welding technology to the machine industry."

The initiators of statement #1 have a chance of success; but #2 is probably doomed before it starts! The latter suffers from fuzzy thinking, the lack of focus, and good intentions unsupported by measurable goals.

KEY STRATEGIC PATTERNS

The business alliance may take many forms. (Yours may be different; do not be afraid to be creative.) These examples illustrate several typical patterns.

- *Products Matched with Marketing and Distribution.* One company has product or service, but does not have the means or resources to distribute and sell. It seeks a partner with excellent distribution capabilities. For example:
  1. A small dairy with a proprietary cheese formula and growing customer acceptance seeks a major supermarket chain or food company with an extensive distribution network.
  2. A foreign manufacturing company seeks entrée into the American marketplace through a well-established retail chain.

3. An American manufacturing company forms a joint venture with an Arabian company to gain credibility and governmental approval to operate in a different economic, social, and political environment in the Middle East.

- *Technology Needing Capital.* Alliances enable smaller technology-based companies to develop products that would take more capital than they are able to generate. For example:

  1. A small electronics firm with a new sensor/control device for the utility industry forms a joint venture with an instrument company, which pays for the research and development in return for the manufacturing rights and an agreement to divide profits.

  2. A small laser optics company uses its technology in a joint venture with a large hospital supply house to create a new diagnostic instrument. The laser company contributes its patents and technical know-how to the venture; the supply house provides developmental capital and receives the exclusive rights to the U.S. market.

- *Manufacturing Seeking Larger Scale of Operations.* Smaller companies may find their volume and size of operations do not ideally fit the type of process required for cost-effective production. For example:

  1. A small chemical R&D company invents and patents a new chemical refinement process, but requires a multimillion-dollar chemical plant to manufacture the product and a large volume user to justify the size of the plant. A joint venture with a major chemical producer satisfies both requirements.

- *Division of Risk.* Many ventures entail too much risk for one business to shoulder, especially if the venture fails. Division of the risk among several entities makes the risk more manageable. For example:

  1. In the oil, gas, and aluminum industries, a chance of a "strike" in raw material exploration is often increased through the use of joint ventures whose greater resources permit exploration of multiple sites. If nothing is found, only a small portion of each company's investment is lost.

  2. In the development of new high-speed integrated circuits, more than a dozen world-recognized U.S. corporations form a joint venture and contribute their best engineers and technical know-how to find the next generation in technology.

  3. In real estate, a large office construction project is beyond the reach of a single contractor unless his function is only that of a

vendor supplying materials and labor. By forming a joint venture, the contractor and his partners jointly assume the risk of the mortgage payments, and, although his short term profit is reduced, he receives long-term cash flow and long-term capital gains from equity ownership.

· *Joint Research or Product Development.* Many new concepts, systems, and technologies are so intricate and futuristic they need huge sums of capital to commercialize their potential. Moreover, these ventures are often highly risky and expensive, with many potential dead ends. For example:

1. Three computer firms join together to research a new computer chip technology. They each contribute equally to the research process, providing human and financial resources, and share equally in the resulting information. None of the participants is prohibited from continuing with his own individual research, and none is prevented from competing with the other using the future applications.

2. A small biogenetics company develops promising drugs to cure a rare disease. But full clinical trials to meet FDA standards are prohibitively expensive. Furthermore, mass production of the drug requires a specialized plant costing millions. The company seeks a large pharmaceutical firm for a partner, who in turn purchases a 30% interest in the smaller company as a preacquisition move, hedging its bet that the technology will prove to be successful.

The strategic analysis is usually done independently at first, with the objective of determining if a partner is truly desirable, and if so, what type of partner is ideal. Then the process of analyzing the strategic elements should be done jointly with a prospective partner to re-test the basic assumptions about strategic synergy to be assured the match will indeed work. If the strategic hurdles are cleared, then a financial analysis should be undertaken. The next chapter outlines the financial considerations.

6

Preparing the Financial Analysis

Money is not the goal; just the best measure of success.

—entrepreneurial saying

Money is the goal; just ask the stockholders.

—investor saying

Money is the resource to gain market share.

—Japanese saying

These three sayings reflect dramatically different perspectives on money. We shall see, through the course of this chapter, how these three perspectives can alter the joint venture's method of allocating financial remuneration or how it can create anxiety among the partners.

Regardless of the alliance's strategic goals, unless there is a financial reward, the venture will not be worth the risk. Each prospective venture must undertake a realistic analysis of the potential returns before sallying forth into the unknown of the future. By undertaking the financial analysis, many of the risks and unknown issues are quantified and a basis established for dividing the rewards.

Yet another goal is accomplished by the financial analysis—by placing a set of financial parameters on markets, capital expenses, and operational costs, a great deal of ambiguity tends to be rinsed out of the venture. And with less ambiguity comes less uncertainty—a distinct advantage in a risk environment.

For many of the more simple, straightforward first-stage courtships, the material in this chapter may seem overly complex, probably better handled by common sense and sheer intuition. Conversely for more complex ventures, this chapter may seem overly simplistic. But for most ventures involving substantial risk and significant capital investment, the issues raised on the following pages should provide a satisfactory level of basic guidance, designed to stimulate questions and encourage more precise thinking.

THREE KEY DECISIONS

The fundamental purpose of the financial analysis is to ensure the alliance does indeed increase financial rewards while it decreases financial risks. Thomas E. McGinty, an experienced joint venturer in the iron and steel industry, has outlined the decision making process used by his firm, the Cleveland-Cliffs Iron Company, to determine whether or not to proceed and with a particular structure for the venture. McGinty recommends that chief financial officers of the prospective partners prepare an analysis to zero in on three key decisions:

- The Investment decision. Is there sufficient return (reward) to merit the initial investment risks? If the answer is yes, then there is merit to the venture; proceed to the next two decisions.
- The Financial Structure decision. Who contributes how much equity, and how much debt financing can be prudently leveraged by this equity?
- The Dividend decision. How much return should each partner receive and how soon?

All these points will be discussed in greater detail in the following pages. The entire financial analysis will be aimed at making these three decisions as prudently as possible.

THE ANALYTIC PROCESS

Financial analysis in an alliance is more than plugging numbers into a computer. It requires hard-nosed research, tough scrutiny of assumptions, and several rounds of rigorous questioning by the prospective partners before the financial answers become clear.

Obtaining Accurate Information

Joint ventures and strategic alliances are, by definition, risky ventures, and therefore fuzzy assumptions, outdated data, and generalizations only serve to increase these risks. Strategic decision makers and operational managers alike should closely examine, re-examine, and cross-examine their assumptions and the data underlying the venture.

Too many joint ventures have failed because too little homework was done on the financial assumptions at the beginning. Joint venture managers who ran into problems frequently acknowledged they had not properly learned about the market, the costs of development, the time involved, and the potential problems they would encounter. While no one can realistically expect to accurately predict the future, the more accurate the information, the less the risk.

Overzealous Estimation

Many joint ventures are inherently similar to start-up companies, and they suffer from the same types of problems that befall start-ups. With the advent of the computerized spreadsheet, almost anyone can "massage" the financial numbers to make a venture work on paper.

Venture capitalists, particularly those specializing in start-up companies, know that the idealistic visions of most entrepreneurs tend to inflate their prospective returns on investment (without which, of course, the entrepreneur would lack the necessary spirit, drive, and intensity to make the business succeed). Through painful experience, venture capitalists, playing the cynic's role, cut through these presumptions. A. A. T. Wickersham, a venture consultant, uses these rules of thumb whenever he sees an entrepreneur's business plan:

- *Costs* estimated by an entrepreneur will usually run *50 percent to 100 percent higher* than projected.
- *Sales* will probably be only *half* of projections.
- *Time* needed to achieve the sales projections will be about *double*.

While these estimates may be exaggerated for more mature business ventures, the danger of overzealous estimation should not be regarded lightly.

Three Levels of Probing

The financial analysis of a joint venture should be done in three steps. It is somewhat like peeling an onion—strip away one layer at a time until you reach the core:

Step 1. Do the preliminary financial analysis *independently* of your joint venture partner to see if it clears the thresholds of return on investment (ROI) required by your company. The preliminary analysis need not be overly complex. This is often one level above a "back of an envelope" analysis to verify that the strategic decisions you are making will have a chance of yielding the necessary financial reward. The accuracy of this first look may be only plus or minus 50 percent. Later, further refinements will be made before the venture structure is put into place.

Step 2. If the preliminary analysis indicates a sufficient ROI, then proceed to a more detailed analysis in *conjunction* with your partners. During this second step—joint analysis—critical divergences in strategic goals may be exposed. For example, one company may place a larger emphasis on market share, and the other company may have significantly higher thresholds for ROI, or require shorter-term paybacks. It is important that these differences be revealed and discussed to determine their impact on the venture.

Step 3. If the second step of the financial analysis clears mutually acceptable thresholds, an *in-depth* final analysis should be made with the intimate involvement of *operational managers*. This is often done in tandem with the development of the operations plan (see Chapter 10). The goal of this last version of the financial analysis should be an accuracy level between + 15 percent to − 5 percent, if possible. Naturally, the accuracy will vary depending upon the type of venture. (Joint research- and development-oriented ventures may not have the luxury of such precise accuracy.) To the projections, a contingency factor should be added, because capital, engineering, and operating costs are usually higher than anticipated. (Seldom are they lower.)

In some industries, such as mining, these three steps may take nearly 10 years, as engineers analyze test borings, as manufacturing plants are designed, and as future prices are projected. In other industries, the full financial analysis may take just a few days or weeks, depending upon the availability of accurate information and the analytical sophistication needed.

Good committee decision making, both before the alliance starts and after it is enacted, will enable participants to engage in wholesome argumentation and debate, like a knife sharpened on a grindstone, honing their thoughts and actions.

By ferreting out problems, by sharpening fuzzy thinking, and by eliminating idealistic visions, the alliance will achieve its first stage of "contingency planning." Once the venture has later reached the operational planning stage, this initial contingency planning will be the foundation for more detailed alternatives should problems arise.

What Factors Should Be Analyzed

Whether or not it is either on the sales or on the expense side of the analysis, always look for "1 + 1 = 3" condition. With a partner, you should have specific sales or production advantages you would not have by going alone. Watch for economies-of-scale advantages, reduction of duplication, and efficiencies your partner possesses that you do not. Your financial analysis should examine at least five specific areas first to properly make the investment decision.

1. Sales Forecasts
2. Capital Costs
3. Operational Costs
4. Projected Margins of Profit
5. Risk Evaluation

It is recommended that future projections not include an inflation factor *unless* the same inflation factor is used universally by all prospective partners. Otherwise, a number of artificially generated disparities may crop up in the financial analysis. Similarly, the same discount/net present value rates, tax rates, and depreciation rates should be used by everyone.

PROJECTING SALES

Sales forecasts are like weather forecasts—they are bound to be wrong by some factor, and only the future will tell the degree! However, without sales forecasting, it will be next to impossible to project future risk and reward levels. As many entrepreneurs say, "Joint ventures are risky businesses, and forecasting future market conditions is the least precise aspect of analyzing risks."

When sales forecasts are off target (and they probably will be), discrepancies will be amplified into the future. Therefore, it is worthwhile to make at least two projections: a high sales and a low sales projection. Then determine if the venture is still profitable at the lower figures. Sales forecasts should be updated regularly—not only while negotiations are going on, but later when the alliance is in full operation.

Example: A cardiovascular medical devices company, with strengths in pumps and monitoring instrumentation, is considering a joint venture with another medical company that has strengths in computers and software. Their objective is to design, manufacture, and market a new heart monitoring system. The proposed joint venture will be a 50/50 deal, with each partner contributing money and resources in the development and marketing of the new system.

The marketing manager of one of the companies prepared a sales forecast using the following assumptions:

1. Units will sell for $125,000 each

2. Total market during next five years will be 240 units

The initial sales analysis was designed to compare the sales potential under two separate conditions:

1. using the joint venture, or

2. each company proceeding independently.

The summary of their projections looked like Table 6.1.

Table 6.1. Sales Analysis

Sales Projections	Using the Joint Venture		Proceeding Independently	
	Units	Gross Sales	Units	Gross Sales
Year 1	8	$1,000,000	0	$0
Year 2	12	$1,500,000	6	$750,000
Year 3	18	$2,250,000	12	$1,500,000
Year 4	12	$1,500,000	10	$1,250,000
Year 5	10	$1,250,000	8	$1,000,000
TOTAL SALES (Units)	60	$7,500,000	36	$4,500,000
MARKET SHARE (%)	25%		15%	

In this example, the joint venture enabled more rapid entry into the marketplace because of accelerated product development, thereby giving the joint venture an ability to ultimately capture a greater share of the market (25 percent with the joint venture versus 15 percent when proceeding independently). This level of sales forecast was sufficient to generate interest in *negotiating*, but would be an unwise basis for *signing* an agreement. Another round with a more detailed analysis would be advisable before finalizing the venture, where the market should be segmented, penetration strategies examined, entry costs analyzed, market research reviewed, and specialized information gathered.

In a very successful real estate joint venture, the partners took pains to understand their specific market before finalizing any agreement. They examined market research very carefully, looking at competitive buildings, other scheduled building projects, zoning requests by competitors, large corporations expecting to outgrow their facilities in the next three years, and rates of absorption of new space.

A list was prepared identifying potential prospectors, their motives, and amount of space needed. Upon completion, the list was subjected to a critical examination. Key decision makers were identified for each of the prospects and potential obstacles to each sale were reviewed prior to the decision to proceed with the joint venture. The partners interviewed potential customers and received commitments from enough customers to pre-lease space prior to the signing of the joint venture, thereby further reducing the risk. Once the project was ready for occupancy, most of the space was already rented.

ESTIMATING CAPITAL COSTS

A careful analysis of costs should be made to compare the expenses based upon both a joint venture and proceeding independently. Does it really cost less for the two companies to proceed together? If cost efficiencies are not present, important questions should be asked about the viability of the venture. The two major areas of cost that should be analyzed are *capital* costs and *operating* costs.

Capital costs are those costs of buildings, land, machinery, equipment, and organization that will be depreciated or amortized over more than one year. For joint ventures, capital costs appear on the joint venture's balance sheet; but for strategic alliances they are divided, each company shows only its share of capital equipment. Technology research and development costs are often considered capital costs by business managers, but current accounting practices may require that these be written off as expenses on the profit and loss statement.

Capital Appreciation or Depreciation?

Accountants can differ widely from financiers in their opinions of what to do with certain machinery, equipment, and property. Normally, machinery and equipment depreciate, and are reported on future financial statements as being less valuable than when they were bought. But the opposite may be true for some types of specialized equipment, such as major technical plants. And although real estate almost always appreciates, accountants insist on depreciating it on the balance sheet!

A tug of war can occur between the accountants who insist that "generally accepted accounting principles" require depreciation of the assets, and strategists and financiers who know that certain assets will be appreciating over time. The strategists will claim the operating statements of the joint venture will show lower profits due to excessive depreciation. The accountants will counter with the claim that depreciation has no effect on the cash flow. In the end, each has a valid point. For those ventures that have a large amount of real estate (manufacturing plants or real estate developments), there can be substantial capital appreciation that should also be factored into the projection of financial returns.

Regarding depreciation schedules: In the financial analysis it is often best to consider actual equipment life, rather than the IRS schedules (which are very likely to change before the venture reaches profitability). These rates can be adjusted later to reflect tax considerations, particularly if a substantial financial return exists from tax shelters.

ESTIMATING OPERATIONS COSTS

Operating costs are usually more difficult to predict than capital costs because they are less tangible than bricks and mortar or equipment. Operational costs usually include:

1. Technology development*
2. Architecture and engineering*
3. Governmental permits*
4. Pre-manufacturing ramp-up
5. Hiring, training, and operational labor
6. Marketing and sales costs
7. Administrative costs

These operational costs may contribute to an initial negative cash flow. The projected accumulation of negative cash flows before break-even will identify the working capital requirements.

Operating Costs Often Overlooked

Each joint venture or strategic partnership has its own internal experts who are effective in estimating capital and operational costs. There are, however, a number of operating costs that are often overlooked. Joint ventures requiring a separate organization may find that one of the parent companies will need to handle certain administrative functions of the joint venture, particularly in its earliest stages. Be sure to build these costs into the venture's financial requirements and include them in the business plan.

Attention should be paid to:

- *Ongoing Legal Costs.* Should in-house corporate counsel be used? Is this a free service or a reimbursable cost?
- *Accounting and Tax.* Will this be done internally by the joint venture, will one of the parents provide this as a service, or will it be done by an outside firm and charged to the joint venture?
- *Employee Benefit Programs.* The parties should review whether or not the employees of the joint venture must be covered by qualified employee benefit arrangements maintained by one of the sponsors for those plans in order for the employees to retain their qualification. Parent companies often shift employees to the new joint venture company. In such cases, pension plans, stock options, and other benefits should be given careful consideration.
- *Payroll and Data Processing Systems.* Who will handle this administrative task?

*IRS regulations may require some of these costs to be capitalized in start-up operations.

- *Insurance.* The entire insurance package of employee, liability, health, and management life insurance can easily be overlooked.
- *Other Support Services.* The venture may need outside consultants in R&D, advanced manufacturing methodologies, marketing, training of salespeople, public relations, and so on. Will these be provided by a parent's in-house staff or by outsiders? Who will pay the bill? It may be advisable to write a consulting contract or service agreement between the joint venture and the parent provider to give evidence of an arm's-length relationship between the entities.

Note: Lost opportunity costs should be considered as a non-quantifiable dimension for the financial analysis.

Example: Using the preceding example of the cardiovascular/computer medical joint venture, a summary of capital and operating costs looked like Table 6.2.

In this analysis, certain developmental economies-of-scale were achieved in the joint venture that were lacking in the independent development because each of the partners had specific engineering skills. The development cost savings totalled $50,000. Similarly, a more rapid technical development enabled fewer operational losses until the joint venture reached break-even ($500,000 with the JV, compared to $600,000 alone), saving an additional $100,000. Based upon this analysis, the financial risk for each partner was reduced from $1.2 million to $500,000.

PROFIT MARGINS

Two profit margins—gross profit and net profit—should be given careful attention. Most joint venture agreements expect that both the gross profit

Table 6.2. Cost Analysis Start-Up to Break-Even

	With JV Partner		Go It Alone
	We @ 50%	Them @ 50%	100%
Development costs	$100,000	$100,000	$250,000
Capital costs	$75,000	$75,000	$150,000
Operational losses until breakeven	$250,000	$250,000	$600,000
GS&A costs	$75,000	$75,000	$200,000
TOTAL COSTS (investment):	$500,000	$500,000	$1,200,000

margin and the net profit margin will be substantially greater by joining forces.

Gross profit is the profit remaining after the direct costs of production of goods and services has been considered, but does not include general, sales, or administrative (G.S&A) costs. Net profit is the profit remaining after all production, overhead, sales, financial, and administrative costs are deducted.

In the case of the previous example of the medical joint venture, gross profit was a critical factor in making the investment decision by the prospective partners. (Other companies may choose net profit as the critical factor.) Gross profit margins were determined to be 60 percent using the joint venture and 50 percent proceeding independently. (*Profit margin* refers to profit expressed as a percentage of sales.)

No single correct set of margins exists for a joint venture. Margins will vary greatly, depending upon the nature of the project and the industry of the partners. For example, in a mature, stable, highly competitive industry, such as home heating equipment, a gross profit margin of 33 percent and net profit margin of 5 percent might be the norm. In this industry, a joint venture producing a 45 percent gross profit margin and a 10 percent net profit would look very attractive.

However, in a fast-moving, technology-based industry still in its early stages—such as biogenetics, where annual research and development costs might average 25 percent or more of sales and gross profit margins are in the 70 percent range—the margins in the example of the mature industry would appear paltry and unacceptable.

Table 6.3 summarizes the margin analysis for our example of the medical joint venture.

This analysis indicates that, while the joint venture gives better gross profit margins, the independent route gives better net profit margins.

Table 6.3. Margin Analysis (cumulative for 5 years)

	Using the Joint Venture		Proceeding Independently
	We @ 50%	Them @ 50%	100%
Gross sales	$3,750,000	$3,750,000	$4,500,000
Gross profit	$2,250,000	$2,250,000	$2,250,000
Gross profit margin	60%		50%
GS&A costs	$375,000	$375,000	$500,000
Net profit	$1,125,000	$1,125,000	$1,750,000
Net profit margin	30%		38%

EVALUATING RISKS

Risk evaluation is one of the more difficult, least precise elements of the financial analysis. After all, how well can anyone accurately determine the contingencies of the future? However, the alternative—doing nothing to evaluate risks—is even more repugnant!

In analyzing a venture, evaluate each of the following risks. If the risk has a relatively broad range—from high to low—you should make an adjustment in the financial analysis to reflect this range. Eight risk areas to consider are:

1. Market risk:
   - Will there continue to be a market in the future?
   - Will the market grow at a rate that will provide opportunities for us to sustain our growth?
2. Competitive Technology risk:
   - Will a competitor develop a technology that will make ours obsolete?
   - Are our gross profit margins sufficient to sustain ourselves in the event of a price war?
3. Completion or Technical risk:
   - Is the venture sufficiently like a predecessor project, technology, or business to ensure that it will work as planned?
   - Might any new technologies throw a monkey wrench into the successful achievement of the venture?
4. Cooperative Environment risk:
   - What is the chance that someone or something (government, weather, labor unions, subcontractors, transportation, etc.) will stop or slow down the venture?
   - Do we have a plan to get around these obstacles?
5. Management risk:
   - Do we have sufficient personnel to carry out the venture?
   - If not, can the proper personnel be obtained on a timely and cost-effective basis?
6. Political risk:
   - Are there any governmental regulations, now or pending, that will interfere with success?

- Will the necessary permits (zoning, EPA, SEC, antitrust, health department, etc.) be issued when needed?

7. Resources risk:
   - Will the supply of customers, materials, or products be available substantially longer than the amortization of the financing?
   - Will the partners have the financial, human, and intellectual resources to see the project through to completion?

8. Capital risk:
   - Will inflation, foreign exchange rates, or government policy dramatically change the value of the investment?
   - What is the chance that our capital will be totally or marginally lost in this investment?

The most fundamental question you must answer again at this point is, "Are these risks less, or greater, with a joint venture partner?" If, after evaluating these risks (along with the costs, sales, and margins), the venture still looks attractive, then proceed with the investment decision analysis.

THE INVESTMENT DECISION

The investment decision evaluates the potential Return On Investment (ROI). In our example of the medical joint venture, the sales forecast was favorable, the cost and margin analyses positive, and risks diminished by venture. But net profit margins were not as strong compared to proceeding alone. Table 6.4 shows the medical venture's investment analysis:

Table 6.4. Investment Analysis (cumulative for 5 years)

	Using the Joint Venture		Proceeding Independently
	We @ 50%	Them @ 50%	100%
Gross sales	$3,750,000	$3,750,000	$4,500,000
Net profit	$1,125,000	$1,125,000	$1,750,000
Net profit margin	30%	30%	38%
TOTAL INVESTMENT COSTS:	$500,000	$500,000	$1,200,000
Return on investment (ROI)	225%	225%	145%
(Cumulative profit/investment costs)			

In this example, a 200 percent cumulative five-year ROI was considered the minimum for the partners, and the independent alternative did not meet that threshold. The joint venture five-year ROI was 80 percent more than the ROI proceeding independently, even though the net profit was less when using the joint venture. This simple analysis was sufficient to determine that the joint venture was the best alternative to achieve the fundamental financial goal of a joint venture: *Increase reward while reducing risk.*

Cost-of-Capital Approach

The cost analysis should include the cost of borrowing money factored into an acceptable rate of return on investment. These money costs may vary depending upon boom or bust cycles, the level of inflation, and rates of exchange for the dollar (more important in international than domestic ventures). What seems to be a reasonable rate of return or cost of money in today's market may become outmoded in the markets of tomorrow.

Larger and riskier ventures require a more sophisticated investment decision analysis, which will result in a *profitability index.* McGinty of Cleveland Cliffs Iron Company recommends an investment decision based upon maximizing the value of the joint venture by making decisions that yield a discounted financial return greater than the company's weighted cost-of-capital.[1] McGinty further recommends using the weighted cost-of-capital approach. (Other approaches can also be used; the most common is the "capitalization rate," but the determination of this rate is quite arbitrary and often subject to individual whim.) This relatively easy cost-of-capital analysis consists of three steps:

Step 1: Cost of Capital. The formula for the weighted average cost-of-capital is:

% of debt × cost of debt × (1 − tax rate)   = % cost of debt
% of equity × cost of equity   = % cost of equity

The determination of the cost of capital works like this: The capital structure of a hypothetical venture permits money to be raised based upon 60 percent debt and 40 percent equity. Also, for this example, assume the current cost of debt to be 12 percent (pre-tax), the cost of equity 15 percent (post-tax), and the federal tax rate 33 percent. Then:

$$\text{Debt} = .6 \times 0.12 \, (1-t) = .6 \times 0.12 \, (.67) \qquad = \quad 4.82\%$$
$$\text{Equity} = .4 \times 0.15 = \qquad\qquad\qquad\qquad\qquad\qquad 6.00\%$$
$$\text{Weighted cost of capital} = \overline{10.82\%}$$

where: t = federal tax rate

Step 2: Discounted Cash Flows. According to McGinty, a joint venture project is financially viable when the total future after-tax cash outflows and inflows (discounted to account for the time-value of money) yield a positive result. (See Table 6.5)

The concept of discounted cash is not difficult to grasp. It simply assumes that a dollar in one's pocket today is worth more than the promise of a dollar in the future. When cash is discounted, it assumes the cash is worth a little less the longer it takes to receive a return. The amount cash is discounted is the weighted cost-of-capital, and the discount rate is usually about the same rate as the interest rate at which the corporation can borrow money.

The following example demonstrates how to discount the cash flows. If the cost of capital is 10.82 percent, then this becomes the investment hurdle rate. The discount factor is determined by the following formula:

$$\frac{1}{(1+i)^n}$$

where: i = investor hurdle rate
   n = year of the investment

$$\text{Example for Year 1: } \frac{1}{(1+.1082)^1} = .902$$

Carrying the medical technology example one step further: Assume the initial capital investment will be $500,000 in the first year only, as calculated in Table 6.5.

In this analysis, it can be readily seen that, while the net cash flows are $1,125,000, the net present value of the cash flows is only $655,375, or about half.

In many joint ventures, especially those having residual value (such as buildings or a solid long-term corporate cash flow), the analyst may also figure a potential sale of these assets five to seven years downstream. In this event, a capital gain, properly discounted for the time value of money, may be added in the investment analysis.

Table 6.5. Net Present Value Investment Analysis (in 000's)

Year	Net Cash Flow (actual dollars)	Discount Factor	Net Present Value (discounted Cash Flow)
1	($500,000)	0.902	($451,000)
2	$250,000	0.814	$203,500
3	$375,000	0.735	$275,625
4	$450,000	0.663	$298,350
5	$550,000	0.598	$328,900
Totals	$1,125,000		$655,375
	Positive discounted cash flow		$1,106,375
	Negative discounted cash flow		−$451,000
	TOTAL DISCOUNTED CASH FLOW		$655,375

Step 3: Profitability Index. The profitability index enables the financial analyst to compare various financial structures and returns. It is determined by dividing the accumulated positive discounted cash flows by the amount of equity investment. Often, this ratio is referred to as the benefit-to-cost ratio. If the ratio is less than one, the project is clearly a loser. The higher the ratio, the better the investment.

In the preceding case, the positive discounted cash flows were $1,106,375, and the negative discounted cash flows were $451,000. The profitability index is:

$$\frac{1,106,375}{451,00} = 2.45$$

This formulation is essentially the same for any major investment, whether it be in technology, mining, or real estate development projects.

Some analysts will want to go farther with these projections, by formulating internal rates of return to compare one project with others. These analyses are sophisticated and go beyond the scope of this chapter.

THE FINANCIAL STRUCTURE DECISION

Determination of the financial structure of the joint venture will vary considerably depending upon the type of legal structure the participants choose. Simply stated, the financial structure decision determines how much *debt* and *equity* will be put into the venture, and in what *ratio*. Strategic alliances established through written contracts will be financed solely and independently by each of the partners, thereby eliminating this decision.

Larger joint venture projects, particularly those establishing a separate corporation, sometimes sell *equity* on the public market or through private placements. *Debt* financing may be available through banks. Insurance companies are also possible candidates for financing projects that generate cash to pay back loans. The critical factors to examine in the financial structure decision are *cash flow* returns, *leverage*, and bankable *ratios*.

Usually bank money (debt financing) is cheaper than equity, regardless of whether the equity is generated internally through retained earnings or through an outside offering. However, too much bank financing can incur heavy negative cash flows from the repayment of principal and interest (as well as have an overloading effect on the balance sheet), and high interest payments can deplete a company's ability to generate a profit. If the debt-to-equity ratio stays at 2:1 or less, banks will probably feel the project is a safe venture.

THE DIVIDEND DECISION

The dividend decision determines the return each partner should receive and how soon. It assumes a positive expected financial return. (If there is no positive return, there should not be a venture.)

To answer the dividend question, you will need to determine how to "divide the pie," which involves a number of structural and operational issues that must be addressed prior to the finalization of the legal agreements. Therefore, it is advisable to look at the entire financial, technical, and human contribution of resources to the venture (these resource contributions are considered later in this chapter and in Chapter 8) before the final dividend division can be made and incorporated into the legal agreements.

One thing is nearly universal in the joint venture world: If you expect short-term financial rewards, you may be disappointed. Joint ventures are for long-term players. Few joint ventures are initiated as publicly traded corporations with their stock traded on Wall Street (with some notable exceptions, such as Tri-Star Pictures) because it is usually difficult to promise positive quarterly earnings reports in short order. Strategic alliances, on the other hand, may provide short-term profits, particularly in manufacturing and marketing alliances, where an existing product is being introduced into a new market by a partner with excellent existing distribution in that market.

Sales Leverage Effect on Profits

Many joint venturers comment about the importance of plowing profits of the venture back into the business in order to reinforce itself, and to ensure sufficient capital for unpredicted changes in the marketplace. For these reasons, it may be more advisable for many joint ventures to look at *market share* as their short run "dividend."

Frequently, compelling financial justification exists for the increased market share strategy because of the "sales leverage effect" on profits. In the following example, a joint venture had recently passed the breakeven point, and the partners had to decide whether to harvest the profit or plow it back in order to capture more market share—in other words, increase sales. Table 6.6 demonstrates leverage of sales on profits.

In this particular instance, a 25 percent increase in sales leveraged a doubling of profits because the joint venture had the capacity to produce more product without changing its gross profit margin or fixed costs.

FINANCING TECHNIQUES AND OPTIONS

Joint venture financing can take several different forms depending upon the size of the partners, their structural relationship, and the size of the venture. Strategic partnerships using a written contract structure will maintain the complete and total independence of each party from a financial and tax perspective.

Table 6.6. Example of Sales Leverage Effect on Profits

	Harvest Strategy	Growth Strategy
Gross sales	$100 M	$125 M
Less sales costs & commissions @ 10%	− 10 M	− 12.5 M
Net sales	$90 M	$112.5 M
Expenses		
Cost of goods sold @ 70%	− 70 M	− 87.5 M
General & Admin. (fixed)	− 15 M	− 15.0 M
Profit	$5 M	$10 M

Raising Equity

Joint ventures formed as regular corporations may issue different classes
of either common or preferred stock. Preferred stock may have specifically stated dividend and profit-and-loss sharing provisions. Those set up
as partnerships usually bring equity into the venture through "limited
partner" investors, and the sponsoring companies become "general partners."

If a larger corporation allies with a small, early-stage business, the
larger partner may also desire to invest in the stock of the smaller company to be sure the smaller company remains solvent, or to gamble on the
stock's value increasing dramatically. This form of investment usually
calls for an option to purchase a majority, or even full control of the
smaller company at a pre-agreed price in the event either the smaller company or the joint venture does exceedingly well. Some arrangements call
for a senior partner to invest equity in increments at a pre-agreed stock
price, on a specific timetable related to technology/product development
milestones.

Debt Financing

Little has been written on the subject of obtaining debt financing for joint
ventures. If your local commercial or corporate banker is called and asked
to finance a joint venture, he will more than likely say the bank is not in
that business. However, large banks and major insurance companies may
have a specialist in the field.

For joint ventures with no previous track record, banks will ask for
guarantees (recourse loans) from the participating partners. The amount
of debt that can be raised will probably be based upon the strength of the
sponsoring partners rather than on the strength of the new venture itself.

Project Financing

If, however, a financial institution can be convinced a joint venture is a
clear-cut business project financially capable of standing on its own, or is
already an ongoing business, then non-recourse loans may be available.
Under these circumstances there may be no need to place the loan as a
contingent liability on the balance sheets of the sponsors.

Similarly, investment bankers may be able to raise equity for "project
financing" based solely upon the economic viability of the project, regardless of the strength of the sponsors. Usually this type of project is distin-

guished by a project asset base that will collateralize the loan to the satisfaction of the financial institution(s) backing the loan. Typically, $25–$50 million is the lowest level that makes project financing worthwhile, although there are instances in the $5–$10 million range. Project financing is appropriate for "big ticket" items, such as large manufacturing plants, commercial real estate developments, mines, and pipelines.

Project financing, by its nature, is complex, time consuming, expensive to organize, less flexible in operation, and requires financially strong participants. Arranging project financing will probably require the services of an investment banking firm, which will handle any private placements of equity and also arrange the debt financing with financial institutions such as insurance companies. The debt portion of project financing can sometimes be arranged by the corporate lending departments of larger commercial banks. These banks will often act as the lead lender, and apportion the remainder of a participation mortgage to insurance companies or foreign banks.

One is best advised to begin arranging for project financing once all the partners are on-board and the project plan is sufficiently complete to clearly define and quantify all the risks. Banks refrain from taking risks.

Joint Research and Development Projects

Projects that involve heavy developmental experimentation are seldom good candidates for debt or project financing unless a governmental entity guarantees the notes on a non-recourse basis. Generally, development projects do not have a risk-free potential to generate cash flow, and a bank will immediately question how the loan will be repaid. If there is a high degree of developmental risk, the project should be handled predominantly with equity financing arranged by the investment banker structured for high risk–high return.

WHAT FINANCIAL COMMITMENTS ARE FAIR?

Some ventures are based upon "soft" contributions of services, licenses, knowledge, expertise, and other somewhat intangible commitments in lieu of hard money. While these contributions are acceptable and often quite valuable, unless there are actual monetary commitments made to the venture, the venture stands a good chance of failing. By making a monetary investment, each party has assumed a measurable level of risk in return for some measure of financial reward.

The methods of putting money into the venture can vary widely:

- One party makes an up-front investment, and the other makes on-going contributions
- Both parties contribute up-front money
- Both parties contribute on-going money

The proportion of financial contributions by each of the parties usually dictates the percentages of ownership and control or percentage distribution of profits to be made from the venture. Typically, the largest contributor receives the largest piece of the action. However, exceptions are made depending upon the leadership structure and the expertise of the partners (see Chapter 8).

HOW TO FIGURE YOUR TAX CONSEQUENCES

IRS Considerations

Each of the three basic forms of business alliance (written contract, partnership, and corporation) has its own specific set of tax implications. This section does not attempt to cover all the tax issues. You should consult an attorney or accountant, particularly because the U.S. Tax Code is in a constant state of flux. The issues presented here are basic considerations intended to reduce exposure to adverse IRS action while keeping "tax surprises" to a minimum.

E. Hans Lundsten, an attorney for the law firm of Adler, Pollack, and Sheehan, advises that tax considerations should not be allowed to "drive" the alliance. The true driving forces should be strategic, financial, and operational, with tax considerations then being weighed to improve the profit and cash flow of the venture.

Taxation of Profit and Loss

Who is taxed on profits and losses depends greatly upon the legal form of the venture.

1. *Written Contract:* The profits and losses are incurred by each individual business in the venture based upon their own internal indi-

vidual profit-and-loss statements. The written contract alliance treats its members as totally independent entities; there is no tax liability to the alliance because it has no separate business entity.

2. *Partnership:* While the partnership is a separate business entity, the profits and losses are allocated directly to the partners, and the partnership itself does not have to pay taxes. Substantial flexibility can be designed into the partnership, enabling some partners to take a larger percentage of profits, and others a larger percentage of losses.

3. *Corporation:* If a regular corporation is established to conduct the joint venture, or if the joint venture is being conducted through one of the partner's existing businesses, the profit or loss of the entire corporation will be taxed at regular corporate rates.

Double Taxation

Joint ventures that set up a separate regular corporation (not an "S" corporation) will have their profits taxed doubly: first, at the level of the joint venture corporation, and second, upon distribution of dividends to the stockholders (member corporations). Corporations that are stockholders of the joint venture corporation may be entitled to a dividend exclusion (normally 85 percent) so that a smaller portion of the distribution is taxable. (This exclusion is not available to non-corporate parties who are stockholders of the joint venture corporation.)

To avoid double taxation, small joint ventures may try to choose the "S" corporation form. The principal drawbacks to "S" corporations are:

1. The exclusion of any corporate stockholders

2. The ability to issue only one class of stock

3. The requirement to distribute all earnings to the shareholders annually, thereby reducing the retained earnings in the venture

For high-growth joint ventures needing to retain money for future growth, it may not be desirable to use the "S" corporation route. One alternative to keep capital in the "S" corporation requires the shareholders to make shareholder loans to the joint venture corporation in lieu of further equity investments. As long as the ratio of shareholder loans to equity capital does not exceed three to one, the IRS will probably not rule that the loans were indeed a disguised equity investment. For these reasons, most joint ventures elect the partnership or regular corporate form.

Loans, Kickers, and Convertible Debt

If one party makes a loan to the joint venture, the IRS may require certain minimum interest rates, which become taxable income to the lender. Equity kickers, stock conversion rights, warrants, fixed and formula price conversions, and the like should be carefully planned to minimize the desire of the IRS to find a taxable gain.

Debt instruments with equity kickers must be carefully constructed to ensure they are not treated as equity, thereby creating a problem where interest is not deductible, and principal payments are not treated as return of capital.

Acquisitions, Options, and Dispositions

If one partner anticipates that it will exercise an option to acquire the joint venture, and the other partner, conversely, desires to sell its interests, an agreement should, well in advance, orchestrate the consequences to pre-empt an adverse ruling by the IRS. Additional consideration should include the liquidation of assets, compensation for services, cost basis of equity in the venture, and so on.

If one partner acquires stock in the other partner when the joint venture is formed, and holds options for future acquisition, care should be taken to ensure no immediate taxable gain to the selling company. Options should be carefully written to avoid any implication that these might be part of an installment sale arrangement, where the option holder is treated as the true owner of the underlying equity, thereby triggering a taxable gain well before the actual exercise of the option.

Marketing and Distribution Agreements

Marketing, sales, and distribution agreements generally have no special taxable implications to the joint venture or strategic alliance, but development or management agreements will probably need tax planning.

Research and Development Tax Credits

Research and development costs, if incurred in connection with expanding an existing business, may be expensed rather than capitalized if they are laboratory and/or experimental in nature. Such costs may also qualify for investment tax credits. Management and marketing expenses as well as start-up R&D costs do not qualify for tax credits.

Start-Up Considerations

Several considerations should be kept in mind when services, property, or rights are being provided to the joint venture:

When one of the parent companies transfers technology, patent rights, or other property or rights to the joint venture, care should be taken to be sure it is an "equity swap" and not a substitute for payment of money that would otherwise be taxable.

The transfer of appreciated property to a joint venture partnership will not generally trigger a taxable gain. But for joint venture corporations, there may be a taxable gain, unless the property was transferred at the time of the creation of the new corporation, shortly thereafter, or in conjunction with transfers by all or most of the other stockholders.

If a new corporation is being formed, start-up expenses are capitalized, not written off as first-year expenses. These can generally be treated as "deferred expenses" and capitalized over a five-year period. However, once the venture is "actively engaged in business," most of these costs may be treated as an operating expense.

Services Provided to Joint Ventures

Services provided to the joint venture in return for equity in the venture may be seen as a taxable exchange by the IRS unless the agreement is carefully drafted. Services and property that are not truly "at risk" in the venture should be provided in such a way as to be received as income when the cash is received. This method can be elected for federal income tax purposes. Property that is both at risk and subject to forfeiture will consequently have little value at the present (should the venture fail), and strong future value should the venture succeed, thereby triggering a taxable gain. If the election is made, the transaction will then be subject to long-term capital gains rather than ordinary income (assuming the IRS recognizes preferrential treatment to long-term gains). *Be sure to consult with a tax attorney or accountant before signing the binding legal agreement!*

USING GENERALLY ACCEPTED ACCOUNTING PROCEDURES

Generally Accepted Accounting Procedures (GAAP), standards often used within the accounting profession, are the rules and disciplines affecting financial reporting. While these rules are approved by accountants, they may differ significantly from the ever-changing IRS tax regulations on such issues as to whether research and development costs are capitalized or expensed. Beware of these differences when the joint venture is formed.

GAAP was established principally as an accounting system for large, publicly traded manufacturing entities, which views income and expenses when "booked" (accrued). Accountants refer to this as an "accrual" system, and only the *accrual* method will be certified as proper by an accountant.

A joint venture will often call for a common financial reporting system, and GAAP will normally be the acceptable method. James Needham of Arthur Young urges all joint venture agreements to clearly spell out the accounting system to be used.

Effect of GAAP on Service Joint Ventures

Unknown to many service companies, GAAP does not recognize the cash form of reporting used by most service companies. (The cash method accounts for a sale only when cash is received, and an expense only when an invoice is actually paid.)

For many small service firms, a conversion to an accrual accounting system may not be in their best interests. Be sure the lawyer drafting the final agreement does not automatically insist upon utilizing GAAP, a requirement that can be an unnecessary burden, creating friction later in the joint venture. This problem does not affect alliances using the written contract format.

Contingent Liability Reporting

From an accounting standpoint, if a bank loan to the joint venture is guaranteed by a partner holding less than 50 percent of the venture's interest, the loan does not have to be reported as a contingent liability on the balance sheet of the guarantor.

PERSPECTIVES ON MONEY

For thousands of years, money has been the universal medium of exchange. Regardless of its universality, money means very different things to different people, and these differences can make a large difference to the alliance.

When negotiating an alliance, it is important to know your partner's perspective on money. If his or her approach toward money is radically different from yours, it may cause frictions and a demand to produce unrealistic results. Several money perspectives to think about include:

Top Line versus Bottom Line.   Younger companies may have a tendency to want fast sales growth, while older companies may seek strong profit margins. These differences could manifest themselves by the younger company desiring to put more resources into marketing and sales, and the older company cutting costs. Well-managed differences could be a "dynamite combination," whereas conflicting differences could be a "dynamite explosion."

Long versus Short Term.   Discordant time frames can be the source of much despair unless they are well defined. Some corporations think of long term as anything longer than five years, but early-stage companies may view long term as two years or less. By the same token, short term may mean six months to one company, and three years to another. Having a clear understanding of how your partner views time and money will help reduce conflict.

In real estate joint ventures, developers expect larger rewards in return for high-risk exposure. More often than not, the developer partner expects to wait several years before the cash flow begins to turn in his favor. Building contractors, as partners, usually expect more rapid cash flow to pay labor and overhead costs for their work crew. They do not normally expect as high a long-term return as the developer. These two perspectives are likely to create frictions, unless negotiated before the agreements have been signed. If the venture is structured to account for these differences, the developer may agree to channel short-term gains to the contractor in return for heftier long-term rewards later in the life of the project. But, as the years go by, the contractor may begin to see the developer taking larger amounts of cash compared to the contractor's rather paltry returns, forgetting the earlier years when his developer partner was on the ropes waiting for bank approvals, investor commitments, zoning clearances, and building approvals. These frictions often result in the partner who feels short-changed, demanding a renegotiation.

"High Grading."   "High grading," a term used in mining joint ventures, refers to going after ore that is highest grade or nearest the top, yielding good profit margins and valuable cash flow. This is comparable to the "run to break-even" strategy employed by smaller ventures, which must beat

the clock before time and money run out. High grading can provide better short-term profits in many ventures, so long as some of the profits are retained by the venture for the long haul.

Reaching "cash flow break-even" quickly is important for more than just financial reasons. Alliances that continually bleed the parents of cash eventually tend to generate anger in the sponsors. The sooner the venture reaches break-even (assuming it is designed to do this some day), the fewer pressures and frustrations on the sponsors. The objective is to make capital investments work advantageously for the sponsors. This goal requires an entrepreneurial style of management, and an understanding that the new venture is much like a new, start-up company suffering from all the critical pains a new company endures. When the venture is continually in the red (and at least one partner expected it to be in the black), a number of disturbing questions will be asked:

· Will this venture manager make the plan?
· If the plan is not achieved, will the entire investment be in jeopardy?
· Where are we going to find more money if it is needed?

If good answers are not forthcoming, the venture may be headed for a crisis.

Is Money the Goal or Only a Resource?   Money is many things to many people. A large public corporation, being driven to manage by the quarterly earnings report, may see money as the goal. This outlook will usually be paralleled by a short-term perspective on money. The entrepreneur, on the other hand, may be using money as the measure of personal financial success, translating corporate profit into personal net worth.

Acquisition-oriented companies look to money as the resource for building their empires. Other companies build their empires through internal expansion by holding powerful market shares in their industries.

Ambiguity and differing perspectives regarding the purpose of money can cause turmoil in the venture. Partners can have differing perspectives, but they should be discussed up front, and the venture should be designed to satisfy these diverse financial appetites.

Investor Returns.   A joint venture will often involve professional investors whose goals may add another set of dimensions. Individual investors may seek risks and returns differing from those of large investment houses or the corporate partners. A clear set of financial goals will keep investors from having false expectations. In addition, it is wise to try to adhere to those goals and thereby avoid being distracted by the sharpshooting of dissident shareholders.

Hard versus Soft Contributions. Hard contributions are directly measurable in actual dollars, including cash, promissory cash commitments, contingent commitments, stock of existing corporations, and the assets and liabilities associated with an ongoing business.

Soft contributions may be just as valuable, but are not as easily accounted for as cash. They include in-kind commitments of skills, knowledge, services, patents, technology, know-how, licenses, and so on.

It is relatively easy to weigh the value of a monetary contribution—cash is easy to count. But non-monetary contributions are far more vague. For example, how are values assigned to a contribution of proprietary information? What is the value of the assignment of key personnel?

Proprietary information may be handled by licensing that information at market rate to the joint venture. By licensing, a concrete value will be placed upon the information, and that value can be calculated as part of the equity contribution. The owner of proprietary information may ask for royalties, which become a preferred dividend payback from the venture.

Be careful when negotiating to watch how players contributing hard assets view those contributing soft assets. All too often, hard-asset contributors may see soft-asset players as "getting a free ride," a condition that could eventually lead to animosity.

The financial analysis and the strategic analysis should dovetail—good strategy should, by definition, be financially sound.

PART THREE

The Structuring Phase

The initial round of analyzing strategic and financial issues should first be done internally within your own company, and if the results are positive, then negotiations may begin, during which further strategic and financial analysis will be done to dovetail with operational considerations.

Integrating the strategic "fit" with the operational "fit" is known as *structuring*. During this phase, the organizational and legal aspects of the alliance are designed and molded to ensure that strategy and operations are marching in harmony.

In this part, the following major themes will be explored:

* Negotiating the Deal
* Structuring the Venture
* The Legal Agreements You Will Need

Managers should concentrate their efforts on more than just the legal and financial aspects of this phase. All too often negotiations are overly complex, and adequate time is not dedicated to the operation of the venture *before* legal documents are signed.

As the strategic phase progresses, the structuring phase should commence. There is usually considerable overlap between the two phases. Chapters 7, 8, and 9 deal with structuring the venture.

7

Negotiating the Deal

A handshake is a deal—as defined by the other party.

—Roy Bonner

Initially, the preliminary ideas for an alliance will often be explored at the senior management level, but deals never get off the ground until CEOs sit down and cut a deal. Once the decision is made at the top, it can then filter down. Otherwise a senior manager may bring the idea to the top without endorsement or commitment until he sees which way the boss is thinking. Donald Trump, in negotiating a joint venture with the Hyatt Corporation, elaborates:

"Suddenly it dawned on me why my deals kept coming apart: if you're going to make a deal of significance, you have to go to the top.

"It comes down to the fact that everyone underneath the top guy in a company is just an employee. An employee is not going to fight for your deal. He's fighting for his salary increase . . . and the last thing he wants to do is upset his boss. So he'll present your case with no real opinion. To you, he might be very enthusiastic, but to his boss he'll say 'Listen, a guy named Trump from New York wants to make such and such a deal, and here are the pros and cons, what do you want to do?' If it turns out his boss doesn't like it, the employee will say 'Yes, I agree, but I wanted to present it to you.'"[1]

Communications can be verbal or written, but there is no need for formal legal documents at this point. Strategic and financial issues will most likely be the focus of initial discussions.

NEGOTIATING TEAM

Do not try to finalize an alliance during the first few meetings; all that is needed is a brief outline of a basic strategy—short enough to be written on the "back of an envelope." If your potential partner is interested in pursuing the venture, a series of exploratory meetings should be held. It may be advisable to bring along the key operational managers who will be responsible for implementing decisions; their early commitment will be essential later. These operational managers will be a good barometer of whether the right "chemistry" exists beyond the CEO level.

Whereas the CEO will be focusing on strategic and financial "fit" in the venture, the operational manager will be measuring operational "fit"—timing, cost controls, communications, engineering, allocation of personnel, and day-to-day problem solving. Rudolf Schwenger of Siemens, AG says, "The cooperation will never work unless you have the support of middle management."[2]

In real estate ventures, the principle is equally important. George Cioe of Gilbane comments:

"CEO's sit down to make the deals, but the deals still need support at the staff level. It is essential to get the middle managers into the middle of negotiations so that the CEO's can moderate. This establishes a role that delegates decisionmaking to the middle ranks, leaving veto and mediating power at the top ranks.

"You cannot possibly name all the things that can go wrong in advance, and the most difficult problems, from the CEO's perspective, will be to make your people in different departments work with the other company's departments as if you are all one company. During the development of the project, everyone is trying to win little victories for their boss, which, at some point, will eventually cause friction. At this point, those top managers who shook hands on the deal can say: 'No, this is the intent of the agreement—this is the way it will go.' Then the project falls into line, and everything goes ahead."

The larger the negotiating team for each company, the longer the negotiations. However, time will be saved once operations commence, because operational managers will "hit the ground running."

Role of the Cynic

An almost natural tendency exists among those considering an alliance to begin "romancing the future," much like entrepreneurs idealizing the potential of their new gadget. Experienced joint venturers understand that negotiations require at least one person to play the role of the *cynic* to counteract these romantic tendencies, and keep negotiations hard-nosed.

Humphrey Neil, the author of *The Art of Contrary Thinking*, states; "When everyone thinks alike, everyone is likely to be wrong—at least in their timing of events . . . Contrary thinking is responsible for [preventing] the delusion of projecting today into tomorrow without thought of what might happen during the night." He goes on to say, however, "it is far easier to be contrary . . . than it is to create original thought."[3] Cynicism alone, while providing a balance for optimism, is not enough. Use cynics to create a dynamic tension with optimists, yielding original, unique solutions.

The cynic's role is not to kill the deal, but rather to look at realities, details, and things that could go wrong. Bankers and venture capitalists are often well trained as cynics to find the hidden pitfalls in a proposal. The cynic should not be a person who is threatened by the alliance.

"Deal killers" are those in the company who are threatened by the prospects of alliance. They fear they should (or do) have the skills that the alliance brings from the outside, thereby bringing the threat of ruining their careers.

When negotiating, look for cynics and deal killers on the other side. You can sometimes tell the difference because cynics are negative but objective, and deal killers are negative but subjective. If you can't identify these people early in the discussions, they will rise to the surface before the agreement is signed. To save time and frustration, the sooner identified the better.

Several years ago, Irving Janis wrote a book entitled *The Victims of Group Think*. In it, he noted major instances of failure in group decision making, such as the decision to invade the Bay of Pigs, where a key policy-making committee made critical blunders because they did not cherish and nurture hard-nosed decision making; they failed to challenge assumptions.

Janis prescribes several ways to avoid the problems of "group think."[4] These methods are extremely applicable to appraising the likelihood of success in an alliance:

· Reinforce critical appraisal and foster an atmosphere that approves of skepticism and critical discussion
· Leaders should refrain from pushing their own view; instead, they should encourage healthy debate, until a decision must be made

- Avoid having a single, insulated group to make the decision
- Create opportunities for experts in the middle levels of the organization to give their critical reviews[4]

To critically evaluate the venture, some companies appoint two groups: an "advocacy team" and a "devil's advocacy team" often led by corporate counsel. One supports and one opposes the venture. Their combined opinions enable the CEO to avoid being seduced by the thrill of courtship, and unwittingly become a victim of "group think."

MUTUAL ASSURANCES AND CONFIDENTIALITY

Do not reveal any information you consider to be proprietary or confidential until both parties have entered into a mutual confidentiality agreement (see Chapter 9 for details). Some large, multinational corporations refrain from confidentiality agreements because their corporations are too large to know who might already be working on a similar field in a laboratory in some remote corner of the world. However, some sort of assurance that confidential material will not be used adversely is important to have at this stage. In lieu of a formal confidentiality agreement, a letter agreeing not to use confidential information adversely may be a good fallback tactic if the players are trustworthy.

If your potential partner does not have an impeccable reputation for maintaining confidentiality, and balks at signing a confidentiality agreement, it might be advisable to find another partner.

There is little purpose in discussing a noncompete agreement at this stage. Later, before finalizing the terms and conditions of the venture, specific products, markets, and locations can be delineated in a noncompete agreement.

The exception to this approach occurs when highly technical, sensitive, and proprietary technical information must be shared between the parties before a decision can be made to seriously consider an alliance. Under these situations, one company may fear the disclosure of sensitive data would give their prospective partner an opportunity to use the negotiations as a means of exploiting the information, then abandoning the idea of the alliance and subsequently becoming a serious competitor.

The prospective partner, however, may need to evaluate the claims of the first company to be sure the technology can truly be used in the commercial applications envisioned by the alliance. In these circumstances, noncompetition issues should be discussed, and may be included in the confidentiality agreement, which specifies the terms of noncompetition if the joint venture is arranged, as well as the expiration term if the joint venture is not consummated. (Again, see Chapter 9 for specific guidance.)

MEASURING YOUR BARGAINING POWER

People who are good at negotiating in adversarial situations may not necessarily be good at negotiating a joint venture. Negotiating a joint venture is not like buying a house or a car. It is more like arranging a marriage. It is far more important to determine if "$1 + 1 = 3$," than to "squeeze the last concessions" out of an opponent. Your objective is to create a "win/win," not a "win/lose," condition. Remember, you will have to rely upon your partners when problems occur. Make sure your partner is with you, and not anxious to regain the advantages they perceived were lost in original negotiations.

This doesn't mean you should be a weak negotiator either. Sell your company and its strengths. Show your partner you are a strong player; you must believe you have something valuable to offer, otherwise your prospective partner will not take you seriously. Don't be afraid to strike a hard bargain on your behalf, as long as it is fair.

You should analyze several key issues in measuring bargaining power:

- How strongly does your partner want a joint venture?
- What resources are contributed by each partner?
- What is the relative urgency for each player?
- What other commitments has each player made that will consume available resources?
- What other alternatives exist for the players?
- How highly do the other players regard your strategic and operational strengths and weaknesses?
- Does the other player think that your involvement will be essential to success?
- Are the expectations for performance realistic?
- Can you actually meet your commitments? Can they?
- How willing are you and your prospective partner to frankly and openly assess each partner's individual strengths and weaknesses?

WATCHING FOR CRITICAL SIGNS

During the preliminary negotiations, you should watch to see if the pre-conditions for a successful joint venture are present. The primary task of this early phase will be to design an overall game plan for the alliance. This process involves transforming the concept into a statement of intent and an operations plan. Ideally, people at other organizational levels of your company will begin working with their counterparts in the other company. This is a critical opportunity to begin watching for signs that indicate whether or not the venture has a decent chance of achieving its potential. There are several things to watch for:

- Does your partner have the ability to achieve results?
- Is the promptness of replies adequate to sustain energy and momentum?
- Is your partner committing top-notch human resources?
- When things need to get done, does your partner make things happen?
- How are problems addressed—by seeking solutions or by placing blame?
- How good is the quality of communications?
- What is the chemistry like between the organizations?
- Is there an ability to have a marriage at multi-levels in the organization?
- Does the level of commitment match the requirements of the venture?
- Is there a real willingness to work as a team?

If your partner performs well on these points, the prospects for a successful venture—while not guaranteed—are certainly higher.

TIMING: DON'T WAIT TOO LONG

There is no hard and fast rule that states how long it should take for an alliance to be consummated. Some types of alliance, such as those between manufacturers and their independent sales reps, are so traditional, easily replicated, and formalized that they often begin and are consummated in less than a week. Other ventures—where the issues are more complex, the stakes higher, and the analysis more difficult, such as the construction of a major chemical plant—may take a year or more to complete. However, if negotiations drag on, if deadlines pass, if meetings are continually postponed, it is very probable that nothing will ever happen.

The opposite extreme is also a problem. Shotgun marriages with the right strategic fit may not work operationally. Avoid pressures to sign an agreement until key operational managers have had a chance to review the venture and meet with their counterparts. It is better to back off or say no than to be railroaded into an ill-fitting alliance.

Perhaps joint ventures are like babies: if a joint venture is to happen, it is usually born within about a nine-month timeframe. But the timeframe can become longer the more complex the internal decision-making process of the sponsors. Smaller companies with streamlined decision making can be frustrated by large corporations until they become educated to the corporate process and decide who has the authority to make decisions. Without a good understanding of the approval process, the smaller company may withhold critical information necessary to trigger a positive decision, accidentally undermining the large corporation's key advocate of the venture.

Dana Callow, a partner in Boston Capital Ventures, which has an alliance with Prudential-Bache, said, "It took us 12 months to structure our relationship. We were careful to meet with a lot of people that might be involved—people with decision-making authority and control of budgets. What was important, though difficult, was educating our partner on how we must operate, especially since our perspective was long-term and theirs short-term."

IBM's Director of Business Development and Practices, J. William Scruggs, comments: "It's very important that you have an open and frank discussion of objectives and of what the measurement of the objectives will be and not leave that to be assumed. . . . We like to establish some reasonable period of time in which we're going to [agree] . . . And either we succeed at it or we decide not to continue and have some generally agreed-to basis on which to make that decision."[5]

POWER AND CONTROL ISSUES

Companies often have very different views toward power and control. For some companies, power is the ability to *get things done*. For others, power is the ability to *mold and control.* And for some, power is the ability to *dominate and enforce.*

An alliance is based upon the ability to *share power.* During the negotiations phase, if one company tends to overemphasize the issue of dominance, it is probable that this dominance will permeate the joint venture, placing one member in the superior position, and relegating the other to either the subordinate or the inferior position. The ultimate long-term consequences are obvious. Strong egos are too tough to stay in an inferior position for long (but they may tolerate being subordinate).

As outlined in the next chapter, sharing power does not imply that all partnerships should be 50/50 deals. There can be, and often should be, a controlling partner—just be sure there is a good reason for the division, and both sides perceive it is fair. It is imperative for the most powerful member of the venture to be sensitive to the needs, values, and style of the other, and for the subordinate member to respect and appreciate the position of the other member.

By the same token, the opposite condition is also a problem: Be ever-wary if power and control issues are dealt with meekly. It may forewarn of a lack of interest or motivation, or that the partners, not wanting to offend one another, are treading too cautiously. The alliance itself must be aggressive if it is to be successful.

One of the best methods of dealing with power and control is not to talk about it in theory, but rather to discuss specific *operational* conditions in detail, such as:

· How are decisions made to select design specifications?
· Who has responsibility for details such as packaging? press releases?
· What authority does the project manager have to allocate funding?
· Who has veto power over what decisions?
· What personnel will be transferred to the alliance?

Answers to questions of this type set the framework for the nonbinding statement of intent, which will be discussed shortly.

Another area for negotiating power and control is determined when the prospective partners must divide the risks and rewards of the venture:

· How are the stock shares divided?
· Who is contributing capital?

· Who pays if things go sour?

· Who receives the greatest rewards? In what proportion?

TRUST AND ETHICAL ISSUES

The Critical Underpinnings

Without high levels of trust, there will be no chemistry, and without chemistry the venture is doomed. Alliances are usually risky ventures. Difficulties are bound to arise, and if communications are not excellent, good problem-solving will not occur to address the difficulties. Inevitably, in an environment of low trust, there will be blame-setting rather than problem-solving; at which point the venture is on its way to oblivion or divorce.

Recently a situation arose in which the parties to the joint venture could have legally avoided payments of a commission to the broker who had brought two of the four parties together. The partners agreed, however, to pay the brokerage fee; their reputations as fair dealers and the tone of the future joint venture were far more important than saving a brokerage commission.

A more dramatic example involved a joint venture between Fleet Bank (one of New England's largest banks), Nortek (a Fortune 500 company), Gilbane (one of the 10 largest U.S. construction firms), and Hinkley Allen (a large regional law firm). The four firms were involved in a joint venture to build a 25-story office complex to house the corporate offices of Fleet, Nortek, and Hinkley Allen. At a price of $63 million, the complex was rather costly. After construction was complete and tenants were moving into the building, at the ribbon-cutting ceremony, one of the partners commented: "Shouldn't we be signing the joint venture agreements pretty soon?" Until that time, the partners' commitment was bound only by their handshakes, mutual trust, and a tremendous working relationship. While this is not the recommended method of joint venturing, it illustrates the critical importance of trust if a venture is to be successful.

Businesses that do not prize the value of their reputations generally do not make good partners. Roy Bonner, former senior executive at IBM, has said, "The partners must consider their reputations as their most important possession." He asserts, "When the Golden Rule is ignominiously referred to as 'He who has the gold, rules' or 'Do unto others before they do unto you,' we will all be done harm. The real Golden Rule was the foundation for Thomas Watson's growth of IBM. He believed he would succeed in direct proportion to the trust customers had in IBM." IBM issues a "Code of Conduct" to all its employees. Several quotes from the document are noteworthy because they are applicable to IBM's strategic alliances:

> "Don't make misrepresentations to anyone you deal with. If you believe the other person may have misunderstood you, correct any misunderstanding you find exists. Honesty is integral to ethical behavior, and trustworthiness is essential for good, lasting relationships."
>
> "Never use IBM's size itself to intimidate, threaten, or slight another person or organization."
>
> "Everyone you do business with is entitled to fair and even-handed treatment. This is true whether you are buying, selling, or performing in any other capacity for IBM."[6]

Avoid partners with repuions for skullduggery, conniving, deceit, and a desire to win at any cost. A properly selected partner gives the joint venture a safe harbor from the rages of cut-throat rules of economic piracy. The reason is quite simple: In a high-risk environment, there is no way success can be achieved by partner assassination. Each knows that success only comes when both parties are teamed together. "Strategic synergy," if properly in place, forms the structural bond that both requires and perpetuates trust and ethics.

Uniroyal's former chairman Beretta had similar experiences:

> "In Japan we entered into a joint venture with the giant Sumatomo chemical company because Uniroyal had the basic technology, but lacked access to the Japanese market, and because Sumatomo also lacked access to the raw materials that it needed.
>
> "Uniroyal found Sumatomo to be honorable people, and we relied on that trust extensively. The everchanging market for petro-chemicals necessitated a system of constant renegotiation. If we did not deal with honorable people, the venture would have been ruined."

Inherently, good partners maintain not only a strong achievement orientation, but they also place a strong emphasis on their people. The development of people engenders trust and loyalty within the staff—a trust that transcends the personal relationships within the company and becomes a part of the corporate culture itself. "Trust happens at the level of the individuals of (our partner's) organization. Our joint venture is with an organization, but it must be supported by individuals," according to Dana Callow of Boston Capital Ventures.

How well will a partner's word hold under the pressures of financial strain? tendencies toward greed? and personal advantage? Experienced joint venturers will often say: "If you cannot trust a handshake, even the best-drawn legal agreement will not be adequate protection." If you don't trust the ability of your partner to perform, don't take up-front money as an insurance policy—this implies a weak agreement, and can eventually become grounds for "getting even" in the future.

DEALING WITH EXPECTATIONS

All prospective partners will have numerous expectations about the future. Most of the expectations will be euphoric—new products, new markets, new opportunities. Some expectations will be apprehensive— questions about job security, unknown risks, or partnership loyalty.

Expectations should be high because, as IBM's Roy Bonner puts it, "High expectations yield high results." James Vaughn, involved in a number of ventures, echoed these thoughts humorously when he said, "If you shoot for the moon, you might miss and only reach a rooftop, but if you shoot for your foot, you'll surely hit it."

Expectations are most productive when stated directly and up front, but, unfortunately, human nature tends to create problems with expectations. Unstated and vague expectations are high energy time bombs ready to explode when the expectation is not met. From a psychological perspective, expectations are always on the edge of disappointment because they are inherently unfulfilled. As unstated expectations fail to be met, the underpinnings of trust begin to erode, the downward spiral commences, communications become ineffective, heated disagreements are likely, as each side blames the other, and the participants' worst fears drive them toward more drastic measures. The best approach is to expect only what is specifically asked for and granted by each party to the venture.

James Needham of Arthur Young suggests that prospective partners think through their expectations up front, continually clarify their expectations, and take care to agree on the value of their respective contributions. "Clear expectations will yield clear results," states Needham. As soon as expectations are stated openly and put into specifics, they are transformed from wishful, passive, and uncontrollable desires into active and driven goals.

For example, in a typical mining joint venture agreement, many expectations of the partners will be clearly spelled out in their agreement: expected rates of production for the mine, expected transfer prices when products or services are transferred from one partner to the joint venture or vice versa, expected time schedules and milestones, expected expenses, expected distribution of earnings and financing of losses. Other less precise expectations may be included in the agreement, but many can be stated verbally or included in the operations plan before commencement of the venture.

PERFORMING PROFESSIONAL DUE DILIGENCE

Investment bankers, large corporations, and venture capitalists all perform extensive "due diligence" before making an investment in a company. They do this to maximize their chances of making a wise decision, and to avoid entering into a deal that will eventually sour.

Nicolas Retsinas' trading firm asks around to find people who are capable and who have a good reputation. "It's like a newspaper reporter who uses two independent confirmations to ensure that the story is true," he says.

Before signing any final agreements, you may want to check on your prospective mate. Some areas to check:

- *Financial Statements:* Do they ensure capacity to uphold financial commitments?

- *Relations with Vendors:* Do bills get paid on time? *and Customers:* Are they satisfied?

- *Court Filings:* Is the company always involved in legal hassles?

- *Industry Reputation:* Is it "quality"?

- *Quality of the Top Managers:* Do they have a good track record? Is there high turnover?

- *Critical Strategic Decisions* in the past: Does the company have a record of excellent judgment?

- *Board of Directors:* Does the board support the decision to form an alliance? Will they support or undermine the CEO?

· *Core Organizational Values:* Do they value integrity, reputation, tough-mindedness, teamwork, loyalty, discipline, adherence to commitments, entrepreneurship, and human resources?

Failure to perform due diligence can result in an entangling alliance whose ending may be painful and costly. Uniroyal's Beretta tells the story:

"Mexican Law prohibits a foreign company from owning over 40% of an industry classified as 'petro-chemical.' Sixty percent must be owned by a Mexican national. We found a small company for whom we had been a supplier of chemical intermediates that they further processed. We thought we knew the company's owner, since we had done business with him for quite some time, so he was a logical person to do business with when we decided we wanted to go forward and begin supplying a broader Mexican market.

"Uniroyal brought in its portfolio of products, technology, and management as its contribution. Soon we spotted a problem when our auditors learned that he was not paying his purchasing agent. When questioned on this unorthodox practice, he replied 'I don't have to pay him, our suppliers pay him!' This caused us to wonder what his other arrangements were. We then discovered he owned the engineering company that received the construction bids. These were just blatant ways of siphoning off funds. He probably had many other methods we never learned about.

"This Joint Venture was difficult to dissolve because we had to find a *good Mexican* partner who would buy his 60% interest to preserve our technology and investment. This is a particularly thorny problem if you need to extricate yourself. Your degree of freedom is limited because there may not be a large number of good replacement partners available."

ROLE OF SPECIALISTS

Lawyers

Many lawyers will state their primary purpose is to protect their clients against unreasonable risks—the most valuable role a lawyer can play. The real question becomes: What is a *reasonable* risk?

Some alliances have never gone beyond the negotiation stage because lawyers began asking the difficult questions about the real risks and how those risks would be minimized. True, overly zealous or very conservative lawyers may occasionally protect their clients right out of an alliance, but more often than not, the probing analysis of a good legal counsel has saved an idealist from a poorly conceived venture.

There is little need for attorneys to be present during the earliest stages of negotiation, but they should be consulted to draft confidentiality and non-compete agreements, to protect against securities and exchange violations, and to ask hard questions about commitments and contingencies so the business participants can prepare solutions.

Perceptive lawyers will also have a natural tendency to find the weak points in a deal and focus 80 percent of their efforts on these issues. In an attempt to rectify fuzzy points or areas of potential disagreement, lawyers may negotiate terminology that tends to drive a wedge between potential partners and jeopardize their future working relationship. Managers should carefully review and weigh this legal advice privately before introducing such rough edges into the negotiations.

A business should avoid bringing an attorney to the bargaining table as its negotiating agent; this only encourages the other side to do the same. Then the negotiations may turn into an adversarial process, with each lawyer protecting his or her client right out of the deal.

Lawyers frequently have a fixation about tax or antitrust issues, or some other specialty in the law. George Cioe, an experienced real estate joint venturer with Gilbane Construction, observed that the "client will often lose the overall picture when lawyers talk about the narrow tax and legal aspects" of a joint venture.

At a recent joint venture seminar, one businessman boasted that he never used a lawyer in putting together his deals because lawyers knew little about business and should not be involved in "mucking up a good business deal." Although this attitude might express frustration with some lawyers who tend to obfuscate issues, this entrepreneur allowed his frustration to replace wisdom! Lawyers have a very real role in negotiating alliances, though that role is often largely behind the scenes.

On the other hand, there is an old axiom in business circles to which seasoned entrepreneurs and experienced lawyers both subscribe: *Never let your lawyer run your business.* J. Peter Olsen, an attorney from the firm of Hinkley Allen, advises: "I don't believe an attorney should make business deals—generally we just aren't good at it. We should be advisors, we should be involved from the beginning, but not necessarily at the bargaining table. But if a business deal goes too far down the road without any attorney's input, it could strain the relationship between client and counsel. The client will think the attorney is not creative and the attorney will feel he is giving awkward advice."

Several seasoned joint venturers have cautioned about young, competitive, overly aggressive attorneys who, when in a room with their equally young and competitive counterparts, tend to dominate final discussions, pick deals apart at the last minute, debate minutiae, and attempt to protect their clients from any and all risks. Beware of these well-meaning missionaries; find a seasoned legal counselor. Contentious lawyers generate large legal fees but cannot sacrifice their own egos for the well-being of their clients.

At one recent deal closing, the lawyers for each of the prospective partners began a series of entangling debates about contingencies, termination clauses, and other details couched in legalese that left the prospective business teammates confused and out of the mainstream of the discussion. Eventually one businessman nodded to his prospective partner; they both stepped out of the room, unnoticed by the rivaling lawyers. Outside the two made whatever arrangements they thought were fair, walked back into the room, and announced their decisions to the lawyers.

Robert Edwards, an experienced business lawyer for the firm of Tillinghast, Collins, & Graham, stated a far more intelligent perspective when he said: "You negotiate the business deal, and I'll protect you from the worst possible legal circumstances. You are the businessman, and therefore you make the business decisions."

When choosing a lawyer, look for one who is not litigious, but who may be confrontive yet diplomatic. If the alliance involves a large corporation, it will be wise to choose a lawyer from a firm with some depth in both corporate and tax law. Small sole practitioners may neither have the experience nor the time to handle difficult issues that might arise in the course of negotiations with larger corporate attorneys. Peter Olsen humorously cautions: "Find a good law firm or you might end up with the fuzzy end of the lollipop!"

Lawyers will tend to focus on negotiations, legal agreements, and deal structure, often distracting managers from looking at fundamental operational issues. During the negotiations period, top managers are wise to assign a person to focus solely on operational issues, and isolate this person from all the legal paperwork pressures.

Accountants

Similar cautions also apply to accountants. Basically, there are three types of accountants:

1. *Tax accountants* expert in IRS matters
2. *Audit accountants* knowledgeable in the rules of financial control and accurate audit procedures
3. *Business accountants* adept at deal structuring and negotiating with investment bankers and lenders

Most alliances should have a lead accountant skilled in the business aspects of accounting available on an advisory team and who can bring in other staff with tax and audit skills. If tax or audit accountants are in charge of the financial specialists, they will often look at the venture too narrowly and miss the more important strategic, structural, and operational issues. Business accountants are more likely to see the big picture and interface more effectively with the rest of the strategic and operational team.

Consultants

Consultants should also be chosen carefully to be sure they are truly appropriate for the task at hand. A consultant strong in strategic planning may not be nearly as skilled in operational management.

If a company has never entered an alliance before, a consultant with joint venture experience may be advisable, although one CEO suggests: "Refrain from bringing in hordes of outside consultants, analysts, and advisors. If you don't have adequate inside resources to make sound judgments, you probably don't have the resources to make the deal work."

GOVERNMENTAL CONSIDERATIONS

While finalizing negotiations, the partners should consider the impact of governmental regulations on the venture. Every government on the face of the earth has mechanisms to regulate business, and formalized joint ventures tend to fall into their realm of jurisdiction more than less formal strategic alliances. (Because a prospective joint venture may cross a number of international boundaries, this book can only provide basic guideline questions that should be asked of proper advisors.) In the United States, some of the critical regulatory agencies are:

1. *Internal Revenue Service.* The IRS will recognize a joint venture as either a separate corporation (if so organized), a partnership (again if so organized), or as nonexistent (if no new entity is formed and the written agreement between the partners stipulates that a separate joint venture business entity does not exist).

   However, tax laws are constantly in a state of flux, and the current U.S. tax law is now a Byzantine labyrinth of convoluted obfuscations designed only to frustrate businesses and even the bureaucracy. Expert advice should be sought on this front. Most lawyers today state that, for tax purposes, they will not guarantee the IRS will refrain from completely redefining the distinction between a partnership and a corporation, however unlikely it may be.

2. *Antitrust Division and Federal Trade Commission.* To ensure market competitiveness, over the last century the United States has passed numerous pieces of legislation to encourage competition by preventing monopolies. These acts come under the jurisdiction of the Federal Trade Commission and the Antitrust division of the Justice Department.

   Generally these laws apply to partners whose combined strength tends to hold a large share of the market. Smaller companies, not collectively holding a dominant market share, will have little or no concern. While not a written policy, a cooperative agreement will generally not attract attention if the market is less than $20 million within the natural geographic borders of the partnership.

   Any restraint of competition between participants, especially concerning price fixing, geographic division or allocation of markets, and consequently depriving the public of the benefits of a competitive marketplace, could be construed to violate the law. Joint ventures cannot be used to deprive other competitors of a vital resource and cripple other competitors.

   The Justice Department has looked upon joint ventures far more favorably than mergers, and has been removing unwarranted regulatory obstacles blocking the formation of joint ventures. They tend to favor specific, project-oriented ventures best. Collaborative research, even among industry giants, is encouraged, particularly when the research is shared among all the joint venturers. J. Paul McGrath, head of the Justice Department's Antitrust Division has said joint ventures "will play a vital role in promoting the growth and international competitiveness of the American economy."

The policy of the Justice Department (which is always subject to change) is currently:

- Size: The joint venture is not too large if enough companies not involved in the venture could finance four comparable ventures. And even larger ventures could pass clearance if the cooperative arrangement would achieve otherwise unattainable efficiencies that would outweigh anticompetitive concerns.
- Benefit: The public economy must benefit from the formation of the joint venture.
- Market: Many markets are viewed as global in size, particularly in research and development ventures. Stricter guidelines are applied in production and service ventures. However, the joint venture between Toyota and General Motors is an excellent example of the flexibility of the Justice Department's interpretation of the size of the market.
- Exclusivity: R&D ventures should not prohibit members from conducting their own internal research.

The Justice Department is open to arguments by potential partners, even in very concentrated marketplaces, particularly if the partners can show gains in production efficiency or the creation of new, competitive technologies.

Joint ventures are not inherently subject to notification, but anything that could reduce the risk of competition could be subject to scrutiny. If, after notification, neither regulatory agency offers objections, then the venture can be formed. Strategic alliances not forming a separate legal entity are generally outside of the purview of antitrust, unless restraint of trade may be involved.

Be careful when forecasting future prices of products or supplies in joint ventures. The Justice Department has taken the position, from time to time, that this may be a form of price signaling to partners who may also be competitors.

3. *Securities and Exchange Commission.* The U.S. Securities and Exchange Commission regulates the amount and nature of offerings of equity to outside investors. If a public stock offering or a private placement of partnership shares is made in addition to the infusion of capital by the corporate partners, certain regulations will be in effect. Also, each state has its own securities laws that must be complied with—a process called "blue skying."

4. *Small Business Administration.* When a small business sells equity to a larger corporation with over $5 million in net worth, *and* the small business holds any SBA-guaranteed loans, the joint venture could become ineligible for SBA loan guarantees. (SBA tends to be lenient if the larger corporation's investment represents 20 percent or less of the small company's ownership.)

5. *Registration of Foreign Investment.* If any foreign business owns more than 5 percent of a U.S. business, it must register under the foreign investment act. A joint venture between a U.S. and foreign company may require registration.

6. *Export Controls.* The U.S. Dept. of Commerce oversees the regulation of exports of products as well as information to virtually every country in the world for the purpose of protecting national security and supporting foreign policy. All business alliances involving U.S. exports come under this jurisdiction. While product exports are of concern *after* the formation of a venture, information exchange *during negotiations* (including plant visits and data transfer) may also require a permit. Seemingly innocent products and manufacturing processes may be strictly prohibited for export to certain countries, and the regulations are modified weekly. U.S. companies forming alliances in foreign countries are also liable for penalties if their joint venture off-spring reveal restricted information, even if a foreign company controls the venture.

If a joint venture is organized or operates in a foreign country, the laws of that foreign sovereignty may prevail. Some countries limit outside investors to less than 50% holding in a joint venture. However, foreign industrial policies are likely to change quickly. Russia, for example, abruptly changed its Joint Venture Decrees in December 1988 to allow up to 100% foreign ownership under certain conditions. The Russians are primarily seeking outside financing, technology, and Western management methods. The Chinese also encourage joint venture investment, but have recently begun revising their policies. Chinese joint ventures have suffered from government bureaucracy that imposes constraints on efficient operations. Workers may be chosen by the government, and the joint venture operators may not have the opportunity to give incentives or fire incompetents. The Communist party may meddle in the affairs of the business, may overstaff the venture, and may place a substantial tariff on workers' wages. Taking profits out of the country may also be quite difficult.

8

Structuring the Venture

A relationship must be for equitable long-term success. Each party must benefit equally.

—Alan Grabene, Micro Linear Corp.

Once the strategic "fit" seems right, the financial analysis is satisfactory, and the preliminary negotiations are underway, it is time to consider the structure of your venture. This process deals with legal issues, organizational frameworks, distribution of risks and rewards, and the interrelationships among the sponsors and the venture itself.

The issue of *control* of the venture can also become a major priority at this stage. In this chapter the control issue is addressed and the options for control are explored.

If prospective partners carefully analyze, understand, and solve the problems of leadership and management while handling the equitable division of risk and reward, the issue of control is likely to be solved easily. However, if the control issue supercedes these other issues, a power game is likely to result, possibly destroying the venture before it begins. Beware.

The fundamental purpose of "structuring" is to successfully achieve three goals:

1. Integrate the *strategic "fit"* with the *operational "fit"* by choosing the right legal and organizational structures.
2. Create the proper *leadership* and *management* to drive the venture to success.
3. Fairly apportion the *risks* and *rewards* of the venture.

THE LEGAL STRUCTURE

Matching the proper legal structure with the alliance is important to ensure the commitments made are properly codified and are tailored to the unique nature of the venture. (The basic options are outlined here, then explored in greater depth in Chapters 9 and 10.)

Options

There are four basic options for the legal structure of the alliance: corporation, partnership, written contract, or handshake. The structure is chosen only after the basic objectives of the alliance are clearly identified, the risks and rewards agreed upon and apportioned fairly between the partners, and the operating principles tailored specifically to the needs of the partners. We explore the four basic options in general here. (Ultimately, competent legal counsel should be involved in the choice of legal structure.)

Joint Venture Corporation. The corporation is the most sophisticated and mature form of joint venture. It is normally structured as a "stand-alone" business and often selected when one or more of the following conditions exist:

- when the joint venture is large or complex enough to require a separate organizational entity with its own internal management;
- if it is advisable to contribute cash directly to the joint venture and, in return for the cash, the joint venture partners receive stock in the new company;
- when the joint venture's goal is long-term.

While this form is the most complicated to design, if the venture is large enough, it may also be the easiest to run.

One management difficulty inherent in any alliance is that executives of two or more companies must cooperate regularly. If, however, the companies form a separate joint venture corporation under independent management, there need be less discussion of the specifics of operations among sponsor CEOs. These operational specifics are then left to the operational managers of the joint venture thus freeing the founding CEOs to focus on strategic issues.

The corporate structure works best when given a certain amount of autonomy in operations, while being strategically driven by the founding partners. If strategic conditions change and the joint venture no longer benefits one of the partners, then stock in the joint venture can be sold, or the partner can withdraw from strategic control, while remaining a shareholder and still reaping financial reward from a successful venture.

TriStar pictures, the joint venture between HBO, CBS, and Columbia Pictures formed in 1982 with $300 million in capital from the founders, has been a notable success. It supplied HBO with an additional source of feature films, CBS with a source of films and a start in the cable industry, and Columbia Pictures with an extra studio and another source of films. TriStar operated on its own, allowing its managers to take advantage of market conditions.

This joint venture was remarkable not so much in what it supplied to the partners, but in how it took shape after two years. By 1984 it had issued securities on its own, so that the three original companies each owned 25 percent of TriStar, and the remaining 25 percent became public stock.

Partnership.   The partnership is a legal structure that simply allocates investment, profits, losses, and operational responsibilities, while maintaining the autonomy of the participants. Smaller, more entrepreneurial companies are more likely to select the partnership form than large multinational corporations.

The partnership has great flexibility in that it can be used when a separate organization with autonomous management is required, as well as when the alliance requires only a coordinating committee and no separate organization. Generally, the partnership itself will *own* something, such as a building, production technology, marketing rights, or manufacturing equipment.

The partnership form is most often selected when one or more of these conditions prevail:

- when the alliance is expected to last only three to five years (i.e., is project-oriented)

- if a separate *business entity* is desirable for the alliance, but a separate *organization* for management of the venture is not currently required, but may be needed in the future

- if high levels of commitment and interaction are necessary for short periods of time

The partnership form is probably the most widely chosen because it has the greatest range of flexibility in what is often an uncertain environment. For example, in high-technology industries with rapidly changing markets, companies must respond quickly to advances in technology if they are to remain viable competitors. A partnership is less complicated and more practical than other forms for what may be a somewhat short-term agreement, perhaps for only 36 months. Real estate joint ventures normally select this structure because it allows for equity participation by financial investors on a limited partnership basis while preserving the management control of the joint venture principals as general partners.

Partnership agreements are also more adaptable to creative allocations of benefits distribution. For example, a minority equity investor may receive a larger share of the distribution of profits if the partners deem it fair.

Tax considerations are the final reason for choosing the partnership form because, unlike the corporation, the partnership is not taxed doubly; the profits flow directly to the partners.

Contract/Written Agreement.   The written contract, even more simple in form than a partnership or corporation, is used to structure a *strategic alliance* because it maintains an arm's-length relationship between the parties. It outlines how revenue is divided, who is responsible for specific performance, who distributes items, confidentiality, and so on, but does not authorize any additional legal layers beyond those issues binding the parties together under contract. In addition, it does *not* establish a *separate business entity* for legal or tax purposes!

The written agreement is frequently used:

- for indefinite or short-term arrangements lasting under three years.
- when there is no foreseen need for a separate joint venture organization.
- when daily or very close coordination of operations is not required for the duration of the project.
- when capital investments are independently made by each of the separate partners within their own sides of the venture.
- when companies have not had prior close cooperative relations, thereby making a true joint venture too bold a move.

The written contract approach also has the advantage of permitting each company president to continue to run his own business with a great deal of autonomy. The character of each company and its individual personalities and styles require little or no change.

Service-based firms with high labor intensity and low capital equipment requirements also use this form of agreement. Sales representatives often use the written contract with manufacturing companies.

The length of the written agreement depends, to a certain extent, upon the level of trust among the partners. In one strategic alliance between a $15 million manufacturing company and a small technology development firm, the written agreement was only two-and-a-half pages long, spelling out the obligations, method of operations, communications, and time schedules. Appended to the contract were specifications for the technology. A year later, after working together, they then formed a joint venture, creating an independent business partnership that required a financial infusion to provide the necessary capital and a sharing of the risks and rewards of the venture.

Handshake.   Surprisingly, the handshake format is used far more often in strategic alliances than one might imagine, even in today's world of lawyers, liability, and litigation. The handshake form will typically be found in these circumstances:

- when the written contract form would otherwise be used
- when there is no need for a separate organization to run the alliance
- during an "interim period" before legal documents are drafted and signed, but when there is a need to commence a project
- when partners have so much trust in each other that legal documents seem superfluous

Generally, however, the handshake form is not recommended over the long haul. People change positions, changes in the economy or the market can put some partners under great financial strain, and memories fade. Add to these factors human nature's tendency to interpret any agreement to one's own advantage, and you can easily see how the handshake form, when used over a long period of time, can end in dispute. (In business law, a handshake can be interpreted as a binding contract.)

To every rule, notable exceptions always apply. In one substantial strategic alliance, a very large chemical corporation joined with a major paper manufacturer and a medium-sized plastics company to design, manufacture, and market a new disposable consumer product. The principals prefer confidentiality, but they confess there has never been a formal written agreement to consummate the pact.

Table 8.1 summarizes the choices for legal structure.

Criteria to Use in Choosing a Legal Structure

Choosing a legal structure should be accomplished with the advice of a lawyer. Each alliance is tailored to the specific prevailing circumstances. The following criteria can be used as a general guide in making the decision:

1. *Simplicity.* Use the simplest structure capable of meeting your needs. Don't form a corporation if the written contract will do.

2. *Number of Partners.* If the number of partners is three or less, and the alliance will probably not last for more than three to five years, the partnership or written contract may be sufficient. As the lifespan of the venture increases and the number of partners increase, the corporate form may become superior.

3. *Expected Longevity.* Alliances intended to last only a few years are probably better advised to use the written contract or partnership form, whereas longer-term ventures are best served when they use the corporate form.

4. *Tax Considerations.* If significant tax shelter is desirable, particularly for technology development where large losses or R&D investment tax credits are anticipated, a tax lawyer should be consulted for specific advice regarding the ways to maximize use of the tax

Table 8.1. Conditions for Choosing A Legal Structure

Alliance Type	Legal Form	Term	Separate Organization Req.	Autonomy	Control	Past Relations
Joint Venture	Corporation	Long	Yes	Med./High	Med./Low	Med./Long
	Partnership	Med./Long	Yes/No	Med./Low	Med./High	Short–Long
Strategic Alliance	Written contract	Short/Med.	No	Varies	Med./Low	Varies
	Handshake	Short/Indefinite	No	Varies	Varies	Varies

shelter. A legal structure that maximizes tax shelter may not be the best form to use to maximize other management efficiencies.

5. *Ease of Management.* Alliances that do not require a high degree of integration of planning, decision making, and operational integration over the long haul can use the written contract or partnership form effectively. However, if a high level of integration is required, only those companies with good abilities or experience with joint venture management should consider the partnership form; otherwise, the corporate form may be better because it forces stronger management.

6. *Capital Investment.* If significant capital investment is required, the partnership form may have far better tax effects than the corporation, but it may be easier to raise larger amounts of capital from the sale of stock in a corporation.

7. *Leadership, Management, Coordination, and Support.* These issues can make or break the alliance. Considerable attention must be given to them, regardless of the legal structure. The management systems should be clearly decided before the legal agreements are formally signed.

THE ORGANIZATIONAL STRUCTURE

Partners must decide how to build an organization that will provide effective leadership and management. The main consideration in any organizational structure will be to maximize its effectiveness. This suggests keeping it simple, with clear lines of authority and easy access to channels of communications and decisionmaking. Remember, alliances are not easy to manage; the more members of the venture, the more complex it is to manage. The first step is to choose between an informal and a formal detached organizational structure.

Informal Organization

The informal option is suitable for all strategic alliances and those joint ventures where a separate organization will not be created. With the informal structure, a *steering committee* or loose confederation of people from within each company is assigned to coordinate functions for the alliance. This informal organization does not require the sponsors to consider the dependency relationship issue that joint ventures with separate detached organizations must deal with.

Formal " Detached" Organization

The "detached" option applies to those joint ventures (partnership and corporate formats) that establish a separate organization owned and operated by the sponsors. Here, the new organization is staffed independently from the sponsoring companies. A board of directors or steering committee is appointed by the sponsors to coordinate activities.

The detached organizational structure is best suited for conditions requiring highly integrated management, long-term commitment, and entailing high levels of uncertainty and ambiguity. The detached structure is also used for ventures expecting to tackle multiple projects or having long-term objectives, requiring extremely close coordination during the entire term of the venture.

DETACHED ORGANIZATIONAL DEPENDENCY RELATIONSHIPS

Strategic alliances and joint ventures that do not set up independent, autonomous organizations need not be concerned about the dependency relationship between the alliance and its sponsors. However, if a detached organization with separate management is established (those using the corporate form, and some partnership forms), the dependency relationship is crucial and must be addressed by the sponsors.

The Right Mix of Autonomy, Support, and Control

The joint venture with the detached organization will initially be dependent upon and subordinate to the parent companies. The nature of this dependency relationship and how it evolves over time will be the result of the proportions of *autonomy, support,* and *control* provided as the venture grows and develops.

Autonomy enables the managers of the venture to take responsibility and be rewarded for their initiative. However, too much autonomy at the wrong times can lead to the venture failing to satisfy the needs for which it was designed, or it may allow the venture to drift too far out of control.

Support is always a critical item. Without it, the venture will be undernourished and probably will wither. Support may take the form of dollars, human resources, technical assistance, access to information, business connections, or effective performance review.

Control prevents the venture from going awry when the projections are not met, or when the joint venture business begins to fail and must be salvaged. At that point, one partner (usually the one with the greatest risk) may need to step in and control the management more carefully. If insurmountable problems emerge, provisions should be made for one party to assume control or buy out the venture.

The mixture of autonomy, support, and control will determine the dependency relationship between the sponsors and the joint venture organization itself. Essentially, detached joint venture organizations tend to follow five patterns of dependency, and sponsors are wise to discuss, select, and guide their venture along the dependency guidelines they feel best meet their needs. Understand, however, that just as a child matures into adulthood, a detached joint venture organization also matures. And, just as the types of control, autonomy, and support a parent provides to a young child are vastly different from that provided to a young adult, so must the sponsors of detached joint venture organizations realize that any long-term alliance will naturally tend to travel through a dependency continuum as it matures. As this passage progresses, the mix of control, autonomy, and support must also change to fit the needs of the sponsors and the venture itself.

It is useful to view the dependency relationship from the perspective of five patterns (see Figure 8.1).

Pattern 1: Dependent/Captive Venture.   The captive venture is akin to a corporate subsidiary except that it is owned by two partners instead of a single parent company. The captive venture is designed to: 1) supply its

Figure 8.1.   Dependency Patterns

Pattern 5.
INDEPENDENT/MATURE VENTURE

Pattern 1. DEPENDENT/CAPTIVE VENTURE	Pattern 4. INTERDEPENDENT/ COOPERATIVE VENTURE
Pattern 2. COUNTERDEPENDENT/ CONFLICTIVE VENTURE	Pattern 3. CODEPENDENT/ CONSTRAINED VENTURE

owners with a product or materials, or 2) be their distribution arm in the marketplace. Owners control the prices, supplies, and markets. The captive venture will be dependent upon its sponsors, just as a child is dependent upon its parents.

If the sponsors of the captive venture are to supply a large amount of the venture's resources (money, personnel, materials, products, and the like), provision should be made to ensure these resources will be of the best quality and will not exceed market prices. Otherwise, the venture will be subject to exploitation by its owners. Under these circumstances the captive will become unprofitable and cause the eventual destruction of the venture, or the relationship between the owners, or both.

This was the principle reason for the break-up of a long-term joint venture between Dow Chemical and Asahi Chemical of Japan. Asahi was to supply the joint venture with low-cost feed stocks. However, after more than a decade of successful operations, the cost of products changed in Japan, and Asahi could not sell at a price competitive to other sources in the United States. Dow wanted to maximize its profits by lowering material costs, and Asahi wanted to increase its sales. Ultimately, the joint venture was terminated by having Asahi purchase Dow's portion of the alliance for $185 million.

The converse is also true for ventures that supply their sponsor with a product. The venture should not supply any products to its owners at prices higher than the market, and the sponsors should not have to respect any agreements to purchase exclusively from the venture if the market price is exceeded. Sponsors should also protect themselves and the venture from being locked into arrangements for purchase or transfer of obsolete or outmoded equipment.

Captive ventures lacking proper cost controls run the chance of becoming fat and flabby as a result of too much isolation and insufficient external competitive pressure. To prevent this potential flabbiness, some sponsors encourage the venture to sell or supply to secondary markets that do not compete with the sponsors.

Example: Two cable television companies formed a joint venture to purchase a wire manufacturer in order to produce coaxial cable for their installations. The two partners were to be supplied the cable at 5 percent below market price, providing the joint venture cable manufacturer could sell profitably at this discounted price. However, if either of the partners could find cable at a lower price, they were not obligated to purchase from their manufacturer—an arrangement that kept their manufacturer competitive. The cable manufacturer was obligated to supply its sponsors first, but since there was excess production capacity, the cable manufacturer also sold cable at full price to other market buyers, thereby enhancing the profit margins and maximizing plant efficiency.

The venture was a success, and the cable manufacturer then made an acquisition of another company, this time a screw-machine company that manufactured the coaxial cable fittings for the cable. The joint venture manufacturer then began penetrating other markets, particularly in the military/aerospace field, until the proportion of business from the original sponsors became less than half of the total sales. By that time the cable manufacturer was contributing to the sponsors not only below-market-priced cable, but also significant annual cash flow.

The captive venture tends to be most effective in large, slowly changing, capital-intensive industries such as manufacturing, oil, chemicals, and mining. In faster-moving industries, such as consumer electronics or computers, a more flexible structure may be desirable. If so, a captive/dependent venture must have the opportunity for transition to another pattern.

Pattern 2: Counterdependent/Conflictive Venture. The conflictive venture often occurs when a captive joint venture is managed by an entrepreneur who desires to break free and become far more independent, in opposition to the owners who want to maintain high levels of control or limit the extent of the venture's operations. The owners often fear the venture will become competitive with the founding companies. In its effort to break free of the "parents," the venture may begin to exhibit an almost adolescent behavior, bucking the control of the sponsors, communicating less frequently, and avoiding close coordination.

This counterdependency can be the natural result of a joint venture designed to provide products or services to the originating sponsors. As long as the sponsors demand the entire capacity of the venture, all is well. But if the market diminishes, or if the venture's managers become entrepreneurial and desire more profits (especially if they are on a profit-sharing plan), or if the manager sees a far greater market that the sponsors do not wish to enter, the venture managers may look to other customers to fulfill their excess capacity.

Example: Two real estate development companies formed a joint venture to market leased space and manage a number of their properties. The sponsors established a separate organization to tackle this activity, and hired an aggressive and entrepreneurial manager who quickly excelled at the task. He established a very effective organization of talented and spirited personnel.

In order to keep these talented people, however, it was necessary for the manager to create opportunities for career growth within the joint venture, which required increasing sales and finding new accounts. Soon it became apparent that this entrepreneurial spirit, so desirable at the venture's conception, now put enormous pressures on the venture because the owners did not want their staff working to help their competitors lease space, nor did they wish to dilute the emphasis on their own properties. The venture's manager proposed that the sponsors purchase more property for him to manage, but the sponsors were not confident of their ability to raise significant equity capital to purchase buildings, and furthermore they wanted to build new structures rather than purchase existing ones.

Eventually, friction increased between the venture's manager and the sponsors. Rather than fire such a successful manager, the sponsors sold the venture to the manager in a leveraged buyout, and signed contracts with their former venture to continue its marketing and management role as an independent entity.

When the sponsors reiterate their desire for the venture to remain captive and passive, a clampdown usually results, and sometimes an order is given to management to begin disassembling their programs. Conflict normally results. More often than not, the venture is then doomed to failure because neither the owners nor the managers can find satisfactory resolution to their desires. Only in the minority of situations is there a happy ending, and when it happens, it is usually the result of the entrepreneurial manager buying the interests of the sponsors.

Pattern 3: Codependent/Constrained Venture. The constrained venture exists when the partners maintain parallel production facilities in their own operations as well as in the joint venture itself, or when one of the partners has not given up its entire product line to the venture.

Codependent ventures are very often an effective method designed as a short-term, interim approach enabling the sponsors to continue production while the joint venture is gearing up production or if the two sponsors are using the joint venture as a bridge to an eventual merger or acquisition. As a safety measure, the partners often maintain their parallel facilities until it is clear that all the venture's production problems are resolved. Then sponsors begin a phase-out, as the venture completes its phase-in.

Problems begin to occur, however, if the sponsors retain their parallel facilities over the long-term. In this event, the venture becomes constrained—a mish-mash, similar to running a three-legged race. The venture is not provided with enough support to survive on its own, not provided with enough autonomy to exist as a real business, and is held back with too much control. This situation usually occurs because the venture was not properly conceived at the beginning; the partners probably had major reservations when they commenced operations. They never fully believed in the venture. Therefore, they hedged their bets by keeping certain critical resources in their own camps. Fear of losing a critical pre-existing strategic leverage point, such as market access or a source of supply, can create the conditions for failure of the venture.

> *Example:* In the medical industry, one very successful joint venture resulted when a medical company with strong marketing and distribution areas joined a genetics company to create a new product to diagnose the AIDS disease. The medical company contributed to the venture an entire division composed of pharmaceutical production facilities, a direct sales force, and linkage to international markets. This unconstrained contribution gave the venture sufficient resources and autonomy to rapidly enter and capture the market, in marked contrast to other far less impressive constrained ventures operated by competitors in the industry.

Pattern 4: Interdependent/Cooperative Venture.   The cooperative venture is probably the most common example of the successful joint venture, when it is sufficiently supported with strong backing from the partners. This interest enables them to exercise careful control while, at the same time, giving the venture's managers the autonomy to be both entrepreneurial and profitable.

Cooperative ventures are often permitted to freely sell to outside markets, but with a "most favored customer" status for the sponsors. The interdependent venture usually maintains a continued strong strategic linkage with the sponsors, and equity capital requirements may still be underwritten by the owners.

> *Example:* A city restaurant had produced its cakes and pasteries within its own facilities for a number of years. However, when the baker planned to retire, the restaurant owners knew their tight labor market

would make it difficult to hire another person for the job. In addition, the restaurant's baking facilities were becoming outmoded and were far too small for the growing business. The restaurant had excellent recipes and a fine, longstanding reputation.

Another very small country bakery about 10 miles away, run by a young entrepreneur who had little management experience, had established a loyal wholesale trade, supplying bread, fudge, and cookies to grocery stores and other restaurants. Like the city restaurant, the country bakery was outgrowing its facilities. The two formed a joint venture, leasing a former pizza parlor that had a number of ovens and a loading ramp in the rear.

At the beginning, the restaurant and the bakery were codependent—each maintained their separate facilities—while a new baker was being trained by the joint venture and new accounts were being solidified based upon the reputation of the two partners. As the joint venture matured, the partners, rather than maintaining parallel production facilities, merged their facilities into the new bakery, contributing fully with their recipes, equipment, and a few personnel. The increased size and scale then enabled them to hire sales and administrative staff, resulting in phenomenal sales growth—a fully coordinated and interdependent joint venture.

Interdependent ventures may not always remain in this mode as market conditions, strategic imperatives, competition, and internal leadership change.

Pattern 5: Independent/Freewheeling or Mature Venture.   The freewheeling venture is not merely born. It is the result of a careful, long-term strategy, nurturing an interdependent joint venture into a self-sustaining level of maturity capable of being spun off from the sponsors. Management will move from an entrepreneurial style into a more corporate management style of operations. The venture, at this stage, is given a high degree of autonomy and low levels of control and support. (See Table 8.2)

The Mature Venture may even be competitive with its founders, a circumstance that does not alarm those secure sponsors who see the mature venture as a means of gaining financial rewards as equity owners and keeping the industry alive through competitive challenges.

Example: Some striking examples of independent joint ventures are Libby–Owens–Ford, Dow–Corning, Owens–Corning, and Tri-Star Pictures. In many mature ventures, the strategic linkage diminishes and

capital growth requirements are satisfied by the venture's internal profitability and balance sheet strength.

LEADERSHIP AND MANAGEMENT STRUCTURE

The "Champion"

Each parent organization must provide support in the form of continued
strategic and *operational* leadership. The person who ensures this support, the "champion," is often a CEO, board chairman, or executive/senior
vice president. In addition to the "champion," a project manager with
expert management and coordinating skills must be selected from within
each company to handle internal operations.

More often than not, the champion then serves on a steering committee
with other representatives of the sponsoring companies and the top members of the venture's operational management team. (These roles are detailed further in Chapter 11.)

The Steering Committee

Crucial to the ultimate success of the venture are good communications,
support, and control by the sponsoring partners. By conducting frequent
reviews of the venture, the partners are able to generate confidence and
trust in one another, thereby maximizing the ability of the alliance to produce the expected results.

For corporate joint ventures, this guidance is provided through a board

Table 8.2. Summary of Organizational Patterns

Pattern	Decision Autonomy	Coordination Required	Owner Control	Support by Owners	Self-Sufficiency	Entrepreneurship
Captive	Low	High	High	High	Low	Low
Conflictive	Mixed	Mixed	Mixed	Mixed	Mixed	Mixed
Constrained	Mixed	Mixed	Mixed	Mixed	Low	Low
Cooperative	Medium	Medium	Medium	Medium	Medium	Medium
Freewheeling	High	Low	Low	Low	High	High

of directors; other forms of alliances often refer to this group as a steering, coordinating, or project review committee. Regardless of the name, the principles of operation are the same. (For the sake of discussion we will call this guiding group a "steering committee.") The steering committee's purpose is to oversee the total project. Its members are responsible for suggesting and approving changes to the operational plan, but the steering committee may not necessarily have the right to reduce its budget without full and complete agreement from the partners.

The number of people on the steering committee can vary, but it is often an odd number—three, five, or seven—weighted slightly in favor of the sponsor who bears most of the venture's risk or who has operational control. Sometimes a third party, such as an experienced executive or technical consultant respected by all parties, is included as a neutral member (or mediator, if one is needed). A prototypical steering committee will be composed of the champions (top support managers from each of the sponsors); venture manager (the first in command as leader/project coordinator involved in operating the venture), and operational or technical managers (the second in command in the venture).

Steering committees usually meet on a regular and predetermined basis, often weekly or bi-weekly, but usually no less frequently than monthly, and at any time requested by a member. (The role of the steering committee is explored in greater detail in Chapter 11.)

Key Personnel

One additional important point should be addressed in joint ventures that set up a separate, detached organization. When each partner contributes key personnel to the venture, the legal agreements should specify what will happen to these valued individuals should one partner exercise a buyout provision, or if a partner chooses to exit the venture. Lawyers will often advise that these personnel should remain with the venture in order to protect the investment, particularly if the people are one of the venture's principal assets.

PROJECT VERSUS GOAL ORIENTATION

Two patterns of focus tend to emerge in alliances, depending upon the nature of the strategy and tasks. *Project-oriented* alliances, such as building construction or the manufacturing and marketing of an existing product, tend to have *higher levels of certainty and clarity*. These ventures, by their very nature, enable their managers to make more definite and specific commitments of money, manpower, materials, and market resources. *Risks are relatively predictable and quantifiable.* Timetables are better adhered to, and roles are generally more specifically delineated. Before beginning the alliance it is obvious to the founders what the specific, measurable results will be required for the project to be considered successful.

Project orientation enables managers to become focused on performance results. For instance, in the health care field, a particular intravenous delivery system might be matched with a particular drug, or a specific electronic diagnostic system might be matched with a particular instrument.

On the other hand, *goal-oriented alliances* tend to deal with much *higher levels of uncertainty,* where the desired result may not be clear in everyone's mind until well into the venture. For example, in the application of lasers into the factory automation industry, a joint venture may identify at its inception a number of obstacles to be overcome as well as some promising potential solutions. However, it may take years for the solutions to become workable, and the technical team may meet innummerable dead ends until a practical solution is found.

These goal-oriented ventures are often research and development related—open-ended affairs with very high risks and lower success rates because of the greater ambiguity and uncertainty levels at conception. Project-oriented ventures are more often described as a "success" statistically than their goal-oriented counterparts. Orchestrators of successful goal-oriented ventures often divide their objectives into very discrete and measurable performance milestones to give the feel and manageability of a project orientation. If these milestones and performance criteria are not met, clauses may be written into the agreements to enable a partner to debark from the alliance, or to allow the alliance to terminate. Many companies with considerable joint venture experience avoid the management difficulties inherent in broad research and product development alliances, leaving those tasks for in-house R&D staffs.

SPREADING RISK AND REWARD

The proper division of risk and reward serves not only the doctrine of fairness in an alliance, but it creates the proper long-term motivation, an absolutely essential ingredient for success.

Why Risk Is So Vital to Success

Insurance salespeople know the power of "fear of loss." Bankers would rather make loans to small businesses secured by the personal guarantee of the owner. Venture capitalists want to keep entrepreneurs lean and mean. What do these three segments of the business community know about risk and reward that is useful to the designer of an alliance?

The insurance salesperson knows that all people fear loss and, for most people, fear of loss is a greater motivator than expectation of gain. The salesperson knows people want to protect their interests and will work hard to pay for insurance to prevent losing the assets they have struggled to obtain.

The banker, whose professional rules require the acceptance of virtually no risk, dramatically increases the chances of getting a loan repaid in full by requiring a business owner to personally guarantee the company's loan or to secure the loan with a second mortgage on the owner's house. The banker knows from experience that the loan stands a far greater chance of being repaid in full when the material possessions of the entrepreneur are at risk daily, and that a business owner will work twice as hard to avoid losing his or her home and material gains.

In the entrepreneurial world, the venture capitalist will refrain from putting cash directly into the pockets of a struggling entrepreneur (through repayments of personal loans, salary increases, and so on). Instead, venture capitalists prefer to channel their investments completely into the company. Even if an entrepreneur has put his home up as collateral for company loans and has every penny of his life savings in the company, few venture capitalists will let their investment capital go toward any form of repayment of personal debts. The venture capitalist knows maintaining these risks will keep the entrepreneur working twice as hard to achieve success and build the value of his company.

Vested Interest Motivation

These illustrations demonstrate the value of "vested interest motivation," one of the vital principles that increase the chance of success of a joint venture. Many alliances have failed when they lost their motivation once the top management of the sponsor changed. It was too easy to pull back from the venture and deploy resources elsewhere because the "threshold of exit risk" was too low.

Paul Lawrence of the Harvard Business School advises that, if long-term motivation by top management is desired, "be sure both long-term risk thresholds and long-term reward thresholds are sufficient to keep the partners engaged." Take away the risk from one of the partners, and the chances are great that the venture will fade away, particularly if one of the individuals who created the venture must leave the parent company.

Before inking a deal, be sure both you and your partner have *vested interest motivation* sufficient to give the entire team the desire to win. Also consider how to keep the operating managers motivated. Alliances frequently will include a profit-sharing provision for their top operations team.

Protecting Your Partner

Earlier, we discussed the importance of ethics and trust. When developing the final structure of the venture, it is critical to understand the risks your partner will be undertaking. These risks are not always financial; many will be somewhat intangible—fear of failure, career patterns in jeopardy, lost opportunities, and the unknowns of how the project's management will fare.

Equally important are the fears and risks of the operational managers. Their career patterns may be dramatically altered; some will experience the agony and ecstacy of entrepreneurship for the first time. Others will be cast into situations with new bosses, new reward systems, and new reporting mechanisms. Along with these changes will come fears and concerns that need to be voiced. When these fears are stated for the first time, either before or after the deal is signed, it is important to understand the reason: Your partner will be concerned about all the things that can go wrong and how you will respond. Undoubtedly you and your managers are concerned about similar things.

The key is understanding your partner's needs, concerns, corporate values, long- and short-term objectives, and communicating your own corporate needs. These concerns must be accommodated, both during negotiations and during operations. It is best to talk over these issues and to understand them well, for they will probably emerge in numerous forms during the course of the alliance. Let's look at a very special set of "protection rules" governing joint ventures and strategic alliances.

Protection Rule #1: Protect Your Partner.   Successful joint venturers seem to agree: *Don't let your partner get screwed.* If you fail to abide by this rule, you will regret it later. Joint venturing is not camel trading in a Near East bazaar. Negotiating a deal is a power expansion game: $1 + 1 = 3$. If you think you can short-change your partner to get a bigger piece of the pie for yourself, or if you think your partner will "do it to you," then get out of the deal before it collapses; because it will eventually be undermined by lack of trust.

Protection Rule #2: Maintain Fairness and Harmony. If, for some reason, unanticipated at the consummation of the venture, one of the partners carries an inordinate burden—perhaps the technology takes twice as much money as planned, labor strikes delay the delivery of goods, or government regulations prevent permits for a new building—then the partners are advised to *consider rearranging the risk-reward ratio to bring the venture back into harmony.* Those new to alliances will be surprised how often this rearrangement of terms occurs based only on trust and a handshake. A partner in a major accounting firm once commented that greed is the motivation for most business dealings. However, greed is a hidden killer; in alliances, cooperation, not greed, creates opportunity for gain.

Protection Rule #3: Protect Yourself. As important as it is to protect your partner, it is equally important to protect your own interests in a joint venture. *Only a fool or a martyr would give away more than is fair.*

Protection Rule #4: Memories Fade. Handshakes are the most admirable form of business agreement. However, as days pass into weeks and weeks into years, the original intentions of the handshake are bound to be forgotten. For the sake of maintaining a successful venture, *put terms and agreements in writing.*

DISTRIBUTION ISSUES

Distribution relates to the allocation of the "4 Rs" of structuring: Responsibilities, Resources, Risks, and Rewards. Ultimately, the central issue in structuring the alliance will be how to distribute these factors fairly. They will need to be tailored to the particular needs of the alliance; each has its own unique script.

The final agreement may be somewhat lengthy, but at the early negotiations stage, most distribution arrangements are conceptually short, basic, and easy to understand. Eventually, as negotiations progress, more detail is examined, organizational issues are discussed, and potential problems are raised for analysis. Several distribution questions should be weighed during the venture's early stages:

- Who invests cash, and how much?
- Who invests time, and how much?
- Who receives rights to:
    market or distribute products?
    manufacture products?
    acquire or license technology?
    purchase future products or technology?
- Who receives tax benefits?
- Who is responsible for specific accomplishments?
- What happens if more money is needed?
- How are the profits (and losses) allocated?
- How is confidential information handled?
- What products are specifically included/excluded?
- What are the patent provisions?
- What are the guidelines for termination or revision?
- Are there any government regulations that should be considered?

The Issue of Control

As the prospective teammates begin to understand who contributes resources, who assumes responsibilities, who takes on risks, and who receives rewards, the foundation is laid for discussion of control. Partners who jump too quickly into control questions will find the negotiations begin to center around power issues without due consideration of the fundamentals of leadership responsibility, resource allocation, risk, and reward.

DIVIDING THE PIE: WHO HAS CONTROL?

Three Principles of Division

Three principles come to bear when partners look to dividing the pie. Each venture will weigh these elements differently:

- *Operational Control.* Whoever is responsible for the results of the venture will want operational control; otherwise, that job is exceedingly difficult. Operational control can be placed in the hands of a minority owner, particularly if they are most qualified to contribute effective management resources to the venture. A special consideration is often given for this contribution, frequently in the form of preferential cash returns (i.e., profit sharing) or a larger piece of the equity.

If one partner has less than 20 to 25 percent of the equity in a joint venture, seldom does that partner receive operating control. These partners are usually considered passive financial investors rather than participating partners. (The exception to this rule is when there are three or more partners, and no partner holds 50 percent or more of the ownership.)

· *Ownership of Equity.* The holder of the largest risk or the largest contributor of cash is commonly given the largest equity share of a joint venture. (Strategic alliances do not have equity interests because no separate business entity is created.) If the largest equity owner does not have operational control, this "power" member will typically insist on being involved in the decisionmaking with the "operating" member, usually through the board of directors.

· *Distribution of Rewards.* The cash flow, tax benefits, and capital appreciation of the venture must be divided, with the largest reward usually going to the parties making the largest contribution toward the success of the venture. When using the partnership or written contract structure, the cash flow, tax benefits, and capital appreciation can be divided in any manner the partners prefer. Publicly held corporations who must satisfy stockholders' demands for quarterly dividends as well as thinly capitalized entrepreneurial companies when they participate in joint ventures may want short-term cash flow, giving longer-term rewards to partners who desire capital appreciation and balance sheet strength. When using the corporate structure for the joint venture, uneven divisions, common in the partnership structure, are more impracticable.

Methods of Dividing Ownership and Control

Joint ventures are faced with the challenge of dividing ownership and control, while strategic alliances circumvent this problem because each member of a strategic alliance must establish the benefits internally for themselves. On the surface, it may appear that the strategic alliance has an easier time dealing with control. But because the issues are sublimated, the strategic alliance avoids directly addressing the issue, and as a result, it can lack the "punch and power" of a well-designed joint venture.

Joint ventures have evolved into three basic frameworks to divide the ownership among the partners.

1. "Superior–Subordinate" division.   *Method of Functioning:* This division is usually a 51–49 split (or other percentages that give one party clear control of the venture, such as 70–30). In this framework, the equity, operational control, and distribution of rewards generally reflect the majority/minority posture throughout. It is used more for high risk ventures. The board of directors is inherently ceremonial and used for information passing.

Advantages: Clearly the advantage in this format is the clarity of decision making, the ability to make rapid adjustments, the understanding of who is responsible and in charge. Generally it has a higher rate of success.

Disadvantages: The minority party may not have long-term "vested interest motivation," may feel railroaded, or may become passive or disgruntled. Under the worst conditions, the majority party may even (intentionally or unintentionally) take advantage of the minority member. It may imply a lack of a clear, unified vision for the venture, or there may not be an effective method of resolving differences.

If one sponsor's operational skills are critical to success and the other's are not essential, then choose this option. Control Data Corporation, with over 80 joint ventures and cooperative agreements under its belt, says that 50–50 deals do not work. They feel the advantages of clear lines of authority provides the "only way to manage." With this method, one sponsor is responsible for operating the venture, and the other sponsors hold the operator accountable for performance.

Use this approach where there are very crisp and distinct corporate or cultural differences, as between a U.S. company and a small third-world company, especially if the foreign partner has little experience and no strong knowledge of the product or technology, and is agreeable to be a rather passive partner or financial investor. The Superior/Subordinate framework is often used in high risk situations where rapid decision making is essential.

2. "Equal Balance" division.   *Method of Functioning:* This framework usually provides a 50–50 split in the entire working relationship (or 33–33–33 in a tripartite venture) and assumes 50–50 contribution, decision-making, and control. In this division, nothing happens unless consensus exists among the partners; all must agree or hash out their differences until there is agreement. It assumes that partners will always be able to work out these differences, and that operational managers have excellent human skills to assist the owners in effective consensus decisionmaking. Both companies are represented equally on the board or steering committee, setting strategy for the joint venture together, and making operating decisions together.

Advantages: The 50–50 arrangement helps promote active engagement by both parties to the venture. This format is best suited to companies having a strong *common vision* for the joint venture, similar corporate cultures, and preferably, a congenial personal relationship at the top echelons. It is used often when both parties have equally vital contributions of technology or expertise. This method ensures each owner's support, resources, and input, and forces commitment to the success of the venture.

Disadvantages: Unfortunately, as seen frequently in partnerships, the Equal Balance division can have serious drawbacks if not carefully managed:

- Stalemate may occur among the partners when disagreements arise. To avoid conflicts, partners may avoid addressing problems. The Equal Balance division requires great skill in problemsolving and excellent relations between the partners. If an intractable stalemate occurs, divorce or buyout may be the only solution.
- Seldom is there ever a real 50–50 division of contribution, leadership, risk, and reward. One partner may perceive the other to have failed in his or her contribution, especially when the venture may not be working out successfully.
- Equal Balance can lead to the assumption that the other party will manage something, and permit problems to inadvertently "slip through the cracks" when both parties make the same erroneous assumption.
- If conditions change too rapidly, shared decisionmaking can become a serious obstacle.

Some managers believe all that shared control really guarantees is the right to fight. On the other hand, Harvard's Paul Lawrence comments that the Equal Balance division forces discussions and keeps the partners in an open problemsolving mode. But, he warns:

"If people cannot seem to get their marching orders clear, if there is vacillation, if the word is inconsistent, if what you are supposed to do

depends upon who you ask, then the 50–50 split may not be advisable
... but conversely the 51–49 split may just temporarily mask more
fundamental problems and create a one-up/one-down relationship. If
the difficulties are grating now, what happens three years from now
when the priorities change?"

Others, such as Arthur Young's Jim Needham, caution against the 50–50
split, advising that it causes many problems and can result in bitter disagreements and business stagnation. Control Data's Chairman, William
Norris, distinguishes ownership from operational control; he says: "Be
sure that one partner is in charge. You can have a 50–50 ownership, but
you have to have it very clear who is going to run it."[1]

Statistically, the likelihood of success for the Equal Balance division is
not as good as the Superior/Subordinate method unless the partners have
a history of working together, or a history of collaboration with others, or
if they come from very similar corporate cultures. Some Equal Balance
partnerships have worked well, particularly when the partners are familiar and comfortable with decentralized decisionmaking, and they provide
the support and time commitment to manage the relationship.

This method keeps the sponsors actively involved, especially if the nature of the venture requires active, full-time involvement—the sponsors
can be ready to adjust, reorient, and adapt faster if they are fully involved
and have understood and supported the decisions that have led to the
present predicament. It requires initial trust and common vision among
the top managers, continued support as the venture progresses, and giving the venture's general manager a good dose of operational autonomy
so he does not get his or her legs tied.

Some Equal Balance joint ventures, to avoid stalemating, will have an
outside advisor sit in on the steering committee meetings to ensure that
problems are thoroughly addressed in a timely manner and that mutually
agreeable solutions are achieved.

3. *"Majority Rule" division.* *Method of Functioning:* This framework is
an adaptation of the equal balance method that brings in a smaller shareholder, usually a minority contributing partner, who acts as a tiebreaker
in the event that the two other partners stalemate. This type of arrangement is often structured as a 45–45–10 split, or some similar variation
(i.e., 33–33–33). Decisions are made by thrashing around a problem until
unanimity and consensus occurs (seldom does the partnership actually
"vote" on a business matter). Skilled managers know that the process of
good team problemsolving serves to build consensus and communica-

tions, resulting in stronger teamwork among the partners. Often this method has one strong operator, but tends to involve the minority partners to a larger extent than the other options.

Sometimes the minority third party is an expert or a neutral who contributes no money to the venture but, because of technical or market knowledge or connections, can be of great value to its successful operation. The expert third party usually receives less than 5 percent of the venture's equity, while a contributing minority may receive a larger percentage.

Advantages: The Majority Rule framework enables both principal partners to remain actively engaged in the venture, like that of the Equal Balance method, without the problems of stalemated decisions.

Disadvantages: The selection of the right minority party is critical. It may also be difficult to keep the minority/third party sufficiently motivated if they may have too small a stake in the venture. If the structure is multipartied (three or more parties), the operational control mechanisms may become difficult to manage unless clear lines of authority and decisionmaking are designated.

Harry Levinson, author of *The Exceptional Executive* and *Executive Stress*, suggests using a third party with no stake in the venture when there are clear structural reasons for bringing things into balance, or when two companies with widely different styles of management are joining together such as a Japanese–American venture.

One of the best reasons for having several partners in a joint venture is to permit the venture organization and its managers to operate at arm's length from the partners. "One of the values of having four partners— none of whom control it—is that control really does reside in the management of the partnership. They understand the venture has to be quick and nimble, and I don't think you can do that if you have to check with four people all the time," says Frank Heffron of AT&T's Covidea joint venture.[2]

The majority rule approach is best if the owners have a past cooperative working relationship, similar management cultures, and high trust among CEOs.

Variations on Ownership and Control

Different versions and variations of joint ventures combine these methods of division. In international joint ventures with developing countries, operational control can be quite different from equity control. Emerging countries with legal constraints preventing foreign companies from owning 50 percent or more of a domestic company has caused the formation of numerous joint ventures where equity control rests with the third-world company, and the operational control rests with the larger foreign corporation. Internal cash flow agreements may allow the foreign company to receive management fees and bonuses based on profit sharing in addition to the proportionate split of corporate dividends to compensate for their extra operational demands.

Although Control Data Corporation (CDC) held only a 46 percent share of its joint venture with the Romanian government, CDC was responsible for its management. Romanian officials later were reported to have asked CDC chairman William Norris if he wanted his share increased to 50 percent, but Norris said that it was not necessary; the venture was working fine.

In the telecommunications joint venture between AT&T and Philips N.V., the ownership is divided 50–50, but the five member board is weighted with three votes for AT&T and two for Philips. This division reflects the stronger interest AT&T has in telecommunication switching equipment versus Philips, which is a diversified electronics manufacturer. The board has authority to decide all matters except large capital investments, mergers, and acquisitions.

Difficulties may also arise, particularly later on, when new people join the venture, or the original founders' vision for the venture fades over time and market dynamics shift. When this happens, the proportions that made sense at the beginning may become grossly unfair several years down the road. At that time, adjustments must be made to the proportions or the venture may be on the rocks.

Success and Failure Rates

Professor Killing of the University of Western Ontario conducted a study that showed the Superior/Subordinate option had twice the likelihood of success (and conversely half the likelihood of liquidation or reorganization) as the Equal Balance option. However, Killing found notable examples of success using the Equal Balance option, and notable failures among the Superior/Subordinate option. (See Table 8.3). It is clear that no right or wrong method exists—only options well designed to fit the resources, responsibilities, risks, and rewards circumstances. Chapter 11 elaborates on essential management issues that can help you make this decision. (Note: Killing did not study the Majority Rule option.)

The ultimate chances of success of the venture are inversely related to the risk involved. The higher the risks, the lower the success rate. Re-

Table 8.3. Performance of Joint Ventures by Type

Type	Number of Ventures	Poor	Sat	Good	Liquidated or Reorganized
Superior/Subordinate	13	23%	23%	54%	15%
Equal Balance	20	55%	20%	25%	50%
Independent or Autonomous	4	25%	0%	75%	0%
Weighted Average	37	36%	22%	42%	31%

Source: J. Peter Killing, *Harvard Business Review*.[3]

search and Development alliances have perhaps the highest incidence of failure because they are designed to address large numbers of unknown variables. Edwin Martin of Hale and Dorr comments:

"Those who have inquired into the subject on a systematic basis have concluded that a majority of the attempted [R&D] partnerships do not succeed, but that the failures usually relate to practical matters or the ability of the developer to attain the specific objectives rather than the failure of the original strategic plan."[4]

SIDE VENTURES

Especially in multi-party alliances (i.e., those with three or more partners), there is always the chance the partners will not be able to reach a consensus on certain key decisions. Many long-term oil, mining, and technology development ventures have solved this problem with independent "side venture" provisions (sometimes referred to as "side payments"). These provisions enable the partners to make acquisitions and engage in new product development independent of the venture, particularly if the venture cannot decide to engage in this activity itself.

These provisions enable two or more of the partners to split off a separate side venture when and if all the partners cannot agree to explore what some may consider an overly risky or unproductive avenue. The independent side venture then has the opportunity to pursue that avenue, and to accept the resulting rewards. If the technology (i.e., oil well, new product, or the like) proves to be productive, a provision may be included for the independent side venture to sell itself back to the original joint venture for two to five times the cost of development, which is normally considered an acceptable risk–reward ratio.

CONTINGENCIES AND CHANGE

Only one thing is ever certain about the future: It will not be what we expected. Even with the best predictions and forecasts, any alliance exists in a risk-prone environment. Therefore, it is wise to have contingency plans in place to handle the unexpected.

An experienced venture capitalist once said that every young business goes through three major crises that jeopardize the very existence of the company prior to landing on stable ground. The same is probably true of business alliances. Before launching the venture, the sponsors should try to predict the crises that might be encountered. An alliance must be flexible enough to change when the uncertainty of the future emerges more clearly. This is why lawyers insist on the divorce and termination provisions in most legal agreements.

Contingency Planning

Two partners in a successful venture in the telecommunications industry recently commented that they always had three plans for their business as it grew: the optimistic plan, the pessimistic plan, and the "Black Sunday" plan. Always knowing the alternatives in the event something might go wrong enabled their venture to keep ahead of the problems, anticipating difficulties before they occurred. This team was composed of flexible problem-solvers who, ultimately, were highly successful, but both the pessimistic and "Black Sunday" plans had to be put into effect at various stages of their business growth in order for them to achieve success.

Contingency planning can take other forms and even be designed into the product itself. In a real estate venture, a development team was renovating an historic mill building. The market analysis indicated its best use to be as a restaurant, which is considered a very risky business by most bankers. The market analysis also saw an emerging market for residential and office use in the area in three to five years. When the architects and engineers were assigned to draw up plans and specifications for the task, their instructions were to design the facility for a restaurant but to configure the plumbing, heating, and electrical systems along with the wall configurations in such a way that, for a minimum cost, the building could be converted into apartments or professional offices at a later date, should the restaurant use fail. When project financing was requested, the bank was far more amenable to the project with this contingency plan in place because it lowered the risk level for the success of the project.

In the electronics industry, similar contingency designs are built into component boards as "core" circuitry to enable the basic engineering and production design to be used for a multitude of other uses, should the need arise.

Phase Shifts

Some joint ventures should shift leadership as the venture progresses through different stages of development. One partner may be the better leader during technological development, and another may be better during the manufacturing and marketing phase.

Real estate joint ventures are also good examples of this shift. During the construction phase, the contractor and developer may play the largest leadership roles, but after construction, the facilities manager and sales/marketing manager may be the leaders.

Changes in the Venture

Opportunities exist at favorable points in time, and when time passes, so do many opportunities. Changes are bound to occur. Industries change; people move to other positions; the sponsor's businesses change direction, expand, and contract; competition is always maneuvering for advantage; and the joint venture is itself changing as it matures. If the owners expect the venture to succeed over the long haul, its designers must enable the organization to continually adapt and flow with the times—to maintain its strategic synergy, its operational leadership, its risk/reward balance, and the vested interest motivation of its partners, all within a dynamic, ever-changing, strategic environment. Like the proverbial oak tree in a gale, the rigid venture will probably be uprooted, while the more flexible venture, bending with the winds of change, has a higher likelihood of survival.

Once the structural issues are resolved between the partners, it is time to begin codifying partner agreements by constructing legal documents.

9

The Legal Agreements You Will Need

Alliances fail because operating managers do not make them work, not because contracts are poorly written.

Kathryn Harrigan, Columbia University

When properly constructed, a business alliance should be worked out clearly in terms of the strategic, management, financial, and operational objectives well in advance of the final legal agreements. This is why most agreements are only 10–30 pages in length, and many smaller ventures are supported by even fewer pages. When compared to other legal arrangements, joint ventures and strategic alliances are a relatively simple endeavor. (Compare this to an equity investment or project financing document, often over 250 pages long!)

Lawyers may play an important role in finalizing the structure of an alliance, particularly the more complex ventures. Simpler arrangements, such as those for a manufacturer's sales representative, have become so regimented as to need little but a cursory review by legal counsel.

A lawyer's assistance can be invaluable in helping the players avoid exploitation of their trust, protecting against fatal decisions, and codifying verbal agreements. However, if brought into the negotiations at too early a stage, lawyers can turn the alliance into a playground for legal sparring. During the early negotiations, leave the lawyers in the background; consult with them frequently if necessary, but keep them out of the direct and active negotiations, except at critical points, like finalizing the ultimate contract (the binding legal agreement). Conversely, alliances that avoid using legal counsel run the risk of building upon a weak foundation, or of being exploited unfavorably.

Typically, the legal process will go through several distinct stages:

1. The statement of intent
2. The noncompetition and confidentiality agreements (these are optional and apply to only some ventures)
3. The binding legal agreement

At each of these stages, important business decisions are made, and ideally, trust grows among the parties.

It has been said the importance of written agreements is directly proportional to the inherent value of the issues at stake. If the partners are contributing valuable technology, products, or property, particularly where large, unrecoverable investments are required, it is far more important to have clear and encompassing legal documents.

Joint venture and strategic alliance legal documents are often more "business oriented" than many other legal business documents. Therefore, substantial thought should be put into a first draft—the statement of intent—by the key business executives involved, before the lawyers start the legal drafting. In this way, the business strategy clearly drives the legal language. The opposite—the legal issues driving the business strategy— can end in frustration, confusion, and ultimately failure to consummate an agreement.

THE STATEMENT OF INTENT

One of the most critical steps in formulating the alliance is encompassed by the drafting of a nonbinding statement of intent. Its primary purpose is to move the negotiations beyond initial talking stages, where the verbal understandings may be somewhat vague or conceptual, to the stage of a clear description of the nature of the alliance.

The statement of intent should be drafted mutually by the principals of each of the parties of the joint venture, without lawyers present (but perhaps having consulted with them earlier). Later, the lawyers will translate this basic document into the final binding legal agreement. The statement of intent should be brief and to the point; generally, it should encompass only four to six pages. Clarity of thought, simplicity of design, practicality of operation, and profitability are essential objectives of the statement.

The statement of intent should cover at least eight critical points:

1. *Spirit and Purpose of the Agreement.* Outline briefly the reasons the alliance is being formed and its perceived mission. Describe any operating principles that will engender communications and trust. State the strategic and financial desires of the participants.

2. *Realm of Activity.* Address what products, services, buildings, or other specific projects will be included and excluded from the venture. Identify the target markets (i.e., regions, user groups, and the like) for the venture, and any markets excluded from the venture that will remain the domain of the partners. If the venture has purchase and supply provisions, state that the joint venture will purchase or supply specific products, services, or resources from or to the owners.

3. *Key Objectives and Responsibilities.* Clarify and specify objectives and targets to be achieved by the alliance, when to expect achieving these objectives, any major obstacles anticipated, and the point at which the alliance will be self-supporting, be bought out, or be terminated. Each participant should designate a project manager who will be responsible for their company's day-to-day involvement in the alliance. If a separate detached organization will be created, the key persons assigned to the venture should be designated, if practical. Responsibilities should be outlined to make it clear to other partners who will be doing what. This plan can be described in further detail in an appended operational plan.

4. *Method for Decisionmaking.* Each alliance will have its own unique decisionmaking process. It is vital to describe who will have the authority to make what types of decisions in what circumstances, who reports to whom, and so on. Without a clear method of decisionmaking and reporting, the alliance may collapse from undermanagement. If one company will have operating control, they should be designated at this point.

5. *Resource Commitments.* Most alliances involve the commitment of specific financial resources, such as cash, equity, staged payments, loan guarantees, or the like to the achievement of the ultimate goals. Other "soft" resources may be in the form of licenses, knowledge, R&D, a sales force, contacts, production facilities, inventory, raw materials, engineering drawings, management staff, access to capital, or the devotion of specific personnel for a certain percentage of

their time. If possible, these "soft" resources should be quantified with a financial figure so that a monetary value can be affixed and valued along with the cash commitments to this internal commitment. In some circumstances, the purchase of buildings, materials, consultants, or advertising will require capital; these external costs should be itemized and allocated between the partners in whatever formula is agreed.

If any borrowing, entry into equity markets (public offerings, private placements, or the like), or purchase of stock in one of the partners is anticipated, these should be noted. In the event that the joint venture needs additional equity infusions, the partners should agree about their own ability to fund the overruns, or enable the venture to seek other outside sources. The manner of handling cost over-runs should be agreed to. Pricing and costing procedures should be mentioned if applicable.

6. *Assumption of Risks and Division of Rewards.* Strategic alliances will cover their risks and rewards internally and not address this issue in the statement of intent. For joint ventures: what are the perceived risks? What are the expected rewards (new product, new market, cash flow, technology, etc.)? How will the profits be divided?

7. *Rights and Exclusions.* Who has rights to products and inventions? Who has rights to distribute the products, services, or technologies? Who gets licensing rights? If the confidentiality and noncompetition agreements have not yet been drafted in final form at this point, they should be addressed in basic form here. Otherwise, if the other agreements have been signed, simply make reference to them.

8. *Anticipated Structure.* This section should describe the intended structure of the venture (written contract, corporation, or partnership) and equity investment. Regardless of the organization's legal form, the terms, percentages, and formulas for exchange of stock should be spelled out if possible at this stage. Any termination provisions should be identified.

If some issues remain somewhat vague, do not be overly concerned; these will be thrashed out as the statement of intent is translated into a binding legal agreement. At the bottom of the statement, include a paragraph similar to this:

This nonbinding letter contains preliminary intentions of the parties to form an alliance based on conditions stated above. Upon review by our respective legal counsel and upon mutual agreement, revisions may be proposed to be included later in a formal, binding legal agreement, which, contingent upon our signing, will legally bind the parties. For the next 60 days, the parties agree to adhere to the principles of this statement of intent until superceded by the formal legal agreement, the extention or modification of this agreement, or the decision to abandon the alliance prior to entering into a formal legal agreement.

The CEOs, after reviewing the statement of intent with prospective operating venture managers, should then sign the letter, which ensures that those responsible for leading and managing the venture understand the prospective deal and are fully committed to its strategy and plan of execution.

THE CONFIDENTIALITY AGREEMENT

Confidentiality is most important where one or more of the parties have very valuable or proprietary goods and services to offer. Entrepreneurs engaging in technology development are especially encouraged to use confidentiality agreements, which keep players from letting stray information damage negotiations at a sensitive stage.

However, even non-tech deals may consider using a confidentiality agreement. Prospective real estate partners, for example, may be concerned that revealing future land and building options, rental price structures, construction costs, and so on can reveal sensitive competitive advantages or trigger other competitors to take preemptive action. Manufacturers, too, may have vital proprietary production techniques or market research data.

Not only does a confidentiality agreement make good competitive sense—it also helps create a trusting relationship. The agreement binds the parties into an ethical operating environment. Potential partners lacking a confidentiality agreement are left guessing about the other party's motives; guessing only creates fears that may ultimately undermine the deal.

Smaller companies with new technologies seeking alliances with larger companies will view the confidentiality agreement as an absolute necessity because it provides the smaller company with intellectual property rights. However, the larger company may, with good reason, resist signing such a document if the larger company is possibly engaged in a similar field of research. Companies like IBM are reluctant to sign a confidentiality agreement, fearing it may restrict the firm's ability to utilize its own research. For a company like IBM, their research network is too vast for any U.S. executive to know what an IBM laboratory is doing in faraway places like Malaysia.

It is common for a "cat and mouse" game to occur at this stage. The CEO of the small technology company won't say anything about his or her product until a confidentiality agreement is signed for fear of losing the "company jewels." Meanwhile, the large corporation's manager is unwilling to sign anything for fear of encroaching on unknown territory within his or her own organization. Often, the problem is solved by placing shorter time limits, perhaps six to twelve months, on the confidentiality agreement if the alliance is not consummated, by limited revelation during the negotiations stage, and by a carefully drawn legal document that excludes "prior knowledge" by the larger firm.

Whether the confidentiality agreement takes the form of a handwritten letter or an attorney-prepared document, Jeffery Stoler of the law firm of Hinkley Allen recommends six issues be addressed:

1. *Defining the Confidential Information.* The agreement must describe the confidential information in sufficient detail as to make it perfectly clear what is within the bounds of the agreement and what is not. The definition must be both encompassing and specific in order to make the agreement enforceable.

2. *Control.* Specific provisions should be included to establish who can know the confidential information and where copies will be maintained. By doing so, the parties are forced to focus on how each company will maintain confidentiality within its organization. It is frequently desirable to have an attachment to the agreement setting forth the form of an abbreviated confidentiality agreement to be signed by persons having access to the information. By doing so, a further degree of control is imposed.

3. *Derivative Works.* For technology-oriented companies, it is often possible to derive other inventions from the source technology. The ownership of such inventions should be dealt with in the agreement. If feasible, include a provision describing notice and transfer procedures.

4. *Fall-Back Position.* In case an alliance is never established, the confidentiality agreement may be the only agreement between the parties. It should contain an understanding regarding products derived

from the technology and other sensitive matters, thereby helping avoid litigation if the remaining negotiations do not go well.

5. *Survival.* The confidentiality agreement should survive, regardless of any further negotiations for an alliance, with a reasonable time period for the provisions to remain in effect (i.e., for as long as the confidential information is not publicly known, or for a minimum number of years).

6. *Relief.* Because it is difficult to establish damages that might result from a breach of the agreement, it is useful to spell out whether one of the parties can request an injunction, and the amount of damages the parties agree are appropriate.

These six issues are ideal guidelines, but, in the event that all points cannot be agreed upon, a partial agreement is better than nothing at all. A sample confidentiality agreement is included in Appendix D.

THE NONCOMPETITION AGREEMENT

Depending upon the arrangements between the parties, a noncompetition agreement may also be negotiated. Due to public policies favoring free enterprise, noncompetition agreements are strictly limited and frequently invalidated by the courts. The basic principal used by the courts is one of *reasonableness.* The best rule of thumb is for the parties to limit anticompetitive aspects as narrowly as possible.

The noncompetition agreement should consider future relationships between the parties. If either is contemplating the ability to license certain technologies or specialized services to others in the future, these intentions should be mentioned in the agreement.

Some lawyers suggest integrating the noncompetition agreement into the confidentiality agreement. This is not wise, because the courts frequently find noncompetition agreements to be contrary to the public interest. Therefore the noncompetition should be separated from other documents in order to insulate those agreements from invalidation.

The noncompetition agreement can be written in business language by business people, or drafted by an attorney. Generally, the best approach is for the business principals to agree to a first draft in layman's terms, and then have an attorney weave the legal framework into it.

Regardless of who drafts the document, it should cover four points:

1. *Duration.* Establish how long the noncompetitive relationship should continue. "Forever" is definitely unreasonable, and even 10 years may be too long. Make the duration only as long as necessary.

2. *Scope.* The noncompetitive relationship should not extend beyond issues concerning the particular technology, services, or reasons for which the alliance is being formed. Do not use the noncompetition agreement as a means of restraining trading opportunities. It is helpful to specifically address other areas where the parties may fairly compete.

3. *Self-Termination.* To avoid possible unfair trade allegations, the parties may find it valuable to put a self-termination clause into the agreement. For technology development, if the technology proves to be in the public domain, then the fairness of the noncompetition agreement will be negated.

4. *No Raiding.* Because the alliance will permit each party to become familiar with the other's expertise, personnel, and trade secrets, it is usually agreed that neither party will "raid" the other, neither before nor after the alliance terminates.

EXCLUSIVITY

Some agreements make arrangements for exclusive rights and relationships between the partners. Alliances should be strict on the exclusivity aspects of the relationship only if a clear and good reason to do so exists at the outset. Many companies prefer to limit their exclusivity narrowly around geography, time, or conditions in order to maximize flexibility in the future. There should be no ambiguity about which markets or products that remain exclusively the domain of the alliance, or remain the domain of one of the partners. One reported reason for more than two decades of the success of a joint venture between Dow Chemical and Schlumberger was that the joint venture is excluded from North American operations where it would compete with the partners.

Caution should be employed if one of the partners insists on using their products exclusively within the alliance. One major computer manufacturer contributed its computer system to a joint venture, but the system was quickly obsolete, and the venture was stuck using inferior products.

Negotiations on exclusivity can take on imaginative dimensions, as this case example demonstrates:

Example: Alpha Manufacturing, a U.S. widget manufacturer, and Major Marketing, an international marketing firm, formed a joint venture to manufacture and market widgets for the Asian marketplace. The widget would be a special low-cost model appealing to a wide variety of Asian cultures. Alpha, however, was concerned that its marketing partner would see the value of the idea and want a slightly different version of the widgets to be marketed in South America and Eastern Europe. If Major Marketing decided to use the expertise it gained in Asia, Alpha Manufacturing's managers thought they should also benefit because they took the initial risks. Alpha Manufacturing proposed an exclusivity clause in the joint venture agreement that called for: (1) any sale of widgets in other world markets by Major Marketing would be produced exclusively by Alpha Manufacturing; (2) Major would not enter into any other joint venture agreements with Alpha's competitors; and (3) Major would not purchase any manufacturing companies that would subsequently copy or produce a version of the Alpha model widget.

Major, while understanding Alpha's concern about exclusivity, balked at the specifics of the proposal, and offered a counterproposal that Alpha found acceptable: (1) Major would offer Alpha the right of first refusal to enter the other markets together; (2) Major would not purchase any competing companies without offering Alpha at least a 25 percent share in the acquisition; and (3) these conditions would prevail for a three-year period.

Each venture will have its own unique script as partners think out exclusivity provisions.

THE BINDING LEGAL AGREEMENT

The binding legal agreement is the final document that operationalizes the joint venture. It should not be too difficult to draft because it should follow the basic format of the statement of intent. A lawyer should review the binding legal agreement before signing. Any issues such as licensing agreements, development contracts, and the like that are not covered in the statement of intent will be more clearly covered in the binding agreement. There will *never* be a perfect legal agreement protecting a partner from all risks. The agreement simply limits and apportions risk; it does not eliminate risk.

Some items, like the operational plan and technical specifications, may not be included in the legal document, to enable operational flexibility in case changes are required. If these are included, they should be as an appendix subject to modification by mutual consent.

The larger the companies involved and the more financial risk, the more detailed the agreement. Alfred Prommer, formerly of Siemens AG, suggests: "The actual agreement has to be clearly defined. If agreements are too broad, they are almost impossible to negotiate. . . . I favor, very much, agreements where you have specific requirements . . . Only agreements in that form—with specific details and with periodic reviews—work well."[1]

Termination Clauses

Joint ventures—because they are closer, more intricate unions—have more complex termination clauses than strategic alliances. Some lawyers devote a considerable number of pages to termination provisions. Sometimes up to 80 percent of the legal documentation will cover issues such as buyout clauses, prices of the buyout, how assets and liabilities are divided if the venture fails or the partners elect to dissolve the operation, what will happen to key personnel, and who owns trade secrets and patents. Moreover, banks and other lending institutions will probably insist on such convenants to provide protection of their collateral. These provisions reflect the 80/20 rule: 80 percent of the document relates to only 20 percent of the important issues. But these "divorce" conditions are essential to prevent litigation in the event of an adverse change.

Lawyers often suggest careful and exact provisions for escaping the relationship for good reasons. According to Edwin M. Martin, an attorney with Hale and Dorr: "Only when [the escape provisions] are in place can the parties work together with a focus on the positive elements, rather than on the methods of finding a way out of a soured relationship."[2]

Some lawyers will include a clause terminating the venture at some point in the future, often seven, 10, or 15 years hence. This carry-over from the provisions of real estate limited partnerships intends to provide investor paybacks within a specified time period. These provisions are applicable when there are substantial financial investors in the venture who demand liquidification of their investment, or if one of the principal financial considerations is long-term capital appreciation that must be retrieved before their tax benefit is foresaken.

However, most alliances should give very careful consideration to the wisdom of these clauses. After all, how can one be sure the venture will not be in an "explosive growth" stage just as the legal provisions call for liquidation? Rather than using these "boilerplate" termination stipulations, it may be better to use "operational triggers" such as certain adverse events, low thresholds of profitability, failure to capture sufficient markket share, or other, more functional criteria.

Another alternative uses "development phasing triggers," which attempt to maximize both partner's interest in expanding the venture through its stages of development, and evaluating success at each development phase. In this scenario, two companies might commence the alliance using the written contract or partnership format, and make an initial financial and operational commitment until some specific, mutually agreed upon performance objectives are achieved that grow the venture from infancy to a more stable point, such as operational breakeven, product introduction, or completion of construction. Neither party may exit or sell its position prior to this point, ensuring that the venture will have established a real value with some form of stable management by this first developmental stage.

As the venture enters its second stage, a partner may sell out its interests *in toto*, first to the existing partners and, if they choose not to buy, then to another prospective partner or financial investor agreeable to the remaining sponsors. During the second phase, the venture is managed as a separate organizational entity, aiming at profitable operations and a fully integrated management team.

The third phase may bring in outside investment capital; otherwise, an initial public offering may be made. As a public corporation, both the founders and the investors now have a liquid means of selling corporate stock to enhance their cash positions.

Joint research and product development alliances use a version of the "development phasing triggers" approach by setting milestones for proving a new technology will be commercially adaptable. Failure to meet any of these milestones may be sufficient reason to terminate activities.

There are two basic options in breaking away, should the need to terminate arise:

1. Dissolve the relationship, particularly if the alliance has no residual monetary value, or

2. Enable one of the partners to buy out the other at a fair market value

Companies may want to exercise termination clauses for many reasons. The most frequent is simply because the conditions that made the venture viable in the beginning have changed. The other most frequent reason is that the venture is not beneficial to one of the partners. Whatever the reason, a clearly written termination clause will avoid costly litigation.

Liability Clauses

Given the uncertain risk of dealing with liability laws, some agreements will contain a liability clause stating neither of the sponsoring parties assumes or is responsible for the financial or legal liabilities of the other. While these clauses will probably not prevent litigation, they may limit the chances of adverse judgment.

Preemptive Rights

Most agreements for joint ventures using the corporate format contain clauses concerning preemptive rights, which are rights afforded under most state laws giving minority shareholders the right to preserve their equity percentage interests by enabling them to purchase additional stock if stock is sold for cash to another party. The specific rights may vary from one legal jurisdiction to another.

In 1987 Britain's General Electric Co. (GEC) formed a 50-50 joint venture with Plessey to make telephone exchanges. The next year GEC and Siemens AG of West Germany formed another joint venture to make a hostile takeover bid for Plessey. Plessey cried foul and claimed this hostile takeover enabled Plessey to exercise its preemptive rights to purchase the remaining stock in the joint venture as a means of making the hostile takeover more difficult. A carefully drafted legal agreement should enable a joint venture shareholder to buy out its partner in the event of a hostile takeover or a major change in the stock ownership of its partner.

The Ultimate Agreement

Regardless of the length, cost, or detail of the agreement, it is only as valuable as the commitment and fairness of the parties behind it. As James Hlavacek of the Business School at SUNY and Brian Dovey and John Biondo, CEO's of small technology companies, have written: "If the parties have to refer to the agreement on a daily basis for direction or to solve many problems, then the joint venture is destined for failure. . . . The negotiations *must* end with both parties feeling they have obtained a good and fair deal. This principle is generally true in any business transaction, but its effect is greatly magnified when you must live together as partners for a long, continuous period of time."[3]

PART FOUR

THE OPERATIONS PHASE

Once the legal documents are signed, the real adventure begins! This is the time to roll up the sleeves and get the machinery working.

Newly created joint ventures are very much like start-up companies, regardless of how large and mature their sponsors are. Add to the start-up challenge the difficulty of managing an alliance that has *two* or more owners.

This next section contains valuable information that will make the alliance more manageable. The critical issues that will be covered include:

* The Importance of the Operations Plan
* Principles and Practice of Alliance Management
* Dealing with Operational Concerns

10

The Importance of the Operations Plan

I thought my partner was responsible for that!

—Lament of a failing joint venture

WHY AN OPERATIONS PLAN IS IMPORTANT

Writing an operations plan is the last litmus test to predict the validity of an alliance. To check if all the venture's "gears will mesh," you should create the operations plan before signing any final binding legal agreements. (Many alliances append the operations plan to the binding legal agreement, with provisions for modification upon mutual consent.)

Some project managers suggest putting the alliance into a preliminary "shakedown cruise" prior to formalizing the legal documents. These managers claim that those who will eventually be running the alliance should be given the opportunity to test ideas and working relationships so that, when the deal is legally consummated, the staff "hits the ground running."

Up to this point, any financial analyses will probably remain somewhat flexible until making a final comparison against an operations plan agreed upon by all the partners. Any major changes to the operations plan may require another review of the financial analysis.

For example, while estimating the cost of a newly designed product engineered to meet market demand, the manufacturing partner of a marketing–manufacturing joint venture found the costs would be 50 percent higher than expected, making it necessary to adjust prices and forecasts.

This increased the necessary financial commitments and lowered the anticipated return on investment.

In another example, this time in real estate, the team designing a construction project did not realize the specified components of a new, advanced heating and air conditioning system would simply not fit in the designated areas. Only when the design team met with the systems engineers to finalize their operations plan and budgeting did they realize the plans would need to be revised. It was a test of their intelligence, common sense, and ability to solve problems together. Yet it was far better to go through this process of revisions *before* the joint venture began than to deal with such surprises afterwards.

Essentially, devising the operations plan with your partners slows down the process in order to:

- establish precise needs and requirements
- ask the tough operational questions and build managers' commitment
- determine if the strategic plan really makes sense when converted into day-to-day operations

While slowing the process down may seem frustrating to hard-driving business leaders, a little planning at this stage will save lots of time, money, and frustrations later. More than once, what seemed to be a good strategic idea failed in operations.

THE TEAMWORK TEST IN WRITING THE PLAN

Equally important in writing the operations plan is the "teamwork test." The operations plan should be written as a "mini-joint venture" between the operational managers of the prospective alliance. If the appointed operational managers cannot write the details of the plan together, then they obviously have slim hopes of managing the venture together. The teamwork test enables operational managers to troubleshoot the plan, check chemistry and trust, smoke out unforeseen personnel problems, determine if the "not invented here" syndrome will smother innovation and, if it has not yet happened, isolate the deal killers from the cynics. This process secures organizational support and clarifies future roles and responsibilities. If this process is accomplished successfully, the future "operational fit" will stand a better chance of surviving the pressures and risks of the venture.

Commitment Check

One reason for failure of some alliances is the lack of commitment of the middle managers to make the venture work. By engaging both top and middle management in the process of formulating an operations plan before the venture begins, commitment is gauged. Even more important, top management will get its first glimpse of what will happen when the middle managers engage gears between the participating companies.

The time needed for the teamwork test also varies according to the size and complexity of the venture and the past relationship of the companies. For the manufacturing/sales rep alliance, this teamwork test may simply involve a meeting with the manufacturer's national sales manager and the regional sales representative to map out goals, the territorial management process, feedback procedures, product warranties, communications channels, commission payment arrangements, and new product ideas.

For real estate developers, this phase may bring the developer, architect, marketer, building manager, and general contractor together for the concept design of the building, schedule dates, and critical problem areas. Several lengthy meetings may be necessary. For a mining venture, engineering studies, geographic surveys, and engineering plans can take well over a year.

ISSUES THE PLAN MUST COVER

Since every venture has its own unique circumstances, the operations plan should be tailored to the specific needs of the venture. The operations plan will differ significantly from venture to venture. However, virtually all joint ventures have common threads covering operational, administrative, and policy issues. Items considered in many joint venture operations plans include:

1. Key objectives and milestones
2. Financial forecasts summary
3. Critical success and risk factors
4. Product performance specifications
5. Service support
6. Competitive analysis
7. Operations management procedures and personnel
8. Marketing and sales plan with sales projection

9. Manufacturing/production/engineering plan

10. Implementation schedule

11. Contingency plan

12. Operational and administrative responsibilities

13. Prices, payments, and ordering procedures

The more complex the joint venture, the greater the need to have a detailed operations plan to avoid confusion and prevent critical items from slipping through the cracks downstream. Operational managers should ensure that the plan is clear, and the partners should agree on the program without hidden reservations.

The plan should contain only enough information to ensure that the practical realities of the alliance will work. For some ventures, only two pages are needed; other ventures simply outline the quality and performance specifications and production schedules. Still other plans for high technology, medicine, or extremely risky ventures may require more detail.

OPERATIONAL REPORTING SYSTEMS

It is valuable for the joint venture to use a mutually accepted reporting system if project coordination is to be carried out effectively. Tremendous amounts of confusion arise when, for example, one company uses a PERT chart and another uses an in-house format; these two partners are thinking in two different operational languages. When logistical or technical problems arise, there will not be a common method of defining the problem, never mind solving it. All operational managers dread the overburden of extra reports; therefore, any system agreed upon should be simple, efficient, and easy to use.

The reporting system should also be clear on tasks, expected results, time frames, communications channels, decisionmaking authority, quality control, product specifications, and managerial responsibilities of all the players.

When the venture involves the development of a new product or the construction of a specific project, the operational steering committee will often establish guidelines for the project manager to review the entire program at various stages in order to ensure that the risk of completion will not be substantially greater than originally expected. Invariably, a final review of the project will determine if it meets specifications.

For example, in a large mining project, the steering committee may review interim reports on the development at the one-third and two-thirds completion stages, or at other critical developmental milestones. But in a product manufacturing venture, quarterly performance reviews may be more appropriate.

Frequently, if the venture is not highly specific/project-oriented (i.e. a broad research program into a new technology), it is common for the partners to authorize the steering committee to terminate the project if progress is not satisfactory at particular predetermined stages. These provisions are normally put in the legal agreement, with clear guidelines for abandonment.

Milestones and monitoring are more precise and critical in *product* development than in *technology* development. For technology development, the milestones are more flexible in order to compensate for the uncertainties that are bound to be encountered; monitoring is usually limited to coordination, assessment, and financial reporting.

When technology is being developed, care should be taken to ensure that it actually "fits" a future marketable design application. Careful thought, coordination, and communications between marketing and engineering personnel are important. In one joint venture, the developer in the U.S. began using a nonmetric standard. Fortunately, the developer's European partner caught the problem early in one of the steering committee meetings, so corrections were made early enough for no time to be lost. If the coordination and communications were sporadic and isolated, it would have been possible for the U.S. company to have completed its technology and manufacturing process before the mistake was identified, resulting in tremendous delays in product introduction timing and incurring costly redesign.

Review reports naturally vary from venture to venture, but most include some variation of this theme:

· Schedule review against key milestones
· Critical issues and deadlines
· Monthly and year-to-date financials versus plan
· Steering committee members' activities on the venture's behalf
· Sales review and forecast
· Customer activity, especially target customers
· Cost and price issues
· Quality review

- Shipment/delivery/completion reviews
- Technical/manufacturing/production problems
- Coordination and teamwork issues
- Next month's expectations

An effective monitoring system keeps energies focused upon the plan, rather than being diverted to dozens of other fascinating potentialities. Particularly in technology and product development, those experienced in the field lament their engineers designing the next version before the first is complete. Similarly, budding entrepreneurs, in their typically expansive manner, find innumerable uses for their products and technologies, failing to focus on immediately achievable target applications as well as distribution systems, applications engineering, and cash flow.

TROUBLESHOOTING AND CONTINGENCY PLANNING

If significant development risks exist in the venture, one of the most valuable areas upon which to focus is the contingency plan. During the operations planning phase, partners may have become enthralled by their own romance, lulled into thinking that sales may be greater than reality will bless, or now, with a partner, all the production problems that used to occur will suddenly halt. The contingency plan is particularly important in relation to *time*. According to William Kirk, president of a small electronics firm involved in a joint venture, "Time is the biggest enemy, and if the product development is delayed or the market introduction takes longer than expected, valuable time is lost. More time translates into a need for additional funding, and is usually unplanned."

The pressures to meet the planned schedule must be maintained. Simultaneously, it will be necessary to have some reserve funding to cover cost overruns. For example, it may be cheaper to hire additional resources in order to meet the plan than it is to accept a slippage. If a slippage is unavoidable, it should be faced immediately and a new operations plan that includes the financial impact upon investment returns must be created.

11
Principles and Practice of Alliance Management

Management is, all things considered, the most creative of all arts. It is the art of arts, because it is the organizer of talent.

—Jean-Jacques Servan-Schreiber

Once the operations plan is complete and the legal agreements signed, it is time to roll up the sleeves, put concepts and strategy plans aside, turn ideas into action, and actions into results. Running an alliance can be frustrating. Coordination must be the rule, diplomacy is a necessity, and the internal politics of allies are often confounding.

Research conducted by Peter Killing at the University of Western Ontario and Kathryn Harrigan at Columbia University indicates that most ventures spend too much time on negotiating and dealmaking, with far too little time spent on how decisions should be made, how operations should progress, and the relationships between partners.

Killing tells the story of a U.S. manager establishing a joint venture with a European counterpart. Although the venture was a success, the U.S. manager belatedly lamented the fact that, during the time the venture was being established, 50 percent of his time was spent on legal work, 30 percent on selecting products the venture would produce, and 20 percent on the marketing strategy. No time was spent on operations planning, management, personnel selection, joint decisionmaking procedures, or communications between the partners.

Harrigan agrees, saying, "Too often, managers are thrown together by owners without thinking through the details of day-to-day operations . . . Because their authority to act for their owners had been poorly defined, the venture's managers could not . . . find a way to get the job of running the joint venture done." Harrigan concluded that "poor performance always exacerbates tensions between the owners and increases managers' frustrations with their counterparts," thus amplifying the venture's chance of failure.[1]

The Seven Operational Management Principles

The seven principles described in this chapter will apply in varying degrees to all forms of business partnerships, depending upon how the deal is structured, its goals, time frames, complexity of tasks, history of cooperation between the partners, and similarity of corporate cultures. There is no one correct solution or answer for every alliance; each one must be designed and managed in its own unique fashion to fit its own circumstances. The alliance's structural design and management style may change over time as the needs and circumstances of the partners and the venture change.

The seven management principles are:

1. Effective Leadership–Management Mix
2. Using Differentiation and Integration
3. The Ambiguity/Certainty Continuum
4. Interface Management
5. Collaborative Decisionmaking
6. Managing Cross-Corporate Relations
7. Personnel Selection

Each of these principles will be explored in detail in this chapter. By understanding and practicing these principles, alliance orchestrators will significantly increase their chances of creating a successful venture.

The principles and practices described here have been tested and researched, but they are only guidelines. They will enhance the chances of success, but only if used in the right combinations at the right times; each partnership must decide for itself what that combination may be. Prospective team members are encouraged to frankly discuss their own scripts and agree beforehand the ways to make the most effective use of their specific talents and to take advantage of varying points of view.

For the sake of simplicity and illustration, this chapter describes operations from the perspective of a joint venture with a separate, detached organization. All these principles are also applicable, in varying degrees, to all alliances but because the detached organizational form is a stronger, more extreme case, it better serves the purpose of illustration.

PRINCIPLE #1
EFFECTIVE LEADERSHIP–MANAGEMENT MIX

There is simply no substitute for good leadership and management in an alliance! Good strategy, excellent technology, an accepting market, fine lawyers, or excessive capitalization will not fill the gap if good leadership and management is missing. When entrepreneurs are questioned about the success or failure of business alliances, the most critical item mentioned is the ability of leadership and management.

It is important to be clear about the differences between leadership and management, for they are related but not the same. They are often referred to synonomously, but there are many important stylistic and substantive distinctions:

- Leaders tend to be pioneers; managers are institution builders.
- Leaders like to make things happen; managers follow through to continue to make them happen.
- Leaders are more emotional and intuitive; managers, logical and analytical.
- While leaders are creating, managers are problemsolving.
- Leadership entails spirit, courage, vision, drive, enthusiasm, imagination, inspiration, selling, breaking through barriers, and overcoming obstacles. Management, on the other hand, involves communication, planning, delegating, controlling, coordinating, problemsolving, marketing, loyalty, choosing between alternatives, maintaining relationships, and clarifying lines of responsibility.
- Leaders are risk–takers who want to create new ventures and drive their imaginations to new limits. Managers are trained people willing to do things the "right" way, to establish an organization that functions the way it is designed. Management keeps the venture on course, with the weight of its tasks evenly distributed.
- Leadership, *as defined by a manager,* is "influencing people to achieve a common goal." But leadership, *as defined by a leader,* is a "burning, persistent, and focused desire to organize people to win a clear and worthy goal." The difference is more than subtle; it is passionate.

- No business, government, or academic institution will last for long without a strong combination of both leadership and management ingredients.
- Success is pursued by the leader as a hound dog methodically tracks its prey—with unrelenting persistence. Managers provide the consistency and continuity to enable success to be replicated day after day.

The Need for a Leadership–Management Mix

The leadership–management mix is very much like the product–service mix in business strategy. Without the ability to provide service to a customer (user training, warranty and repairs, spare parts, etc.), a product is barren, worth significantly less in the eyes of a customer. Similarly, management and leadership together are like a horse and rider. Every alliance cries for leadership and management, and the partners must know how to provide an experienced, well-trained team with both characteristics.

Leaders must forge their own distinct culture for the venture—customer and staff relations, organizational and team values, commitment to results, the ability to solve the very problems that are the venture's primary risks—out of the parent cultures.

The business alliance must be led and it must be managed. It needs a powerful combination of the two; it must be done with the right people in charge, for it will not happen by itself. People tend to a have a mixture of leadership and management abilities in their own personalities. Some people have more of one end of this spectrum than the other; others fall in the middle. Choosing the right person with the right mix for the right position is vital to the ultimate success of any venture.

Champions

Leadership in a business alliance is personified by the sponsoring CEOs and their designated "champions," who intensely believe in the purpose of the venture, provide it with nourishment and support, and passionately desire its ultimate success. The success of the alliance must be pursued by the champion with a missionary's zeal. This champion must possess an entrepreneurial spirit where the business goal is his or her personal dream. Day-to-day operations of the alliance are left to the venture managers.

According to Edwin M. Martin, a lawyer for Hale and Dorr in Washington, "Probably the single most important factor for the success of a corporate partnering relationship is an individual within the sponsor who believes in the project, has the confidence of the principal executives of the (other partner), has an understanding of the (project), and the technology involved, and has clear access to and the confidence of [his or her own] CEO. This individual also needs to have enough time to work within (his or her own company) and closely within the (partner's company) on the project."[2] Thomas Peters and Robert Waterman, authors of *In Search of Excellence* state: "The champion is not a blue-sky dreamer, nor an intellectual giant. The champion might even be an idea thief. But, above all, he's the pragmatic one who grabs onto someone else's theoretical construct if necessary and bullheadedly pushes it to fruition."[3]

When deciding to develop a new product at Texas Instruments, the number one criterion is the presence of a zealous volunteer champion. After that comes market potential and project economics, running a distant second and third.

The champion provides the link between the joint venture and the sponsoring company. Champions often meet informally among themselves, working out potential problems and ensuring the commitment of their respective organizations. They must provide continuity and support. Many top managers tend to be deal makers, but do not follow through on the maintenance of the venture once the deal is cut. The champion does not forsake his or her offspring.

If the champion must move on to some other job, a replacement should be someone acceptable to all partners because, in the person-to-person world of the joint venture, there is a marriage between the people as well as the companies. Often, when a champion moves to another company, there will be a very real need to re-sell the alliance to the new person before he can really be a zealous replacement.

Peters and Waterman comment: "Champions and systems of champions are the single most important key to sustained innovative success."[4] A system of support consists of product champions, executive champions, and godfathers. Each has a critical role to play in the alliance.

Product Champions. A good product champion is part zealot, part fanatic, and part polished manager. He will passionately defend the new venture, but at the same time be strong and smart enough to be a good leader, a good manager, and a good persuader. This person is not a lunatic or a wild-eyed stargazer. He or she is persuasive, practical, and respected. A person with these qualities is the best choice for a venture general manager. But product champions must have strong, consistent, and reliable support from executive champions within the sponsor companies.

Executive Champions.   Invariably, this person is an ex-product champion. According to Peters and Waterman, "He's been there—been through the lengthy process of husbanding, seen what it takes to shield a potential practical new idea from the organization's formal tendency toward nega-tion."[5] The executive champions are usually not the final decisionmakers in large corporations, but stand at the senior vice-presidential or divi-sional level. They are a vital bridge between the sponsor corporation and the joint venture itself; indeed, they play a major support role with the venture general manager.

Also, executive champions' power is strong enough that they influence major decisions within their own company, and they can have important face-to-face impact on key decisionmakers in the other parent company.

Godfathers.   The "godfather" is typically an aging leader who provides the role model for championing—setting the corporate culture for risk-taking so that the other lower-level champions have corporate support. William Norris of Control Data perfectly fits this description, having "fa-thered" over 80 cooperative ventures within his own organization, and having played a major role in orchestrating the joint research venture at MCC.

The Role of the Venture Manager

The term "venture manager" is really a generic term. People who fill these roles have a variety of names, including general manager, project man-ager, program manager, product manager, and systems coordinator, de-pending upon the venture and the style with which the sponsors are familiar. (The term "venture manager" will be used here for consistency.)

The operational, day-to-day involvement of executive champions and godfathers in joint ventures will vary, depending upon the size of the sponsor. In most large corporations, the champions and CEOs stay out of the day-to-day operational decisionmaking, preferring to give that role to the venture's designated general manager.

It is the responsibility of the venture manager to oversee the venture's day-to-day operations. The venture manager ensures that the project is driven to success, and in a manner that keeps the motivation of the par-ticipants in high gear. In many respects, the venture manager will re-semble a chief operating officer (COO).

The venture manager's role is vital because most all communications and coordination must go through him. He is both an operational manager and a *catalytic coordinator*. It is a special role not suited to the average manager. The venture manager, in conjunction with the executive champion, must be capable of maintaining a level of excitement and harmony between the members of the venture, both at the steering committee level and among more diverse members. The champion and the venture manager together help maintain unity among the partners. Harvard Business School's Professor Paul Lawrence suggests that project managers "fire up key questions which will force the partners to make policies and decisions" that tend to unify the joint venture.

Regular corporate overseeing is usually delegated to the executive champion. Most experienced venture managers from large corporations say they prefer to have their parent CEOs keep out of day-to-day operations, only providing top level support and quarterly monitoring of progress.

Larger joint ventures will have one general manager in charge of the operational leadership of the venture. Smaller ventures that do not entail a separate organization need to assign a project manager from each of the sponsors who will be responsible for their company's achievement of goals and tasks.

Some companies involved in highly technical joint ventures actually appoint *two* project managers—a business manager and a technical manager—from each company to coordinate activities. The business manager's role is to orchestrate all project coordination meetings, conduct periodic performance reviews, oversee all pricing arrangements, ensure quality control, handle confidentiality and disclosure procedures, deal with product licensing issues, and coordinate with the technical manager on any changes that occur.

On the other hand, the technical manager is responsible for product engineering and manufacturing specifications, packaging, production delivery schedules, product inspection and testing, warranty procedures, repair services, and coordination with the business manager on any technical matters.

Managers should be designated early in the negotiating stages so that the partners can begin to understand each other's perspectives, goals, styles, and working relationships as early as possible.

Venture Manager's Authority

William Perkins, a professional project manager formerly of General Electric and a member of the Project Management Institute, advises:

"Be sure to give the venture's manager the authority, with his steering committee's approval, to shift budget dollars to deal with downstream changes. If manufacturing needs more money because of a major engineering change, the venture manager would be hamstrung if he had to go back to the parent companies each time he needed approval."

Properly empowering the venture's general manager is vital to success of the venture. In his study, Killing found two "worst case" situations where the manager made no meaningful decisions, spending most of his time collecting information for, and making presentations to, his board of directors. The manager complained that, "In no area was either parent willing to defer to the other's knowledge or expertise. I felt I was dragging an elephant behind me whenever I tried to do something."[6]

In another situation, a German company entered into a venture with a developing nation. Although the German partner had operating control of the venture, the Germans made an unusual decision and hired a general manager from the subordinate partner, apparently to "curry favor" with the local government. The general manager was ineffective, and expressed his frustration when he said:

"I was in a very peculiar and often frustrating position, since I did not control the major parameters of the business. We made most of our purchases from [the controlling partner] at a price fixed by them, again at their price. Product mix, and even the production schedule, was beyond my control. My number two man reported to his superiors in Germany every day; but because of the language problem, I never knew exactly what was being discussed. Because of the difference in parent pay scales, he was being paid even more than I was."[7]

Needless to say, this venture failed.

Venture managers also have a responsibility to manage the "interfaces" between diverse and differentiated parts of the venture. More will be said on this responsibility later.

Venture Manager Selection

Venture managers should have line management experience rather than staff or consulting experience. Line managers are driven by getting jobs done on target, on time, on budget, and at top quality. A joint venture staffed by too many experts and not enough "shakers and movers" is bound for hard luck.

In Equal Balance partnerships, especially those with only two partners, it is often advisable to select a venture's general manager from outside the partnership. Few managers can maintain neutrality when their past employer is still their supervisor. Be not deceived: Venture managers are not blessed with an easy task, and the greater the number of joint venture partners, the greater the complexity of the venture manager's task.

PRINCIPLE #2
USING DIFFERENTIATION AND INTEGRATION

What Is Differentiation and Integration?

Tasks in any organization are *specialized* for the work group to maximize its effectiveness. In a restaurant, chefs cook food and waitresses serve customers. In a hospital, doctors and nurses attend patients and administrators coordinate. In a manufacturing plant, marketing and salespeople service customers and production personnel transform raw materials into finished products. Without this type of specialization, people would be disorganized and out of harmony.

Organizational *differentiation* is a term that looks at the total differences between the specialties within a working unit. The more specialization of tasks, the more differentiation. The more complex the functions, the more differentiation.

For example, plumbers are less differentiated from electricians, than lawyers are from deep sea divers. Electronics technicians are less differentiated from electronics engineers, than chemists are from architects. Marketing executives are less differentiated from salespeople, than manufacturing production supervisors are from truck drivers.

The more highly differentiated the parts of an alliance, the more the alliance cries to be integrated/coordinated in order to be successful. For example, when a joint venture is composed of an investment banking firm, a gas line owner, and a law firm (for the purpose of establishing a gas commodities clearinghouse), the three groups look at the world from radically different perspectives. They have highly differentiated skills, needs, frames of reference, and operating procedures. Without very strong *integration*, the venture will lack the operational synergy, the linkages, the organizational unity, the drive, and the focus to be effective.

Dimensions of Differentiation

At Harvard Business School, Professors Paul Lawrence and Jay Lorsch have been studying the phenomenon of coordination in complex organizations for over 25 years. They have devised an organizational framework for analyzing differentiation and integration in order to find better methods of managing the process of integration of specialized functions. They have identified several dimensions of organizations; we have modified them here to fit the unique circumstances of joint ventures and strategic alliances.

1. *Organizational Structure.* How different are the organizations of the parent companies? Do they differ significantly from the structure of the joint venture?

2. *Time Orientation.* Do the partners have radically different pressures on how they utilize time? Will the joint venture's perspective on time differ significantly from any one of the partners?

3. *Personal Relationships.* Are there strong personal relationships between the CEOs of the partners? Are personal relationships significantly stronger within the management hierarchy of one partner than the other?

4. *Industry Orientation.* Are the industries of the partners similar or radically different? Will the industry of the joint venture be radically different from that of either of the sponsors?

5. *Rate of Change in the Environment.* Is there a significant difference between the partners regarding the speed with which their technological or market environments change? Will the joint venture's environment differ significantly from the partners?

6. *Ambiguity/Certainty of Information.* Is there a disparity between the two partners regarding the clarity, preciseness, and specificity of the information needed to be successful in the joint venture? Is the venture itself basing its decisions on clear, precise, and specific information?

7. *History of Collaboration.* Do the partners have a tradition of working together? If not, have they had a successful pattern of working with other partners?

8. *Coordinative Business Culture.* Do the partners have a natural style of management that complements a cooperative alliance? Does their style require them to work closely with other compa-

nies, or are they largely independent operators? Will their management styles clash with or within the joint venture?

9. *Social Culture.* Especially for international ventures, do the social values and norms of the partners differ widely? Are there major language barriers? Can clashes be expected within the alliance because of these differences?

10. *Complementary Technical Skills.* Are the technologies and areas of specialized competence between the partners similar or compatible? Do the experts within each of the sponsors understand the others' technical language?

By carefully analyzing these 10 dimensions, an alliance's designers can quickly determine the level of differentiation present and the level of integration needed to make the venture most effective.

Example: Real estate joint ventures are notable for their relatively high rate of success. If the prototypical real estate venture were rated for differentiation, these conclusions might be reached:

1. *Organizational Structure.* Most companies dealing in real estate development are in the construction business and are hierarchical in design (except architectural firms, which are usually collaborative). Overall, there is relatively little differentiation on this dimension; therefore, integration can usually be accomplished by adding information channels within the existing organizational hierarchy.

2. *Time Orientation.* Pressures to perform in real estate usually require rather fast response because of weather, availability of subcontractors, and the pressure of a clock ticking away on the mortgage payments until the project can open its doors and receive positive cash flow. In this area, there is little differentiation among the partners. However, government agencies needed to give approvals and permits run on an infinitely slow time clock, so high levels of integration are needed between developers and government authorities. Liaisons and personal connections, as well as political favors, are often used to bridge this high level of differentiation. Here, the integration is not needed *within* the venture, but external to it.

3. *Personal Relationships.* Usually real estate ventures are localized affairs. The presidents of the partner companies are often friends,

belong to the same clubs, and have extensive mutual friends and professional associates. Their personal affairs are already integrated locally and socially.

4. *Industry Orientation.* Joint ventures in real estate are, almost by definition, within the same industry. Even when a construction firm moves to a new locale, no significant change in industry procedures occurs because all construction is governed by a national (BOCA) building code. Again, there is little differentiation here; and much integration is provided by industry-wide standards and rules.

5. *Rate of Change in the Environment.* Although changes are numerous in the technology of building construction, they tend to be incremental in nature. Never has there been a major or fundamental change within a short period of time in this industry, as there has been in computers, consumer electronics, or biotechnology. Therefore, this dimension exhibits high stability and, consequently, low differentiation.

6. *Ambiguity/Certainty of Information.* Virtually all buildings are constructed with a universal blueprint language, and construction follows this detailed information. There is little ambiguity in this area; therefore, little differentiation exists. Again, integration is provided by a standard, industry-wide language.

7. *History of Collaboration.* Even if the prospective partners have not actually worked together, they have already learned collaborative behavior because collaboration is required between all subcontractors on a construction job. On this dimension, the differentiation level would be moderate if the partners have no working history; otherwise differentiation is low and integration of information is almost a natural process.

8. *Coordinative Business Culture.* The real estate construction industry, as a whole, requires firms to work together. Masons must interface their work with electricians, who must interface with plumbers and heating specialists. Overall, the industry is based on coordination. Here again, the differentiation rating is low, and the procedures for integration are based on age-old traditions.

9. *Social Culture.* Joint ventures involving architects with engineers have a lower differentiation level (because their professional cultures are rather similar) than those involving architects and plumbing contractors. Similarly, a development firm familiar with

supervising union workers in New York City will have far greater difficulty venturing in rural Vermont than in downtown Chicago. Therefore, the level of differentiation will vary by project location.

10. *Complementary Technical Skills.* Construction materials are all designed to be installed with labor trained through the apprentice system, the technologies are designed to interface together, and few of the technologies are so advanced that they cannot be understood by a moderately intelligent generalist. On this dimension, the venture rates a relatively low level of differentiation.

This brief analysis demonstrates that a real estate joint venture starts off in a relatively integrated environment, and only routine coordinative mechanisms may be necessary to integrate the venture effectively. Some of these additional coordinating mechanisms might be:

1. Good information for tracking and scheduling systems
2. Clear rules and procedures for decisionmaking
3. The addition of a project manager and one or two assistants to help with liaison functions between specialized work groups if the project is sufficiently large.

Given the relatively low level of differentiation that needs to be handled in a real estate venture, it should be apparent why internal management problems typically do not destroy real estate ventures, and why they statistically have a good track record of success.

In the next example—a three-way joint venture between a company strong in research and engineering, another company with a worldwide salesforce, and a third company with excellent manufacturing abilities— the sponsoring partners were faced with the problem of choosing a venture manager who would have excellent abilities to pull a diverse group of people together and get them to work in a common direction.

Using the Lawrence and Lorsch framework, the prospective partners drew up a chart and saw job positions with very disparate outlooks on business. These disparate outlooks would probably have caused frictions when the people involved tried to solve problems together. (See Table 11.1).

However, by careful selection of the integrating mechanisms and coordinators with professional experience that covered a broad diversity of

Table 11.1. Differentiated Job Perspectives

Key Jobs	Organizational Structure	Time Orientation	Personal Relations	Environment Orientation	Rate of Change	Certainty of Information
Research	Low	Long	Permissive	Science	High	Low
Sales	Medium	Short	Permissive	Customer	High	Medium
Production	High	Short	Directive	Plant	Low	High

these orientations, the designers of this alliance were able to bridge the key differences in orientation between the members.

Integrating Mechanisms

There are two great dilemmas in joint ventures. First, the reason for joining forces is the unique areas of *specialization* of each of the partners (differentiation). Second, the joint venture—to be successful—must attain a strong unified position (integration). Lawrence and Lorsch are very direct about this dilemma.[8] To paraphrase:

> When groups in an organization need to be highly differentiated, but also require tight integration, it is necessary for the organization to develop more complicated integrating mechanisms. The basic organizational mechanism for achieving integration is, of course, the management hierarchy. In organizations with low differentiation, we have found that this is often sufficient to achieve the required intergroup collaboration. However, organizations faced with the requirement for both a high degree of differentiation and tight integration must develop *supplemental* integrating devices, such as individual coordinators, cross–unit teams, and (liaisons) whose basic contribution is achieving integration among other groups.

Essentially, there are five methods for improving integration within a complex organization:

1. *Rules and Policies:* Increase number and clarity of rules, policies, and written procedures to deal with new situation
2. *Hierarchy:* Funnel decisions into existing chain of command to avoid confusion
3. *Planning and Information Systems:* Create centralized planning

and computer analyses, centralized files, and up-to-date sources of information

4. *Excess (slack) resources:* Provide more people or machinery to fill the voids in staffing or production

5. *Lateral relations:* Make more effective use of lower-level expertise, create better communications between lower echelons.

The first four methods have been dealt with extensively in numerous other management books. However, the last method, lateral relations, is vitally significant to the unique circumstances of joint ventures. Without a sound understanding of how this fifth dimension interplays with the other four, the designer of a business alliance will miss an important though sometimes subtle factor in building successful cooperation.

Lateral Relations

Lateral relations simply refers to the reduction of the number of decisions referred upward, thereby increasing the capacity of the organization to process information. This function is most useful when the decisions are qualitative in nature, not just numbers-oriented. Its fundamental premise is to utilize direct contact between experts who share a problem, rather than send decisions up and down a cumbersome chain of command (which, in a joint venture, may be a bit convoluted) that may not be equipped to deal with the issues.

Author Peter Drucker says business confederations need to deal person-to-person to compensate for the cultural differences between partners. Because these partnerships are more highly specialized in a narrower range of products, players must speak a similar language, regardless of their corporate or national cultural backgrounds.

Jay Galbraith, author of *Designing Complex Organizations*, suggests people whose career paths have included lateral transfers from one department to another will be more effective in managing lateral relations. He says, "Managers having interdepartmental experience communicate to a larger number of colleagues [and] they are also more likely to perceive the presence of conflict" than other managers.[9]

The Role of the Coordinator/Integrator

Drucker suggests that in an alliance, because no one company is in charge, no one is in sole control. He adds, because autonomous organizations such as joint ventures cannot be commanded but must work together, the critical skill is *coordination*. When it is critical to have innovation, close integration between work groups is essential. Lawrence and Lorsch call this vital coordinative role an *integrator*.[10]

According to Lawrence and Lorsch, integrators are individuals whose skills enable them to increase a venture's ability to specialize in what it does best, while at the same time coordinate these specializations into a unified organization working for a common goal. In their studies, these researchers found the most effective complex organizations in rapidly changing environments had key individuals who integrated/coordinated the diverse management functions to achieve a unified effort.

An integrator is similar to most general or division managers with "line" authority over functional departments. But, in the most effective complex organizations, Lawrence and Lorsch found *several* people performing the role of the integrator, even though *only one* may have ultimate authority.

Job Titles

The researchers found that the job titles for integrators included product manager, program coordinator, project leader, business manager, planning director, systems designer, and task force chairman. Job titles are not nearly as important as the skills exhibited to pull the organization into a team. The best coordinators have certain skills, particularly in communication, conflict resolution, scheduling, problemsolving, and financial controls. Effective integrators are generally adventurous, humorous, and flexible, not rigid or overly methodical.

Coordinative/Integrative Skills

Lawrence and Lorsch found that, to be most effective, integrators need to feel they are contributing to the important decisions of the organization based on their competence and knowledge, not because of their positional authority. In fact, it was learned that, in most cases, these people do not have much positional authority at all, and exhibit most of their influence through personal persuasion. Their persuasive power is based both on their personalities and competence as experts. Ultimately, their styles can prevent internal dissension and possible stalemating, which can destroy a diverse team.

Another important characteristic of an effective integrator is the ability to relate to the diverse perspectives of the variety of specialists within the organization. For example, research and engineering personnel hold a longer-term view that revolves around science, concepts, and technology. This attitude greatly differs from that of the production manager, whose whole work ethic is built around rapid decisions, efficiency, and practical application. Effective coordinators are able to pull diverse interests together; managers best suited as coordinators can handle great diversity.

The players in the alliance most in need of integrative skills are the champions, the general and project managers, and the corporate liaisons. For example, Ross Systems, Inc. of Palo Alto is a financial software firm with extensive cooperative marketing agreements with Digital Equipment Corporation (DEC) of Massachusetts. Ken Ross, Ross Systems' president, found an excellent integrator to manage the relationship between Ross and DEC by hiring a former DEC employee who knew the "behind the scenes" rules and procedures.

In a real estate joint venture, the individuals concerned with marketing a building are probably unlikely to be naturally adept at communicating with the construction supervisors. In this case, the architect or developer may take on the integrator's role to bridge the communications gap.

Both architects and developers usually have their roots in organizations that are not hierarchical in nature and their task orientations require a broad understanding of a myriad of issues, thereby increasing their likelihood as successful integrators. Table 11.2 indicates the key job positions within a joint venture which require leadership, management, integration, and technical skills.

Effective coordinators see the "big" picture and talk the many languages of the venture. Integrators at the upper echelons use a variety of leadership styles to get the job done, picking a style that matches the situation. They are able to focus goals into a common vision, maximizing the use of diffused resources.

The Liaison Role

Another coordinative role is that of the liaison. Liaisons are established when the volume of communications contacts begins to become too difficult to manage, especially if information is normally referred upward in the organization and might tend to become bottlenecked.

Liaisons serve as buffers between the venture and the sponsor organizations. As Norm Alister commented in *Electronic Business*, liaisons are "often the only force capable of keeping the form-shuffling bureaucratic 'memo-masters' from tying up the new venture in mountains of red tape."[11]

Table 11.2. Key Positions and Skill Requirements

Job Positions	Critical Skills			
	Leadership	Management	Integration	Technical
Sponsor CEO/Godfather	High	High	Medium	Low
Sponsor Sr VP/Exec. Champion	High	High	Medium	Medium/Low
Venture Manager/Project Champion	High	High	High	Medium
Functional/Technical Managers	Medium/Low	Medium/High	Medium/High	Medium/High
Corporate Liaisons	Low	Medium	Medium/High	Medium/High

The venture's manager is often one of the joint venture's liaisons, primarily responsible to the venture itself. The sponsoring partner's liaison, referred to as a "corporate liaison," is primarily responsible to the sponsor.

In smaller ventures, the liaison may also be "double hatted" as the champion. Stratus Computer has had a long-standing and highly successful strategic alliance with IBM, in which IBM sells Stratus computers and together they work on developing networking software. The president of Stratus, Nicholas Bologna, a former IBM employee, serves as champion and Stratus liaison to IBM, who, in turn, assigns an IBM liaison to Stratus.

Between Stratus and IBM, all requests for information are channelled and supervised through either a project manager or technical liaison on either side. No other people may initiate or respond to information requests. This rule limits information slipping over the transom or being mismanaged. Only four IBM employees are authorized to issue these information requests, thus preventing Stratus from becoming deluged with red tape. IBM is very careful in its choice of liaison personnel, being considerate of the different needs and concerns a smaller partner will have.

If required, IBM will increase the number of liaisons for larger joint ventures as it did when it set up its initial alliance with ROLM. In that instance, liaisons were assigned to specific areas, such as manufacturing, system development, and finance. They serve as "two-way funnels," tracking relevant information and providing resources on both sides of the alliance.

According to J. William Scruggs, director of business development and practices at IBM:

"Each of [our liaisons] have great personal knowledge and personal contacts throughout IBM. It could be access to manufacturing systems that we have, or perhaps IBM has solved a specific technical problem or he could make available some of the things we're doing in terms of software. So it is an efficiency or time-saving concept. The people who are most effective at that tend to have a very broad knowledge of IBM, and even though they might be the liaison in a specific function, they have the breadth of knowledge that goes to other areas, and they seem to have widespread contacts throughout IBM."[12]

Liaisons should have helpful attitudes and lots of contacts. Effective liaisons are the mid-level "interdepartmental deal makers," trading favors and linking information. The best ones are not self-centered but organizationally-centered. This is not the prototypical "organization man" who passes information up and down the chain of command; it is a job for a seasoned insider.

Jay Galbraith cautions to be sure liaisons are rewarded for supporting a joint venture outside their regular career paths. Be sure they are not rotated in and out of this position too frequently. He gives the example of how *not* to send a signal to the rest of the organization:

Boss:	"It's your turn in the barrel."
Liaison:	"I'm too busy."
Boss:	"It'll be okay; it won't be for long."[13]

PRINCIPLE #3
THE AMBIGUITY–CERTAINTY CONTINUUM

The ambiguity–certainty continuum refers to the relative amount of clarity within the joint venture environment. Joint ventures are designed to overcome risks. If the risks are measurable, specific, and easily defined, a modicum of certainty exists in the risk environment.

However, if the conditions are similar to the conditions in one of the ventures mentioned earlier where the partners saw themselves faced with "solving a triple simultaneous equation with all unknowns"—the unknown formulation of the actual product, the unknown kind of machinery that would produce that product, and the unknown of market demand—then we could conclude there is an ambiguous, and therefore risky environment in which the alliance would operate. The greater the uncertainty of the task, the greater the unpredictability and, therefore, the greater the amount of information that must be processed among decisionmakers to achieve a given level of performance.

Similarly, if the companies involved have not worked together closely in the past, the greater the uncertainty in team relations and, therefore, the greater the need to focus on and maintain close working relationships. Anyone who has been involved in sports competition knows significant time is needed for any team to "jell." If the partners' teamwork is untested, the organizational structure must adapt to this condition.

Options to Deal with Ambiguity

Conditions of high ambiguity will call for more information to be processed, more collaboration, increased lower-level decisionmaking, and stronger lateral relations. Partners have three fundamental sets of choices to make in order to deal with highly ambiguous situations. The first set of choices aims at *risk reduction*. The partners can scale down the venture to a smaller, less risky size, or phase the project into risks that are clearer and more certain to be successfully conquered. The partners could also step away from the alliance and begin with a less formal cooperative venture, such as a licensing agreement, a joint marketing program, or sharing research data, all requiring less integration of functioning.

The second set of choices focuses on *consolidation*, where one partner takes operational control and assumes most of the risk, figuring that the advantages of internal decisionmaking and internal resources outweigh the increased complexity of coordinative sharing of information, decisionmaking, and control. The subordinate partner may still make resource contributions to the venture, but only within the framework designated by the superior partner.

The last set of choices addresses an *organizational* solution that maximizes the resources of the partners, believing that, without the full contribution of knowledge and expertise by both the partners, the risks will be overwhelming.

If the venture's partners choose the organizational solution, they should begin to analyze their risk situation by examining some of the conditions described in Table 11.3 and determining the appropriate management functions to match their conditions.

While few ventures are completely oriented to one end of the Ambi-

Table 11.3. The Ambiguity–Certainty Continuum

Ambiguity ◀—————————————————————▶ Certainty
Conditions

Dynamic change	Stability and predictability
Innovation required	Routines required
Unanticipated problems	Anticipated problems
Developments outside organization control	Developments within organization control
Information unclear or inadequate	Information clear and adequate
Management Functions	
Collaborative management styles	Hierarchical/task-management styles
Decisionmaking at lower levels	Decisionmaking at higher levels
Mature personnel needed at all levels	Mature personnel needed at higher levels
Looser structures needed	Tighter structures needed
Shared decisionmaking	Decision-dominance of one partner
Predominant lateral information flow	Predominant vertical information flow

guity–Certainty spectrum or the other, the spectrum will assist you in developing a set of management functions that relate to the specific conditions within which your venture is designed to operate. If some parts of the venture are clear and crisp (i.e. as in the production phase) but other parts are highly unknown (i.e. as in the marketing phase) then the continuum would suggest production organization may be more centrally organized and hierarchical in nature, but the marketing organization may need be more collaborative.

As times change, new conditions of ambiguity arise in organizations. Unanticipated problems, developments outside the organization's control, and unclear or inadequate information are just some situations that may drive the venture to reexamine its management functions.

Problems and Opportunities in Managing Ambiguity

Ambiguity presents a special condition to a manager: it creates the potential for counterdependence, conflict, and creativity within work groups— all at the same time. When a situation or condition is unclear, groups will naturally attempt to impose some structure on the problem in order to attain a better level of understanding. As a result, a group will either look to its leader to provide direction, support, and solutions, or it may decide to reject its leader—"We can handle this ourselves"—especially if the members do not think the leader can handle the problem. If they feel overwhelmed by the problem, they may feel out of control, resulting in anxiety, frustration, blame, and confusion.

A real dilemma faces the manager at this juncture. On the one hand, ambiguous, complex situations generally call for decentralized decision-making and lower-level autonomy; on the other hand, the psychological needs of the team demand structure, direction, and discipline—and the sponsors want performance, not confusion. This dilemma is particularly acute when dealing with personnel who are used to highly structured, unambiguous working environments. Richard Clawson, Program Manufacturing Manager for Ford Aerospace and Communications states: "Experienced manufacturing people tend to emphasize rules and focus on following them. Where flexibility and innovation are needed, [their] mechanisms are rigid, and to make matters worse, [they] tend to formalize behavior [because] constant ambiguity drives everyone crazy. The lack of order causes fear of the unknown, and under such highly unstable conditions, the whole operation becomes immobilized. Managers, who also operate formally, tend to panic. Witch-hunts begin, fear mounts on top of fear, the situation goes from bad to very bad to worse to impossible."[14]

The manager must do *something*. Left unchecked and undirected, these highly ambiguous situations, particularly in the earlier stages of an alliance, can lead to the formation of stereotypes and generalizations, which can then escalate into conflict. If unaddressed, these conditions will spread and polarize the alliance right down party lines.

At this point, the manager must intervene with a structured process of problemsolving that redirects the anxiety onto a course of creativity. Some methods for achieving this redirection are:

- Delineate several optional courses of action, letting the group suggest additional alternatives, and force the group members to deal with choosing an alternative to which they will be committed.
- Restructure the work group to cope with the ambiguous condition by decentralizing or recentralizing decisionmaking, increasing or decreasing information flow, creating more or fewer liaisons, or breaking the desired results down into smaller, more realistic goals.
- Put more valid information into the problem, break assumptions, and put boundaries around the problem by defining the worst possible outcome.
- Break stereotyping (unfreeze people) by introducing new information that conflicts with old data.
- Display no tolerance for inappropriate blaming; reinforce the "team culture" of the alliance.
- Explore more effective methods of controlling the variables (i.e., lobby with local officials, employ a specialist, use a more standard formula).
- Establish more clear ground rules about teamwork, cooperation, communication, coordination, and commitment.

Clawson recommends using high level liaisons with broad knowledge to provide support and to "go into the trenches, observe what's happening, and observe what employees are saying. They need to open their minds and think. Most important, managers should provide rigid systems for rigid situations, and flexible systems for flexible situations."[15]

Organizational Management Style

To maximize effectiveness and to deal with the variables of the ambiguity–certainty continuum, the management style of most alliance organizations will be some combination of the hierarchical and the collaborative styles. Generally, few alliances are successful with only one style or the other; there should be a mix for the alliance to have enough power to function. Obviously, if the partners choose the Superior/Subordinate structure, they will have more hierarchical elements than collaborative ones. If the Equal Balance structure is chosen, the venture will rely more upon the collaborative and less upon the hierarchical.

Some alliances may emphasize completely different management styles in different phases of operations or within certain divisions of operations. Table 11.4 highlights some of the distinctions between the hierarchical and collaborative styles of management.

You should remember, however, that at the points in the organization where groups with major stylistic differences must work together, conflicts are bound to occur. Someone with good integrative skills should mediate the "interface."

PRINCIPLE #4
INTERFACE MANAGEMENT

Every manager has had some previous experience with "interface management," even without calling it by name. The point of contact between two internal departments—or any differentiated groups, for that matter— is called the *interface.*

Interfaces: Where Problems and Complexities Lie

Manufacturing executives know of the frustration they experience when dealing with issues between the engineering and production departments. Engineers are often at odds with the production manager because production does not give engineering enough lead-time, or production is lowering the product quality by cutting corners. Production personnel complain that engineers will not "get practical," and production steams when the sales department promises unfeasible delivery dates, regardless of how valued the customer might be.

Chief technical engineers also know about interfaces. They can always predict that problems will occur where different technologies must interrelate. For example, when designing robots the points at which the mechanical systems must interface with the electronic sensing systems are the areas the designers know difficulties will emerge. Again, where the sensing system interfaces with the computer control system, they will

Table 11.4. Hierarchical and Collaborative Management Styles

Dimensions of Management structure	Hierarchical	Collaborative
Authority		
Guidelines:	Policies, procedures, rules	Standards and behaviors accepted by work unit
Leader role:	Guides work unit	Builds mutual trust, support, and cohesion in work unit
Influence:	From leader to group	From work unit to its members
Direction:	Leader directs work unit	Work unit directs its members
Decisionmaking		
Interpreted as:	Precise	Guidelines for work
Binds the individual:	To the leader's decision	To the work unit's decision
Power for implementation:	Leader or organization	Work unit and its cohesion
Enforced by pressure from:	Leader and organization	Within work unit
Communication		
Listening:	To leader's ideas	To work unit's ideas
Sensitivity:	Toward leader	Among work unit members
Directionality:	Downward by instruction/advice	Lateral by mutual influence
Style:	Gives directives	Asks guiding but poignant questions
Conflict		
Disputes are:	Controlled by leader	Avoided by work unit
Resolved by:	Leaders or policy	Work unit by consensus
Activities determined by:	Leaders	Consensus between leader and work unit
Competence located in:	Leaders	Work unit membership
Planning and evaluation done by:	Leaders	Work unit
Commitment is to:	Leader's tasks and needs	Work unit's tasks and needs
Primary relationship between:	Leader and sponsors	Leader and work unit
Roles are:	Fixed or constant	Flexible, depending on work unit's situation or tasks

experience difficulties. With near certainty, problems and complexities will lie at the interfaces, whether the interfaces be organizational or technological.

Interfaces are simply examples of *differentiation*. Every company composed of more than one department experiences these conflicts because, when we specialize, we create differences in frames of reference, time perspectives, points of view, needs, values, and operating pressures. The principle of interface management says that *most organizational frictions occur at interfaces* between specialized work groups, and the role of the coordinator-integrator is to manage the interface to maximize people's abilities to get the job done. In alliances, *the greater the differentiation of partner membership, or the greater the complexity and specialization of task functions, the more problems will emerge at the points of interface.*

Integrator's Problemsolving Role

The first task in interface management is to begin identifying the interfaces before the organization goes into full swing. In this way, points of potential conflict can be isolated beforehand and personnel can be assigned to the integrator's role to head off potential problems.

When problems emerge—and they will—the integrator's role is to manage the decisionmaking, not necessarily to make the decisions. (Clearly, in times of crisis or urgency, the integrator may become the decisionmaker.) To be effective in a highly ambiguous environment with mature people on staff, the integrator will bring key individuals together to build consensus, help the groups mutually diagnose problems, and stimulate creative solutions that maximize meeting each group's needs, while at the same time insisting that the venture's goals be met.

As Jay Galbraith says in *Designing Complex Organizations:*

> "The integrator's role is not to make the best decision, but to see that the best decision gets made. . . . He must be able to listen to a proposal in "marketing talk" and restate it in "engineering talk." Thus, the use of integrators achieves coordination without eliminating the differences—languages, attitudes, etc.—that promote good subtask performance. . . . The behaviors of line managers which are described as strong, quick, and decisive would be considered dogmatic, closed-minded, and bull-headed if exhibited by an integrator."[16]

Managing Conflict

The effective integrator will not bury conflict that emerges between work groups. Instead, the integrator sees conflict as an opportunity to transform tension into creative solutions. Granted, those experiencing the conflict may not naturally gravitate toward this attitude, but it is the skill of the integrator to bring people together, listen carefully, establish a framework to develop mutual understanding, and guide the groups to see the larger picture when developing solutions.

Nearly all strategic alliances and joint ventures are built on the premise that most decisions will be reached by some form of consensus. Consensus is not majority vote; rather, it is an understanding by all involved that everyone has had a chance to put their ideas on the table. While there may still be some disagreement, the team then agrees to move on for the good of the venture.

Integrators should also be firm in clarifying which actions will not be tolerated when conflict emerges. Those who begin by blaming, accusing, or hurling inflammatory remarks should be properly reprimanded. The integrator must not be soft on discipline and must insist upon maintaining a corporate culture based upon teamwork.

Conflicts can occur at all levels of the alliance, from the bottom to the top. Researchers Harrigan at Columbia University and Killing at the University of Western Ontario both found that, when companies begin to grow dissatisfied with each other in unsuccessful ventures, they seldom confront the problems openly with their counterparts. However, venture managers and sponsor CEOs who were able to put differences and problems in the open had a better chance of turning the alliance in the direction of successful achievement.

The "Hidden Ball Trick"

Because lines of authority are not precise in an alliance, there will often be confusion or ambiguity concerning who is responsible for accomplishing a specific task and what exact role the participants should play. For example, several years ago, the federal government's General Services Administration brought in a new director from private business to attempt to straighten out a rather tangled organization. The new director had not been on the job long when a particularly sensitive problem emerged requiring rapid action. He called in his right-hand man and stated: "I want whoever is responsible for this problem in my office at two o'clock this afternoon."

Promptly at two o'clock, 17 administrators paraded into the director's office. Puzzled, the director asked his assistant why there were so many people for the meeting. The assistant replied that all 17 were the people responsible for the problem. The director, somewhat befuddled, explained that this may be how things are handled in a bureaucracy, but in private business, one person is responsible, not an entire organization.

Similarly, designers of the alliance should be cautious not to create a Gordian Knot that strangles decisionmaking and operational integrity. This can happen if partners, in an effort to create teamwork, attempt to involve too many people at too many levels in too many decisions.

Responsibility Charting

Responsibility charting has been designed to reduce ambiguity at the work group interfaces. One of the first tasks of the steering committee is to clarify roles and responsibilities to prevent people from tripping over each other. This process defines how people should act in relation to the other players, and the key decisions they must make. This task is far more functional than simply assigning titles to job positions because it gets to the meat of the critical issue: Who is responsible for what? And how does their working relationship interact with others?

Richard Beckhard, retired professor of MIT's Sloan School of Management, advises using a system of responsibility charting to overcome the potential confusion of interlocking management. This technique should be used if any chance exists for ambiguity or overlapping of roles, confusion as to who is in charge, or mixed loyalties.

Beckhard recommends bringing teams together to formulate and disseminate the responsibility charts prior to actually making these decisions. Key players should be involved in developing a consensus regarding role assignments, matching each major decision or task with the individual or organizational unit necessary to carry out that operational decision or task. Each individual is then assigned a specific functional role (and only one role per person for each task). See Table 11.5

The role categories Beckhard suggests have been expanded to meet the needs of joint ventures: (These categories can and should be modified if needed to suit the needs of your situation.)

Table 11.6 illustrates this procedure in a joint venture between a marketing firm and a manufacturing company that established a small detached organization for coordination of manufacturing and distribution of their products.

In this example, broad tasks are divided between organizations. If desired a further refinement of the charting then splits the broad tasks into specific activities and assigns one person to be *responsible* for that activity, while more than one person can have daily *accountability*. Be careful not to have more than one person responsible for any task or decision.

Table 11.5 Responsibility Charting System

Functions	Code
· Responsibility for carrying out programs	(R)
· Keep informed (after the decision)	(Info)
· Input (before the decision)	(Input)
· Support (be involved, but not responsible)	(S)
· Veto Power (implies approval power)	(V)
· Accountable (on a day-to-day basis)	(A)

Table 11.6. Sample Responsibility Chart

Task	Steering Committee	Joint Venture Company	Marketing Company	Manufacturing Company
Develop operations plan	R	S	S	S
Develop product specs	V	R	S	S
Engineer the product	S	V	Input	R
Establish manufacturing budget	V	Info	—	R
Manufacture the product	Input	Input	Info	R
Pricing and costing	R	S	S	S
Purchase materials	Info	Info	—	R
Establish sales quotas	V	Input	R	Info
Train sales reps	Info	S	A	Input
Design literature	V	Info	R	Input

Otherwise, each person will assume the other is responsible, and operations will quickly disintegrate.

Roy Bonner, retired IBM manufacturing troubleshooter and currently a management consultant, strives to hold only one person responsible for achieving a specific, measurable result. He feels that the venture's reputation is dependent upon holding to these commitments. "A group is never responsible," he states, "only a person."

PRINCIPLE #5
COLLABORATIVE DECISIONMAKING

No alliance can succeed at the task of coordination without teamwork. *Teamwork* is not just a trendy word; it is the basis for using "chemistry" to advantage, it is the manifestation of "synergy," and it is often "salvation" in times of crisis. But, as those familiar with teamwork in athletics will attest, teamwork comes from practice, continued working relationships, trust, fairness, consideration, organization, and discipline.

Making an operational decision in an alliance can be cumbersome if the partners lack teamwork. What should normally be simple and straightforward can become complex and convoluted if the partners do not have a strong common vision for the future of the venture, or if they disagree regarding authority to operate the venture. And, if too much time is needed to make a decision, competitive advantages may quickly slip away while the partners are pondering.

Teamwork cannot flourish at any level unless teamwork exists at the top echelons of the venture itself. In addition, experienced venture managers will tell you that the more players and the more organizations, the more difficult the task of managing. Coordinating these responsibilities and activities will require some form of board or committee.

The formal decisionmaking structure will vary from alliance to alliance, depending upon the legal structure, the frequency and amount of contact needed, and the sponsors' personal preferences. Corporate joint ventures may have a board of directors, which usually meets quarterly, and a management committee made up of the top venture managers and one representative (often the executive champion) from each sponsor, which meets regularly. Partnerships may have a partners' committee and a policy committee. Written Contract alliances may have a coordinating committee. The names are far less important than the primary functions. For the purposes of simplicity, we refer throughout this chapter to this variety of coordinating entities as the "steering committee," illustrating the coordinative function it serves.

The Steering Committee's Purpose

The steering committee is an operational committee and the principal focal point of top management team activity. The committee has five major purposes:

1. *Policy Guidance:* to provide direction and support directly to the venture through the sponsors' representatives
2. *Performance Review:* to measure progress against some mutually agreed upon standards
3. *Pressure:* to put continued pressure on the venture in the form of support, planning, and the expectations for performance

4. *Problemsolving*: to identify and solve problems in the event of unforeseen difficulties, needed resources, and so on

5. *Partnership Relations*: to maintain communications, understanding, trust, and fairness

At the outset, the steering committee should set the pace by clearly defining roles and operational reporting channels. The level of operational autonomy of the venture manager should be specified and agreed upon by the steering committee and the venture's owners. When problems do arise, the responsibilities for solving those problems should be placed at a pre-agreed level in the organizational framework.

William Kirk, the president of a small electronics company engaged in a joint venture with a larger manufacturer, has several tips for steering committees as the alliance begins to get underway. *First*, he advises that there be an honest discussion, up front, on how the owners expect the venture to be run. *Second*, they should address the issue of what happens when something goes wrong. "No one has passed this way before, therefore something is bound to go awry!" he warns. *Third*, keep the sponsors committed and supportive by giving each steering committee member a project to accomplish with a completion date.

The steering committee will be the focus of activity for maintaining high sponsor commitment, and the mechanism for converting goals into specific accomplishments.

Steering Committee Composition

Some steering committees choose an even number of people to ensure plurality for any decision. In the event of a tie vote, more negotiations must occur. To prevent a deadlock, other committees choose an odd number of people—three, five, or seven—weighted slightly in favor of the sponsor who bears most of the risk in the venture.

The rank of steering committee members does not vary too much from venture to venture. It usually includes at least one high-ranking, influential person from each of the sponsors. This person is usually the sponsoring company's "champion" of the venture. If a second representative of the sponsor is on the committee, it will usually be a high-ranking manager representing a functional department that is the sponsor's "lead" or specialty department for the venture (i.e., marketing or manufacturing or engineering).

Representing the venture itself will be the venture's head person, and often one or more of the venture's key management personnel. These personnel are referred to by a variety of names depending upon the type of organization; some of their titles are general manager, project manager, systems coordinator, program manager, and product manager. (The generic term "venture manager" is used here for simplicity.) Sometimes liaisons will also be on the committee. Most steering committees have the authority to call anyone to attend meetings to give their input on technical or operational matters.

The schedule for steering committee meetings varies from venture to venture. Some meet weekly and others biweekly, but seldom less frequently than monthly. Most committees have a provision for meeting at any time requested by a member.

Executive Champion's Role

It is absolutely essential to have the venture's champions represented on the steering committee because they help the venture overcome potentially serious problems and pitfalls. For example,

- Any unclear or unrealistic goals imposed by the sponsor can be clarified and focused. The champion is the policy representative of the sponsoring company and is the venture's primary and regular connection to the sponsor's top decisionmaker.
- Many ventures have suffered from poor integration of the venture's products into the sponsoring companies, often because of the "not invented here" syndrome. To overcome this, the executive champions often assume the role of product integrator.
- In the event the corporate liaison is stymied at lower levels, the executive champion helps find internal resources within his or her company that can assist with the venture.
- Finally, each sponsor is usually responsible for committing certain support to the venture. The executive champion is responsible for watching the "people process," making sure quality people are helping the venture achieve its goals and ensuring the venture receives the proper level of corporate attention from the sponsors.

Smaller companies venturing with large companies may not have many hierarchical levels of involvement, so the smaller company CEO is frequently "double-hatted" as the "executive champion" and may also be the corporate liaison, while the larger-company counterpart may be a divisional manager.

Selection of executive champions is a very important issue, as Edward Roberts, professor at MIT's Sloan School, and also an accomplished technology entrepreneur, comments: "The large company . . . has to take on a very special interface management relationship, . . . [they] have to very carefully select people . . . for the role of relating to small companies . . . to have gentleness, diplomacy, and an ability to work with somebody much smaller than they are without making you feel it." In Roberts' venture between his small medical firm and the massive EG&G, Inc., EG&G's CEO Bernard J. O'Keefe had the right personality as an executive champion. "He was patient. He sat in board meetings and took a lot of crap. He didn't lord the fact that he was running a billion-dollar company over five guys that were running a million-dollar company. . . . He made offers which he allowed to be rejected. He wouldn't push."[17]

Responsibilities of the Venture Manager

A venture manager must know that the success of the venture will be highly dependent upon the long-term good will and support of the sponsors. Even if the venture is dominated by a shareholder with greater than 50 percent control, it is important for the venture manager to avoid being heavy-handed and to refrain from driving a wedge between the partners.

Peter Killing tells an exemplary story about a 50–50 venture. In this particular cast, "the eight-man board consisted of four executives from the American parent, three from the German parent, and the general manager, who was a former employee of the German company. The manager made it clear to both parents that, should any issue come to a board vote, he would vote with the German parent executives—even if he disagreed with them—thus creating a four–four deadlock. In other words, all issues would have to be negotiated. Yet, in 14 years of his administration, no issue has ever been put to the board for a formal vote."[18]

The venture manager must build a "common vision"—a bond of similar perspectives and values about the overall venture—shared by the rest of his operational managers if they are to be effective. If no cohesion is found at the steering committee level there will be no unity at any other level in the venture.

It is highly advisable that the venture manager be involved in designing the operational aspects of the partnership at the earlier stages of negotiations. One of the reasons for difficulties in alliance management has been the lack of commitment of the venture manager once the sponsoring CEO turns the venture over to the company's operational side if the manager was not involved at the negotiations stage. If changes in personnel need to be made, they should be spotted very early.

Teams and Task Forces

To complement the venture's normal formal organization structure, most venture managers also find it quite valuable to form task forces and teams, particularly when they must address interface management problems or highly ambiguous challenges. Task forces and teams are a key element in the coordinative management style that makes precise use of lateral relations. As a general rule, task forces and teams are formed when informal contacts alone cannot solve a problem and it is necessary for three or more organizational groups to be involved in the solution.

Task forces are ad-hoc groups formed for a limited time. As Jay Galbraith suggests, the task force is a temporary patchwork used to shorten communications lines in a time of uncertainty.

Task forces must communicate regularly with the established chain of command to integrate information with those having regular line responsibility. However, do not let the regular managers become frustrated because they feel the task force has put them out of the communications loop. Task force members should communicate regularly with these managers.

Teams cross functional lines and are made up of diverse experts or lower-level managers to solve recurring problems where the resources to solve the problem are not at top echelons. The team provides functional managers with a broader flexible staff to augment their own specialized crew.

Assignments to teams should be made on the basis of having relevant information and the authority to make commitments for the functional groups they represent. Teams often are made up of liaison personnel specifically assigned to a team because of their particular skills in coordination. Some members of teams are assigned to meet regularly, whereas some members attend only on an "as-needed" basis.

Teams and task forces tend to create better coordination and communications at the lower levels of the alliance, as well as between the partners and the venture itself. For example, a successful joint venture was formed between an electronics systems company and an aerospace company to bid on a sophisticated missile control system for the U.S. Navy. They won the contract. After producing units for over a year, the venture decided to bid on a project for the Army. A technical engineering task force was established that brought together technical resources from both sponsors, plus technical systems engineers and the production manager from the venture's staff. The task force was assigned the job of completing all bidding requirements, and reported directly to the steering committee through the venture's general manager. The venture won the bid. The task force was then converted into a permanent team to bring the product through the engineering phases, into production and, subsequently, through field trials.

Task forces and teams require additional human resources and, therefore, staff support to be effective. These staffing and resource needs are too frequently left out of the planning process.

Organizational Structure and Personnel Functions

No ideal organizational structure exists for a joint venture. However, the following diagram will provide a basic "wiring diagram" outlining some of the fundamental relationships. (See Figure 11.1)

Milestone Management

Most joint ventures establish clear milestones against which to measure progress, and thus help bring a project to fruition. The steering committee's role is to outline the framework of interim project reports, to conduct

Figure 11.1. Organizational Relations Between Joint Venture and Sponsors

Sponsor A	Joint Venture	Sponsor B
CEO	---communications---	CEO
Division Manager Champion	---communications---	Division Manager Champion
Project Manager		Project Manager
Corporate Liaison	Steering Committee	Corporate Liaison
Operational Managers	Sponsor Division Managers	Operational Managers
	Venture Manager Key Project Managers	
	Teams Task Forces	

periodic performance reviews, to ensure that time deadlines are met, and to review the completed project.

Management consultant Roy Bonner advises being extremely accurate on timing and having a means to track progress precisely. He says, "If you can't measure it, you can't manage it."

When the joint venture involves the development of a new product, or the construction of a specific project, the operational steering committee will often establish guidelines for the venture manager to review the entire program at various stages. This review ensures that the risk of completion will not be substantially greater than originally expected. Invariably, a review of the final results of the project will determine if it meets specifications.

For example, in a large mining project, the steering committee may review interim reports on development at the one-third and two-thirds completion stages or other critical developmental milestones. If any major impediments loom that require significant increases in capital investment, the steering committee will call a board of directors meeting to determine if the project should proceed or be abandoned, or to see if any one of the partners desires to withdraw while the others proceed. Similar provisions are part and parcel of many joint research and development projects in high technology.

William Perkins, a professional project manager, comments that the project evaluation and review system should be simple and practical. PERT (Project Evaluation and Review Technique) and CPM (Critical Path Method) will only work "if you have the time, the money, and the people to make it work," he says. Otherwise, choose a simpler, easily managed system. If unforeseen problems arise in meeting critical milestones, managers must have a means of obtaining resource commitments from the steering committee or the sponsors. This procedure should be planned in advance.

PRINCIPLE #6
MANAGING CROSS-CORPORATE RELATIONS

Maintaining the relationship between the partners is more than just a nicety. By capitalizing on an effective working relationship, the venture achieves the synergy that makes "1 + 1 = 3." High "relationship factors" in an alliance enable the partners to gain or take advantage of operational as well as strategic synergies. When the relationship is working, the chemistry between the partners enables them to work more closely as a team and more creatively in their problemsolving.

The time and human resources necessary to manage a partnership can be high, and venture organizers must be prepared to make commitments to the relationship as well as the operational aspects of the venture. Without coordinators and integrators in place, without using teams and task forces, an alliance may flounder. Leaders should look to the future and anticipate demands and pressures, and design their operations accordingly.

If such commitments push the venture to the limits of a realistic allocation of resources, the organizers should consider using a Superior/Subordinate control structure that centralizes operational leadership in one of the partners, thereby diminishing the need for cross-corporate relations. If this choice is made, there will be important sacrifices in the synergistic advantages of the venture. Another alternative is to narrow the scope of the venture, thus leveraging available resources more effectively.

Coordination and Control

Coordination between the partners becomes increasingly more vital when the frequency of contact should be regular, and when: (1) there is no separate organization through which the venture operates; (2) there is a strong need to share information and resources between the partners; and (3) the venture is intended to be highly captive for the partners. When designing the operational organization of the joint venture remember that, *if coordination between the partners must be high, then control must also be high.* In addition, *high control conditions are mandated when the risks are high.* All joint ventures should have strong financial control systems in their early stages of development.

When there is a high need for control overlayed with the need for strong entrepreneurial management, beware of a potentially "hypertensive" environment. High levels of outside corporate control may conflict with an entrepreneurial manager's style, causing friction and frustration. In these circumstances, discussions beforehand are advisable.

Different corporate cultures also have different thresholds of control, since they may have widely varying needs for information and centralization of decisionmaking. These control issues can conflict if a partner has a far different threshold of control.

Columbia University's Kathryn Harrigan comments:

Alliances "are especially difficult for managers within firms that instinctively overmanage their subsidiaries and for managers that are unaccustomed to techniques for managing cooperation. A regular flow of requests from owners' managers to the venture's managers for figures, status reports, and other information fairly overwhelms the venture managers, especially if the joint venture is small and the inquiring owner is large. When frustrated managers in sponsoring firms slam against the constraints of the matrix organization they created for monitoring their venture, they do not change their control mechanisms. Instead, they layer in more and more people and procedures to solve their personality conflicts with the venture's managers or with their partners by buffering them from direct contact with them. As the situation grows more hidebound, owners lose track of the original benefits that motivated the venture's formation."[19]

Sponsors should be alert to overburdening their alliance managers with excessive reports and requests for information. Quality information is more useful than worthless details.

Differing Corporate Cultures

The venture management task requires coordination across corporate boundaries. This problem is somewhat difficult to solve because different cultures, reward systems, missions, management styles, and organizational structures can create confusion and sometimes impotence if not managed by a sensitive leader. Peter Killing cites a good example of a Canadian manager whose top management team was made up of people contributed by the three partners in the venture:

"In one division, I discovered I had insulted a senior manager by going directly to a subordinate to get some information. In his previous company, the hierarchy was very strictly observed, and if you wanted information you asked at the top and the request was relayed down until someone could answer. Then the answer came all the way back up. I'm used to an operation where you go directly to the man who can answer the question. Employees of another division are disgruntled with the bureaucracy they find here. They are used to a small, entrepreneurial organization. What we regard as the facts of life, like the time taken to get an approval, they look at with surprise and dismay."[20]

These problems could have been avoided by carefully structuring the venture at the beginning and properly selecting personnel. Some managers suggest that key members of the management team be sent to one of the other parents for a period of time for "corporate cultural indoctrination" prior to formalizing the venture. The hope is that they will learn how the "operational fit" will be once the venture is functioning.

Private-public-nonprofit ventures are among the most difficult to manage because of major differences in organizational cultures. Thomas Tanury, a successful entrepreneur and creator of the Thin Films Research Partnership between six large corporations, two small companies, a bank, a research institute, two universities, a utility, and a state and a federal agency summed up this difficulty:

> "It is very difficult to deal in these very different environments. Not only do we have different organizations with different people and different egos, but added to that are the vastly different cultures with widely disparate motivations. We are constantly educating them to think the way we think—and we are learning to think their way too. But the universities and government agencies are far slower and more bureaucratic than we are used to. If we worked at their pace, it would take forever to get anything done."

Michael Lauro, the partnership's venture manager, adds: "We must understand their powerbase and their values so we can play their songs with their tunes."

International ventures can also have critical communications and cultural value problems. Ventures with developing nations may also introduce aggravating problems of low education and competence within the venture's workforce that American and European managers are not accustomed to, and may find rather repugnant.

Corporate Allegiance

If the venture manager remains attached to the parent company and is assigned to the alliance as a secondary or collateral responsibility, the venture will not receive the attention it needs. Managers should have major operational control and be primarily concerned with the venture's interests.

Exit Barriers

If the partners are highly differentiated, the partners should consider using shorter-term alliances with low exit barriers because the partners may have very different or incompatible long-term objectives. If sponsors feel locked into an unholy alliance, the result may be irreconcilable differences within the alliance.

Negotiating Skills

In the event that conflicts or differences of opinion begin to emerge between the partner companies, the venture manager, the champions, and the CEOs must be ready to play diplomat, negotiator, and problemsolver to bring the parties together. If the parties have irreconcilable differences due to fundamental changes in their strategic environments, then the management team should begin designing a transition strategy (see Chapter 14).

The term *negotiating* here does not mean overpowering the opponent or getting as much out of the other company as one can. If problems arise, negotiating must center upon maintaining trust, ethics, diplomacy, consideration of the other team, understanding another person's perspective, patience, tolerance of other values, dealing with unspoken insecurities, and willingness to cooperatively resolve any and all differences of opinion.

Phase Shifts

It may be advisable to plan a change of venture managers and sponsor liaisons if the venture goes through distinct and highly differentiated phases, similar to a relay race where the first runner runs 100 yards and passes the torch to the second runner. In a real estate venture, a first-phase venture manager might have construction skills; the second-phase manager might know marketing, building management, and maintenance.

The Alaska Pipeline joint venture requires each of the owners to rotate operational responsibility. It is much like having a "lateral promotion" to provide a broader perspective and understanding of the nature of the alliance.

Meetings

Steering committee meetings should be held on a regular basis to evaluate progress and solve problems. Some venture managers advise shifting the location between companies on an alternating basis. Others advise holding the meetings at the location where "the action is" if the venture's focus moves to different locations during its life cycle. Meetings at remote locations are only advisable when it is necessary to devote extensive time and thought to strategic planning and performance evaluation.

Maintaining Trust and the Win–Win Perspective

Establishing and maintaining trust is one of the most important factors in the continued success of the joint venture. This means frank communication, meeting commitments, and informing people as soon as problems arise that might delay schedules.

If the venture runs on hard times, or needs more capital or other resources, the partners must still see themselves as winners or the frictions will become too severe for the partners to remain committed. When partners lose their power, they withdraw, regress, become belligerent, blame, and lose that narrow focus that gives them energy and commitment. Keep expectations open and carefully defined in advance.

Creativity and Support

Many business partnerships are, for all intents and purposes, start-up companies, and thus require all the resources that start-ups require. Managers can become quite frustrated when they know the venture is ready to take off toward success but, because of haunting doubts, the sponsors withhold the vital resources needed to capture the opportunity. These resources can be money, materials, personnel, access to technology, or sometimes simply the confidence of the owners and the autonomy of the venture manager to make operational decisions.

One company that has been very successful in joint ventures insists that, once the decision to proceed has been made, the alliance will receive all the resources and assets necessary to make it a success as a separate, independent company. The management team is selected for its ability to take the venture from ground zero to success, and is then given autonomy without day-to-day operational interference.

Support may simply be to provide the right technical people to make a new product or technology work. In a joint Canadian–British venture, communications had to be done by telex, telephone, and letters because a critical technical engineer was not provided. When the technology did not work properly, frustrations erupted, and important timing was lost— resulting in loss of market share.

Support must continue to come directly from the top management of the sponsoring companies. CEOs should think of a corporate alliance with the same consideration given to a subsidiary or a new acquisition.

Ron Whittier, Vice President of Intel Corporation, says: "You have to make a major investment of the senior management—between the presidents of the corporations—in strategic alliances or they don't work. . . . The management sets the general tone for cooperation . . . it's generally understood that it's a fundamental part of our strategy."[21]

Norm Alister of *Electronic Business* counters: "The truth is that many top managers are enamored of making deals and bored with maintaining them. It is also true that some firms have made so many deals that it is impossible for management to have more than a remote acquaintence with day–to–day operations."[22]

Training and Teambuilding

After selecting key personnel, it may be very helpful to have a teambuilding session to clarify issues, focus efforts, and establish workable reporting systems. A neutral outsider is often called upon for a teambuilding session as the project begins to get underway. This neutral third party should be agreed upon by all partners.

Harvard's Harry Levinson urges the use of a sophisticated teambuilding program to enhance the venture's chance of success. He recommends that, during this process, several key points should be covered, including the mission of the venture, expectations each member has of the other, problems they should anticipate, and how problems will be resolved. Levinson continues; "If people are not brought together at first to get on the same wavelength, they will take more time later. Many managers don't realize this. They get started on the task, and forget focusing on the team."

Dow Chemical's success in joint ventures is, in part, attributable to their own crosstraining of managers to communicate and coordinate across internal corporate boundaries. These skills are then easily adapted to joint venture situations using functional teams led by people with good integrative skills.

PRINCIPLE #7
PERSONNEL SELECTION

Find the Very Best

Skilled personnel will make the critical difference for most alliances. As the venture gets underway, if the partners find their strategy or structure is not on target, or if conditions place heavy pressures on the venture's stability, skilled managers have a far better chance of success than if of mediocre caliber.

Business partnerships must be treated as though they were start-up companies. Weak management will lead down the rapid road to failure. Remember the first rule of venture management: "Far better to have a Grade A management team and a Grade B product, than a Grade A product with a Grade B management team."

Highly skilled, top-level people whose decisions are valued and trusted by the sponsors constitute an essential ingredient for success. Companies not willing to put top-notch people in charge of the venture are probably lacking some element of the all-important "vested interest motivation." A lack of commitment to the venture, or a significantly low risk and/or reward ingredient, is usually the reason for betting on second-string players!

Beware the sponsor who plays his second string in this game. Many joint ventures have failed specifically because the sponsoring companies had appointed second-rate managers to positions, figuring the joint venture was a good "dumping ground" for people who did not work well in the parent organization.

Choose personnel whose goals and skills match the needs of the venture rather than people skilled in a specialty unrelated to the venture, in the hope that it will become a good training ground.

Finding people with excellent integration/coordination skills as well as superb operational management abilities will probably be a most challenging personnel selection task. Roy Bonner insists that managers be "customer-oriented" even if they are on the production floor. Manufacturing managers need customer contact in order to know when customers must have an order delivered, to develop solid delivery schedules, and to assure a firm adherence to price levels.

The Selection and Appointment Process

If the partners do contribute key personnel, be sure the type of personnel will mesh within the operational framework of the venture. If the venture draws its functional managers from the sponsors, the venture's general manager should have the final right to hire—and fire—these people. Otherwise, the functional managers will continue to give allegiance to the parent rather than to the venture, and if this happens, the venture manager will not have a cohesive management team.

Bobby Inman, former U.S. Navy Admiral and Deputy Director of the CIA who now heads MCC, the massive computer research collaborative, had the power to accept or reject people sent to him by the sponsoring companies. He insisted on having only top-quality people and, in fact, rejected numerous candidates until the sponsors realized he was serious. Eventually he developed the quality team he desired.

In one venture in which the functional managers were "donated" by the sponsors without the final approval of the venture's general manager, major difficulties arose. According to the story recounted to Professor Peter Killing by the venture's manager:

"You cannot use your organizational position, because you are not sure where the loyalties of those below you lie. The people who work for you are not necessarily appointed by you, so your hiring, firing, and promotion powers are limited."[23]

Career Paths

Key personnel must be devoted to the alliance first and foremost. If their priorities are focused in other corporate directions, internal management problems are inevitable. Joint ventures are frequently outside the normal career paths of those appointed to the position. Unless the venture can provide long-term growth opportunities, the sponsors run the risk of having venture managers become an anomaly, an organizational outcast, marooned. Many advise making the joint venture assignment part of an employee's regular career path.

Some experienced joint venturers advise that the middle-management positions in the joint venture should be relatively short-term to enable a cross-pollination of new and creative ideas, which may be carried back to the sponsoring companies. Sponsors must also decide if the venture is a "revolving door" for the manager—an assignment for a brief period of time followed by a return to the parent company—or a "one-way street" where the employee returns only if victorious.

Key operating personnel should have previous experience in at least two of the venture's functional specialities in order to assure that middle- and lower-level experts and specialists regard these managers and integrators as having a degree of competence. Obviously, for these reasons, the role of the integrator is not a good selection for a new, unseasoned management trainee.

According to Professors Lawrence and Lorsch, because integrators often attain high degrees of performance by indirection, they often fail to receive the credit they deserve for making things happen. To compensate for this inequity, some joint ventures provide additional motivational incentives for key managers by offering a share in the venture's profits.

Ten Traits to Look for

Discussions with successful venture managers reveal a number of traits found in top and middle echelon personnel that are particularly desirable for venture managers, and to a lesser degree to lower-level coordinators and corporate liaisons.

1. *Courage.* Because joint ventures are inherently risky, courage is an essential ingredient for key personnel. As one venture manager so eloquently said: "This is a risky business, and we need staff which can rise to the occasion by looking those problems square in the eye, and, with great confidence, convince everyone we will master the problems before we run out of time and money." Thomas Tanury, executive champion of the Thin Films Research partnership, pointed out: "We've been aggressive and unconventional. Most people think what we've done is outrageously risky because they have great fear of the unknown—they are inherently conservative, stepping backward rather than forward when challenged."

2. *Decisiveness.* Time is one of the greatest opponents of those who play the field of risk. To defeat time requires decisiveness: an ability to make timely and correct decisions. This factor comes with experience, and is not normally found in the uninitiated.

   However, it is important to differentiate between the decisive leader and the "hip shooter." The decisive leader consults with staff, receives ample early warning signals, plans for contingencies, and acts accordingly. The hip shooter makes quick decisions but bases them on inaccurate, untimely, or incomplete information.

   Thomas Watson, Jr., looked for intelligent people with "common sense" when he was at the helm of IBM, saying, "common sense allows managers to make a decision, but too much intellectual depth may allow them to see too many variables—and therefore make no decision."

3. *Persistence.* Persistence and dedication to winning are vital leadership factors for the project manager as well as for other key support staff. In choosing key personnel, preference should be given to those who do not accept defeat easily and, when faced with defeat, rebuild their plans, act creatively, and move forward to the coveted prize of success.

On one manager's wall is a poster by an anonymous author, which describes this trait so well:

Nothing in the world can take the place of Persistence . . .
Talent will not; Nothing is more common than unsuccessful men with talent . . .
Genius will not; Unrewarded genius is almost a proverb . . .
Education will not; The world is full of educated derelicts . . .
Persistence and determination alone are omnipotent
The will to "press on" has solved, and always will solve
The problems of the human race.

4. *Fairness.* Another vital trait involves the ability to see the entire picture of the joint venture, and then treat people and their respective organizations fairly. Distinctions between white-collar and blue-collar workers tend to be minimized in alliances.

    Integrity, often referred to by partners and staff members, is a factor that enables the structure of a venture to be reformulated when it is not fair to one of the partners.

5. *Discipline.* Because partnerships inherently deal with ambiguity both organizationally and operationally, successful managers must have a strong sense of discipline, which provides a structural framework for the ambiguity they must handle.

    This discipline may manifest itself in a variety of ways, including holding weekly meetings, an adherence to strict testing procedures, or meeting deadlines and commitments. The discipline factor is often associated with a personal sense of self control, because without *self* control, leaders have little chance of controlling others or their operations. Any manager who will be proactive, rather than reactive, must have the discipline to plan and work closely with others. The self–control factor should be distinguished from rigidity, however, which takes persistence to the extreme of stubbornness, and discipline to dictatorship.

6. *Organized.* Successful joint venture leaders tend to be extremely well organized and able to delegate responsibility to others within their span of organizational control. These leaders appear to have the ability to *master detail* while maintaining the *vision* necessary to see the larger, long-term picture. Moreover, they tend to be willing to take *responsibility* for action, for mistakes, and for any problems in the project.

7. *Humble.* Leadership in a joint venture often requires directing without having full authority because there is often no direct line

of command across corporate boundaries. Therefore, certain traits—humbleness, diplomacy, and asking the right questions to make others think of the solution—tend to be most effective.

A *sense of humor* can break the ice, establish rapport, and foster teamwork. Humble people tend to set a good example for others by "getting their hands dirty" or by being willing to do anything they ask of others.

8. *Resilient.* A vital trait involves the ability to bounce back from defeat, from seemingly insurmountable obstacles, or from a lack of progress. As one person stated, "I attribute my resiliency to my ability to see failure as an opportunity to refine my sense of humor, and I never take myself too seriously."

9. *Cooperative.* Cooperative effort is essential for joint venture success. A leader must be able to induce people to work together, to marshall human resources for creative problemsolving and timely accomplishment of goals. Being cooperative implies being communicative; the two go intimately together. Thomas Watson, Jr., said his father's success in the founding of IBM was his perceptive ability to understand his impact on other people, asking frequently, "How does what you say affect others?"

10. *Power expanders.* Power expanders are leaders who create the right conditions to make others around them feel more powerful and effective. This unique trait, while often mentioned, is extremely hard to quantify and difficult to replicate by formula. A power expander will generally give great guidance to subordinates, focus on helping subordinates solve their own problems, and stay out of subordinate's details unless necessary. Joint ventures are usually designed as dynamic, fast moving organizations, and power expanders tend to have less reliance on formal rules, find ways for lower levels of the organization to reach decisions, and exercise wider spans of control.

12

Dealing with Operational Concerns

The job of managing business is managing morale.

—Thomas J. Watson, Jr., IBM

Joint ventures and strategic alliances are probably more prone to problems than are other business ventures because they not only tackle higher risks—they also require coordination between independent business entities. Ventures can be expected to have crises, just like any other start-up business going through its growth cycle.

If a crisis point is reached, the sponsors must evaluate whether the failure is *strategic* (such as a change in market conditions), *structural* (has one of the partners lost interest or commitment?), or *operational* (is the problem in leadership, management, support, marketing, or production?).

Strategic problems, usually the most vexing of all, may call for a complete reevaluation of the venture and either a restructuring or termination.

Structural problems, while thorny, may require only a redivision of risks, rewards, and management. Equitable division and control is the main issue here. (If the alliance experiences strategic or structural problems, Chapters 13 and 14 address those difficulties.)

Many operational problems can normally be solved without structural or strategic realignments by bringing teams together for problemsolving sessions. This chapter addresses operational issues and concerns.

EARLY PREVENTION OF PROBLEMS

Clearly, the best way to limit operational problems is to take strong *preventative action*—a result of careful planning far ahead of time. Three approaches are suggested.

1. *Evaluate Potential Problems Regularly.* Have venture managers meet frequently with their key advisory teams to discuss potential problems *before* they occur. The old adage "An ounce of prevention is worth a pound of cure" still prevails. Determine what factors are likely to create problems. If the problems seem very likely to occur, ask if the problems are surmountable or insurmountable.

   Reevaluate the risks, break them down into manageable components, and organize for a succession of incremental victories. One venture manager suggested this process was analogous to the riddle: "How do you eat an elephant?" The answer: "One bite at a time."

2. *Develop Contingency Plans.* Each partner should know his or her role, risks, and responsibilities in the event problems occur. Particularly in fast-moving markets and highly risky ventures, a strong contingency plan may spell the difference between success and failure.

   Have three plans ready to go at all times: (1) an optimistic plan, (2) a conservative plan, and (3) a "Black Sunday" plan. With each adverse turn of business events, some aspect of one of the plans can be counted on to help save the day. The plans don't necessarily need to be written down but, "when the enemy attacks, the platoon members need to know their battle station assignments."

   In an alliance in the food service industry the operations manager handles the ever-changing daily conditions of the restaurant trade by training his staff well. Before every major event, he advises his team to anticipate every single problem that could realistically ruin the affair. Then employees are expected to work closely together as a team. If one of the problems crops up, each knows how to help their teammate and to move quickly to remedy the problems. During the event, he roams the dining room and kitchen watching for any small indication that a problem is emerging—cold food, slow pickup of orders, a waitress becoming burdened by the needs of a special table, a refrigerator beginning to lose temperature, or a myriad of other minor problems that are constantly brewing. At the first sign of a problem, he pounces like a cat on a mouse, taking firm corrective action.

Also, do not overlook a potential opportunity when forced to implement a contingency plan. For example, in a recent real estate joint venture, a reluctant seller on an abutting property threatened to delay a major development but, when offered an equity position in a joint venture in return for the contribution of his land, quickly become a staunch advocate.

If a thorny engineering problem may substantially delay the project when developing a technology, consider using only a portion of the technology for introduction into the market, followed by the rest of the technology later.

3. *Establish an Early Warning System to identify when problems are beginning to occur.* The early warning system approach has been used effectively by many alliance managers. The following list represents typical signals warning an impending problem:

- *Back burner.* When one or more of the parties doesn't give top priority to getting the job done, look for the lack of "vested interest motivation" of one of the partners or of a key individual.

- *Missed deadlines.* This failure will normally be the result of insurmountable problems, poor planning, poor resource allocation, or poor management. If it occurs, watch for a spiralling progression of problems throwing the venture off course.

- *Role confusion and conflict.* If the team doesn't know its assignments, the job will not get done. The venture manager is responsible and must clarify roles and expectations immediately.

- *Winners and losers.* If one party thinks it got the short end of the stick, the venture will fail because the structure is wrong and there is insufficient "vested interest motivation" for continued success. Realign for parity.

- *Cost overruns.* Early-stage cost overruns may signal serious problems in risk analysis and planning. Left unattended, the venture may be bled dry of financial resources, creating friction between the partners. Smart managers get on top of these problems immediately.

- *Missed goals, milestones.* An effective monitoring system determines how well goals and milestones are being met. Any early deviation from these plans will be amplified over the long haul. The steering committee should address early deviations immediately.

· *Missing communications.* Establishing good communications is essential, and venture managers must be held accountable for this function. Be careful managers don't "shoot messengers bearing bad news," for this will only stifle good communications.

EXPLOITING THE "CHEMISTRY FACTOR"

Earlier, the issue of "chemistry" was discussed as being the intangible but essential ingredient of the alliance. During operational management, chemistry becomes paramount.

Chemistry is both the *cause* and the *result* of a successful alliance. It is a potent tool deriving its strength from the unification of common business goals and psychological harmony. Chemistry works on two levels. At the first, most rational level, the alliance is formed because each party lacks certain skills and resources that the other party has. When partners are properly matched, the missing elements of one partner are provided by the other: "$1 + 1 = 3$."

But beyond this elemental rationale, at a second level, something else happens. When together in a room trying to solve a problem, minds in harmony—for some reason best explained as "psychic"—tend to become elevated, excited, and creative. This excitement is often described as "synergy" or "dynamic tension"—and it works. When structure and strategy are in harmony, when trust and integrity are prevalent, when enthusiasm and desire are heightened, and when leadership and management enhance human effectiveness, chemistry is in action.

Those who have experienced chemistry know the power of this force, which creates a dynamic environment for a "sixth sense" to emerge, enabling the design of unique, creative solutions. When unleashed, chemistry enables partners to generate new answers to problems that they would never find alone.

Using chemistry in creative problemsolving is one of the greatest advantages joint ventures and strategic alliances have over more traditional business structures. Inherently, the joint venture provides a staff of experts available to tackle unique and seemingly insurmountable problems. Without a strong inspirational champion and without venture managers who can bring expert resources to the table in a coordinated and harmonious manner, chemistry in problemsolving may go untapped. Without firm direction and proper selection of personnel, these experts may engage in unproductive ego conflict.

SOLVING PROBLEMS WHEN THEY OCCUR

Every alliance will run into problems; it is inherent in the process because, by definition, business partnerships tackle elements of the unknown. Wherever there are risks, there are bound to be anxieties and, often, conflicts.

Therefore, good venture managers and integrators should have excellent abilities at solving more than just mechanical and technical problems; they need to be able to solve personal conflicts as well.

Operational Problemsolving "Rules of Thumb"

Venture managers often mention four useful rules for problemsolving in alliances:

1. *Deal with problems quickly; don't let them fester.* Some problems seem to solve themselves or go away, replaced by bigger problems. But if the problem continues and conflict begins to get in the way of everyday operations, the venture manager must act—sometimes very subtly, sometimes abruptly.

2. *Work through problems together; placing blame on the other party will doom the venture.* Unless the problem is urgent and time is crucial, most venture managers will let their staff talk out the problem in detail, enabling a full discussion of the issues. Good integrators have exceptional listening skills, enabling people with a problem to talk it through carefully. Once the problem is clearly spelled out, the integrator will guide a discussion of alternatives, and will carefully generate a consensus decision to gain an acceptance by the entire team.

3. *Make a commitment to action; don't procrastinate.* Once the solution is found, effective leaders are neither passive nor shy. They take the initiative, turn on the heat, and aggressively pursue the objective. Commitments are set, milestones established, timetables agreed upon, and results ultimately achieved. Often this characteristic is referred to as "deadline driven."

4. *When in doubt, communicate; no alliance has ever failed because of over-communication.* Establishing clear, accurate, and timely communications in a cooperative venture is not an easy task, and the complexity increases as the number of partners increases. Effective managers are sensitive to communications across corporate

boundaries, ensuring the right person is doing the talking to the right people. They are also aware that certain specialists may be junior in the management hierarchy, but their closeness to operational problems gives them the best perspective.

SUPPORTING TEAMWORK

Most alliances are built on teamwork—all for one, one for all. The venture manager often must gain results through an interlocking set of teams. This means fostering a team culture or climate.

Teamwork is a way of life. The team leader will not be an egomaniac, but instead a high achiever who sees his or her greatest achievement as pulling a group together so that all members can display their best individual talents in a cooperative framework. Yes, there can be "superstars," but the superstars arise because their team avoided blaming each other, refrained from backstabbing, and abstained from crashing in a crisis. One thing venture managers seem to agree upon: avoid hiring "primadonnas"; they never can work well in a team.

Team Guidelines

Effective venture managers speak of creating a corporate culture within the alliance that makes teamwork and cooperation a way of life. Some guidelines they suggest are:

- Give the team a sufficient amount of responsibility for members to gain satisfaction.
- Provide the team with a complete work task so that, when completed, members know it was done successfully, and they can be held accountable for it.
- Allow team members to inject their ideas before they start tackling a project; foster creativity for them to solve unknowns.
- Managers must oversee teams, but without meddling or becoming overbearing. This is usually done by focusing on results, boundary conditions, and obstacles, and encouraging creative solutions rather than dictating processes and procedures.
- Provide teams with timely feedback, encourage good communications, and supply proper resources (but not too many resources,

which will encourage waste and complex solutions; and not too few, which will undernourish the group).

· Keep both the team's goal and the "big picture" of the alliance in focus at all times so the team doesn't become too ingrained, introverted, detailed, and parochial. Teamwork requires team members to do whatever is necessary to get the job done, regardless of position, company affiliation, or job description.

· Put a quick end to ego-centered, anti-team behavior. Leaders should be quick and sharp in intervening when an individual's or clique's behavior (i.e., rumor spreading, "me-first," "us versus them") begins to disrupt the team culture. Emphasize that teamwork is not just a nice word, but a fundamental value upon which excellence is built.

Teamwork may not come naturally; it is an art requiring practice, thought, discussion, recommitment, and then more practice. Regularly during the venture, the alliance manager should continue the teambuilding program whereby teammates remain involved in committing to goals, dealing with expectations, establishing roles, setting communications channels, and outlining expected results.

If Problems Persist

If operational problems go unchecked, sponsoring companies become anxiety ridden, often jumping into the middle of the venture management picture, demanding reports, sending in investigators, and tightening financial controls. Then the venture manager's ability to function worsens as decisionmaking becomes more difficult, and a downward spiral may doom the alliance.

When faced with such a condition, sponsors should call a "summit" meeting of all the partners to address the problems and design a set of solutions that will constructively bring the venture back on course. Independent nipping at the manager's heels by individual partners will probably have negative effects. If leadership is inadequate, the partners will have no choice but to make a change in personnel.

PART FIVE

TRANSFORMATION

No venture is expected to operate without problems; problems are inherent in any risk environment. This section is intended to provide guidance on how to prevent problems from overwhelming the alliance. However, there will be certain circumstances when strategic or operational considerations will require a change. Rather than let the venture fail, it is usually wiser to *transform* the venture into something new and more viable to suit the future demands. The main themes of this section are:

* Problems and Pitfalls in Strategy and Structure
* When to Change the Terms

When problems occur once the venture is into the operational stage, first look for an "operational fix," described in the previous chapter. But if the operational fix is ineffective or inappropriate, then other strategic or structural problems exist that are addressed in this final section.

13

Problems and Pitfalls in Strategy and Structure

*Far better it is to dare mighty things, to win glorious triumphs
even though checkered by failure, than to take rank with those
poor spirits who neither enjoy much nor suffer much because
they live in the gray twilight that knows not victory nor defeat.*

—Theodore Roosevelt

If problems occur that cannot be cured by operational adjustments, then
invariably they will be strategic or structural in nature. The following
strategic and structural issues, while not all-inclusive, represent the
broad range of difficulties that can occur in strategy and structure leading
to less than satisfactory results. All of the following problems can be
avoided or diminished with careful analysis and good planning. These
problems fall into categories of mission, strategy, technology, market, organization, management, finance, business culture, and chemistry.

MISSION ISSUES

Mission-oriented problems are a result of inadequacies in the alliance's
primary purpose, its very reason for existing. If the alliance's objectives
are unclear or ill-defined, the chances of success are nil.

Good relations between the partners are essential, but without clear,
concise business arrangements oriented toward concrete, achievable
goals, good relations only bring warm, fuzzy feelings at first; then as the
venture deteriorates, good relations turn sour. Alliances that tackle specific, definable tasks (i.e. project oriented) tend to suffer less from this

malady than their more ambiguous goal-oriented counterparts. More emphasis on specific, measurable, achievable, time-specific goals can help remedy this condition. Some types of mission-oriented issues are:

- **Tunnel Mission** is a term describing an overly narrow avenue of concentration. Clear and sharp focus is normally a great attribute in any business venture, but too narrow a focus can easily miss an unexpectedly moving target.

  For example, a real estate joint venture was building an office complex. Once the complex was ready to be rented, sales skyrocketed, and the partners wanted to build a second complex. Unfortunately, the adjoining land had just been purchased by a keen competitor. Because the office developers were too narrowly visioned, they missed the broader opportunity and failed to negotiate a future option to buy the adjacent land at the outset.

- **All Things to All People** is just the opposite of tunnel mission. Combining the strengths of two partners does not omnipotency make. It is simply unrealistic to assume that any joint venture can conquer a multitude of diverse hurdles too soon.

  For example, three small advertising firms, one strong in public relations, one strong in media, and the other strong in market research, formed their alliance as a preliminary move prior to a potential merger. They expected that sales would increase threefold over the next 12 months as a result of their tremendous talents, primarily by landing large corporate accounts that normally go to larger advertising firms. Slick presentation materials were created, and a few good accounts were landed, but, overall, sales were disappointing. The venture targeted too many corporate markets where the principals were not well known and had not established a solid reputation. A number of years and the eventual merger were required before the marketplace developed confidence in the team.

- **The IBM Illusion** occurs when it is assumed that, because IBM (or any other major company for that matter) did something successfully, it will be the right thing to do in a multitude of other situations. The joint venture and strategic partnership format is like clay in a sculptor's hands; it can and should be molded to suit a variety of specific needs. Copying another's unique creation is not necessarily the key to success.

  For example, two small computer companies, struggling to break out of their financial woes, decided to form a joint venture, thereby increasing their capabilities in manufacturing and marketing, and reducing their overhead. They had both read of the strong market growth projected for the medical market, and designed products for this market. Not being able to afford consultants or lawyers, they designed their own structure for the joint venture based on an article they had read describing two giant computer companies. While the joint business plan was fascinating on paper, it did not work because it lacked a number of critical elements that should have been addressed (the most critical being financial contingencies, which were nonexistent). When overruns occured, working capital was insufficient. None of the management team was experienced at joint venturing, which caused terrible management communication problems. Eventually, a manager from a large corporation was brought in to straighten out the difficulties, but this person's management style was not oriented to the smaller, faster-moving, less bureaucratic entrepreneurial environment. By the time the product was introduced, it was inadequately designed to meet the needs of a marketplace with which neither company was familiar. The venture failed.

STRATEGY ISSUES

Strategy-oriented problems manifest themselves when the fundamental strategic aims and objectives of the joint venture are flawed. Frequently, the strategic aspirations of the partners were greater than were possible within the scope of the competitive marketplace. Even with careful planning and analysis, an alliance may miss its mark because the industry moved in the other direction. As an example, a business partnership in the consumer electronics industry that tried to advance eight-track cassette recorder products in the 1970s would be a total failure by the 1980s.

Having a good secondary strategy and a contingency plan are essential, particularly in rapidly changing markets. Some ventures are simply constructed too quickly, without enough thought to the details. It may be too easy to jump on the partnership bandwagon without carefully thinking through the strategy, structure, operations, and potential problems.

Albert Einstein was once asked how he would spend his time if he was given a problem upon which his life depended and he had only one hour to solve it. He responded by saying he would spend 30 minutes analyzing the problem, 20 minutes planning the solution, and ten minutes executing the solution. For those overly prone to jumping into action, a bit more planning would be worthwhile.

Some examples of strategic problems are:

· **The Future Isn't What It Used to Be.** A strategy perfect now may be a future disaster. Never assume the future will simply be a replication of the present; instead, assume competition is forever maneuvering for advantage. Timing can be paramount in any business venture. Successful alliances are built on sound competitive strategies timed for the right moment.

For example, two machine tool companies formed their joint venture to combat major Japanese incursions into the U.S. marketplace. Historically, the Japanese had been known as great copiers of American technology, looking for competitive advantage primarily through lower prices. The U.S. joint venture was aimed at lowering price points through better manufacturing technology, and the partners expected the Japanese to be consistent with past history by further lowering costs. Instead, the Japanese competitors reversed their field, increased prices, and at the same time improved quality, reliability, and performance. The American joint venture was caught flat-footed and continued to lose considerable market share.

· **The Simpleton Syndrome** occurs when a partnership is formed to cover up fundamental weaknesses in either one of the partner's businesses or the strategy itself—all in the simpleton's "hope" that the alliance will cure these fundamental ills. Alas, "hope" is the simpleton's opiate; optimism untempered by constructive cynicism is delusion. The field is filled with too many risks for anyone to be an optimist for too long.

For example, two small electrical contractors formed a partnership to bid on government jobs. Neither contractor was very good at handling administrative paperwork, a prerequisite for any government contract. However, each had a fine reputation in the community for quality work, and the principals personally knew and liked each other. One of the contractors, however, was also in serious financial difficulty, due to another subcontract with a larger general contractor who had serious legal difficulties. This electrical contractor hoped to use the alliance to get some "lucrative government jobs" that would ease the financial pressures. Instead, the administrative weaknesses within the cooperative venture resulted in substantial delays in government payments, which only exacerbated the electrical contractor's already miserable financial condition.

· **Diagnostic Deliriums** result from too much planning and analysis, and too little commitment to action. As when the centipede who trotted his hundred legs in unison, ever so quick, was asked how he could move all those legs with such great coordination, he stopped to analyze the phenomenon, and found himself paralyzed, unable to move. Too much analysis of a problem without parallel action can leave the players without a "can do" attitude.

For example, one marketing strategic partnership was in the planning stage for over a year. The parties planned strategy, planned tactics, planned financing, planned target markets, planned staffing, planned, and then planned some more. The principals seemed to enjoy all the jaw-boning and thinking, but never made a commitment to action; they talked and talked of courtship and marriage, but the marriage was never consummated. Finally, a competitor heard about their idea, jumped at the opportunity, and the talkers decided to abandon their plans.

· **Early Abandonment** of a venture may not always be wise. Persistence is often a tremendous virtue. Knowing how long to continue the struggle and when to abort can mark the difference between success and failure.

For example, in a classic case of coitus interruptus, Uniroyal was engaged in a joint venture with an Indonesian company making latex for rubber gloves, condoms, and balloons. The market had not materialized as expected. Uniroyal decided to sell its interests to its partner. Within months, the AIDS epidemic became public, the condom market exploded, and the demand for latex rubber skyrocketed. Persistence and vision would have yielded great rewards.

TECHNOLOGY ISSUES

Technology is one of the fastest growth industries in the world, but it is fraught with high risks. Perhaps the highest risk is represented by a new company bringing a new product into a new, developing market. If everything is perfectly timed, and the product meets a clear customer demand, then—as was true for Apple Computer—the rewards are phenomenally high. But difficulties arise when vital technological risks have been underestimated or the market's response to technology has been overestimated. The playing field is littered with the bodies of venturers who made these errors:

· **Hi-Tech Seduction.** While technology has provided the basis for many successful and creative joint ventures and strategic alliances, and undoubtedly will continue to do so for many years, technology can also induce its developers to over-use technology, resulting in customer confusion and poor reliability.

For example, in the telephone industry, one venture applied advanced computer technology to smaller multiline switching systems used in hotels and businesses. The high-tech system was capable of performing dozens of functions, filling a large user instruction manual, it did almost everything except dance and wash the dishes. Unfortunately, the salesforce sold the product before the manufacturing bugs were worked out, which resulted in delivery of an unreliable product filled with performance problems. Even after the product operated properly, users found it was too complex. All the extra functions were confusing, requiring extensive training to use the system. The multifunctioned high technology was a high-tech nightmare.

· **"Not Invented Here"** syndrome is seen frequently in engineering and manufacturing alliances. Engineers often have a nasty habit of torpedoing technologies by denigrating designs created outside of their own laboratories.

For example, in a computer joint venture between a hardware and a software company, the hardware engineers constantly rejected software designs because the hardware engineers were unfamiliar with the software's structure and design. Rather than learn the new system or find constructive ways to improve it, the engineers chose the negative approach, which created frictions between the parties and unnecessarily delayed the project. Not until a new project manager with a good background in both technologies was appointed and, in a friendly fashion, laid down the law about cooperation, was the program put back on track.

· **Invention Before Profit.** Technology engineers are intense people dedicated to their special interests and profession—a concentration of energy that often yields excellent rewards. However, it is common for engineers to become carried away with continuous refinements to a new product rather than bringing a reliable initial version to market quickly.

For example, an energy management company signed a strategic alliance agreement with a systems control company to develop a new energy controller for the electric heat industry. The chief engineer for the systems control company was a brilliant designer, highly proficient in his profession. However, the controller device, which should have been designed and manufactured in less than 12 months, took nearly three years. The delay was caused by endless revisions. Each time the marketing and sales staff of the energy management company brought potential customers to see the near-final prototypes, the chief engineer would demonstrate the inadequacies of the latest design and sell the customer on a future, "improved" version, undermining the sale on the current model. When the finished product was finally introduced to the marketplace, the competition had had a product on the market for over six months and had gained a major competitive advantage in market share.

MARKET ISSUES

Market problems occur because customers or competition have been repositioned, lead times to closing a sale are longer than expected, or demand is significantly less than anticipated.

Business partnerships are, for the most part, aimed for the long term. Yet, long-term planning cannot account for every maneuver and whimsy in the marketplace. The agreement must be flexible to deal with such events. If the venture cannot reposition itself in the market, be prepared to terminate the venture.

Some examples of market problems are:

- **Market Entry Timing** can be everything. Moreover, the development of a new market can be very long and very expensive. "Early entry" risks should be an important concern when one or more of the following indicators is *lacking*:

  1. Customers must be *ready*, have a strong *need* for a product *and* a strong *desire to buy* at an affordable price.

  2. Using the product must create very satisfied customers who will buy again and/or refer others through word of mouth.

  3. There must be a reasonable method of economically distributing the product into the market.

  If any one of these elements is missing, a very expensive process of market development will be necessary, entailing considerable financial outlay.

For example, since the early 1950s, communications companies have been promoting video telephones that enable the user to see the person to whom they are talking. The Japanese have entered the market in recent years. But despite new technologies, new players, and new promotions, the market simply has not developed. Money cannot yet buy this market.

Late market entry is equally frustrating because, at the time of entry, demand is already satiated, price margins are shrinking, and market position is dominated by others. Unless a venture can provide a dramatic improvement in price or performance, late market entry will be costly and probably unproductive.

Renault's joint venture with AMC never yielded success because its auto product was neither a price nor a performance breakthrough. The product lacked market distinctiveness. The General Motors and Toyota joint venture produced one of America's most reliable, best-built cars—the new Chevy Nova—but unlike its nearly identical Toyota counterpart, the American version lacked the distinctiveness U.S. buyers associate with an American car.

· **"Foreign Intrigue"** is a version of the "grass is greener on the other side of the fence" syndrome. A company experiencing success in its domestic marketplace may look at another country as a potential market, only to find foreign intrigue was really economic disappointment.

For example, a European instrument manufacturer was seeking to expand its market and attempted a joint venture with a U.S. sales firm to distribute a digital precision instrument line imported from Italy. An agreement was signed, a warehouse site selected, and financial commitments put in place. However, the European partner failed to understand its primary U.S. competitor had a steel-hardened grip on the marketplace, with over 85 percent share of the market. The U.S. product was considered the standard in the industry, even though—when compared to the European competitor—it was a technologically obsolete analog device. The venture was failing from poor sales until the product was repositioned to have both an archaic (but accepted in the marketplace) analog readout and a digital interface that could be fed into a computer.

· **Forecasting Follies.** Market forecasts can have a tendency to be terribly understated or overstated. Unless conducted by an experienced market researcher, sales projections can lie more profusely than a crooked politician or an iconoclastic economist.

For example, alliances in the robotics industry have watched sales forecasts fall far short of projections year after year. The market for robots has never met expectations, principally because the customer demand is highly specialized and centered around specific, custom needs. Money invested based on these forecasts has seldom seen a return on investment.

ORGANIZATION AND MANAGEMENT ISSUES

Organization difficulties stem from problems in the organizational structure and usually are connected to some management deficiency, such as personnel not suited for the job. Alliances must be operated by people, which can be the venture's biggest asset or its biggest obstacle if improperly chosen. Running a partnership with more than one master increases the venture's complexity "exponentially by square of the number of partners," according to one seasoned joint venturer. Alliances must not be dumping grounds for the sponsoring company's "also-rans."

The converse can also be a problem if the parent company's very best employees are put in the joint venture. People may begin to think that the joint venture is where all the fun is, where all the really good jobs are, where the president's interests are, and where the best career growth is. Time should be spent to ensure the correct "operational fit" between the partners, dovetailed with the optimum selection of personnel.

Some examples of organization and management issues:

- **Delegation Deadlock,** one of the most frequently experienced problems in joint ventures, is the difficulty of determining who is in charge or responsible.

   For example, two small plumbing and heating contractors formed a joint venture to bid on a large downtown office building. Neither had ever been involved in a joint venture, and both contractors were accustomed to making quick decisions by themselves. After winning the contract, they became frustrated because of difficulties mutually deciding who was in charge of certain aspects of the project, to whom the work crew reported, and who was responsible for handling change orders. They failed to appoint a project manager, avoided establishing an operational steering committee, and never gave any real power, authority, or leadership to the joint venture. Finally, one of the partners agreed to take operational control, and eventually the alliance began to function.

- **Who's on First?** Remember the classic Abbott and Costello routine? It symbolizes the utmost management malfunction: not knowing who has the responsibility for achieving objectives and solving problems. It is a close kin to "delegation deadlock."

  For example, in an international joint venture between a U.S. corporation and a South American firm, the U.S. company was required to hold a minority interest in the joint venture due to the national laws prohibiting foreign corporations from holding a majority interest in a domestic company. Much to the chagrin of both the venturers, the terms of the agreement did not address managerial control issues adequately. The Latin Americans were relying on U.S. management expertise and technology to make the venture work. Just after the venture was initiated, the U.S. champion was hired away by another firm. By the time his replacement was on board, the joint venture was several months old, and the Latin American manager had filled the breach and taken control, driving the venture into a direction for which the U.S. partner was not ready. Equipment of the wrong specifications had been ordered, personnel were hired without proper qualifications, training programs were not in place, and financial controls were nonexistent. The U.S. firm was reluctant to insist on assuming management control for fear of further aggravating a delicate situation, especially because the U.S. firm was a minority owner of the venture. Things went from bad to worse until the two companies' presidents sat together to map out a reasonable and proper solution. In the meantime, considerable money and time was lost, and team morale was at a low. Eventually the U.S. managers were sent in to manage the venture and, subsequently, to train their Latin American counterparts.

- **Partner's Peril.** Some companies and people are just not good partners. Regardless of well-intentioned efforts, good organizational structure, and a well-conceived strategy, the partnership just will not work.

  For example, three consulting companies joined forces to provide strategic planning, financial, and marketing services to small fast-growth technology companies. The strategic planning partner had experience with alliances, but the other two partners had none. After less than a year of operation, the venture was in disarray: The financial and marketing partners could not get along, each wanting to control the venture, neither having trust in the other's abilities. The presidents of each of the dissenting companies were accustomed to making decisions themselves and were not willing to adhere to a joint, committee-oriented decisionmaking process. Later they decided to terminate the alliance.

· **Trapped in the Iranian Desert.** Several years ago, when President Carter was dealing with the hostage crisis in Tehran, a military force was transported into the desert outside the city to attempt a hostage rescue mission. It ended in a disaster because the various military units had not worked together before. They failed to coordinate their activities well, and many problems—like sand getting into the helicopter motors—had not been anticipated in advance of the maneuver. Problems like these happen in business alliances, too.

For example, the computer science department of a prominent university developed a technology to translate voice commands into written words via a computer program. The technology looked promising in the laboratory, and a joint development agreement was signed with a small private technology development company. The university's computer science engineers would finish the software programs, and the private company would convert the technology into a marketable computer-based product. However, the university's applications engineers worked at a far slower pace than the private company's timetable necessitated to stay on schedule. Then a multitude of other problems emerged: Local dialects were a problem for the computer to translate; adapting the university's computer program to match the numerous computer systems in the private marketplace proved to be far more complex than anticipated; the initial target market was less than enthusiastic once the pilot tests were over; and the sales cycle took about three times longer than anticipated. The technology company could not establish an effective distribution system for the product once the product was perfected. IBM then decided to enter the market. The venture lost money, bleeding the financial resources from the small technology company, which eventually declared bankruptcy after losing over $1 million.

· **Organizational Inertia.** At their inception, joint ventures to a large extent (and strategic alliances to a lesser extent) are start-up businesses. As such, they need "shakers and movers" to get them going. These people are high achievers who believe in breaking goals, for whom time is not a limitation but a challenge; they desire results and can inspire others to desire the same; and they hold to budgets dearly.

For example, in a private–public partnership alliance established to revitalize a declining commercial downtown area, the initial project manager was selected from the city's planning and economic development department for her skill in designing large-scale urban renewal programs. This individual was adept in dealing with political leaders, policymakers, and professional administrators. She was well liked and well respected by those in her profession, as well as those with whom she came into contact. But after five months of meetings, discussions, subcommittees, hiring of consultants, and considerable expense, the business members of the steering committee were frustrated that there were no tangible results. They pressed for a change in personnel, but the city officials were quite satisfied with the manager's performance, primarily because there had been no controversy to this point, no adverse publicity, and no negative reactions by the vocal political opposition—all political pluses. But the business leaders knew far more should be done. They also knew that seldom do good public-sector administrators make good private-sector project initiators. They knew the price they would pay for the decision to hire an administrator would be organizational inertia. If a change were to be made, the trade-off would be the expense of conflict with the public sector. This failure to discuss the goals of operational management between the partners before the venture began was a serious flaw.

· **Functional Synchronization.** Ventures not requiring close coordination on a daily basis may be prone to serious problems synchronizing the elements of each stage of development.

For example, five companies formed a joint enterprise to design and develop a control system to monitor and regulate bacteria-fighting chemicals in swimming pools. One partner was assigned to design and manufacture a dispensing system utilizing standard, regularly available parts. The second partner was to develop a marketing and sales program. A third partner was to ensure proper financing for the venture. The fourth partner was to develop a sensing device to determine when the swimming pool had too much or too little of the bacteria-fighting chemicals. A fifth partner was to ensure that regulatory approval was obtained from U.S. government agencies and any prevailing state agencies. No strict time deadlines were established, and no experienced project manager was designated. Rough goals and time desires were spoken about, but no regular project meetings were scheduled. It was hoped that the first prototypes would be ready for a trade show eight months hence. Three years later the project was finally reaching the point where serious marketing programs could be established. The venture was out of synchronization, primarily because no one was in charge of timing and deadlines. Eventually, the venture successfully introduced the product, but only after one of the partners, almost by default and motivated by frustration, took control, saw the emerging market opportunity, and "drove" the venture to success.

FINANCE ISSUES

Financial tensions come from monetary issues that have not been properly diagnosed and analyzed. Particularly with smaller companies having highly leveraged positions, a joint enterprise can be a terrible drain on its resources unless the agreement is structured to provide cash to the smaller company. When a financial crunch occurs, objectives seldom are achieved successfully, animosities grow, and trust is strained.

Will a large corporate partner support the smaller one during a crisis, or will it take over ownership? Proper due diligence by sharing financial statements can help prevent or diminish the chances of this problem.

A list of typical finance-oriented issues might be:

· **The Cost Overrun.** One of the most common problems faced in high-risk ventures is the problem of the cost overrun. They seem to gnaw at the heart of so many ventures because of the developmental risks at the core of many plans. The best methods of addressing the inevitable cost overruns are: first, build contingencies into the budget; second, make provisions for these events in the agreement; third, have a decisionmaking process for reviewing the validity of each overrun, and fourth, create a control system placing a limit on expenditures if they start cycling out of hand.

Underestimated costs are likely to pervade many alliances. Any industry is vulnerable, whether it be hi-tech, mining, hospitals, or construction.

For example, a building general contractor and real estate developer formed a joint venture to renovate six Victorian buildings in a Midwestern city. Initial estimates were made for the renovations. Unfortunately, the developers were delayed because they underestimated the time for obtaining the necessary zoning and environmental permits, putting a halt to the renovations. This time delay did not halt the bank from demanding interest on its construction mortgage. By the time the permits were issued, the state government had enacted more stringent fire code regulations, which required several of the buildings to have sprinkler systems, adding an additional 10 percent to the renovation costs. Then, once construction restarted, certain unanticipated structural deficiencies were found that had to be corrected. The time delays cost the project its lead tenant, who was forced to find other space elsewhere. By the time the project was ready for occupancy, the costs were 45 percent over budget, which left the partners with a substantial loss rather than profit.

· **Make It In-House.** The decision to make a product in-house or buy it from an outside source can be a complex one. Many companies lack sufficient financial data to make a good "make-or-buy" decision, and the presence of the partnership may make this more difficult.

For example, two manufacturing companies—one in the aerospace industry and the other in the electronics industry—formed a venture to bid on a military radar control system. The electronics company was recently purchased by two young MBA graduates with strong strategic and marketing skills. Having formed the joint venture soon after buying the electronics company, they were unaware of the tremendous inadequacies of the pricing and costing methods used by the former owners. Therefore, the government bids for the new product were based on highly erroneous costing methods. The joint venture won the contract, engineering design was completed, and production commenced, at which time the electronics company management began to realize the terrible losses they would sustain by fulfilling the contract. Finally, a management consultant was called in and the problem was identified, but by then the company was too deeply in debt to recover. Rather than lose the contract, the other partner purchased the manufacturing rights, subcontracted the production, and fulfilled the commitments to the military.

· **The Money-Grows-on-Strategic-Plans Syndrome** is the financial version of the "diagnostic delirium" and the "forecasting follies." Financial forecasts should be based on hard data and include cynical or conservative estimates. A risky project will often take twice as long to bring to fruition, use twice as much capital, and capture only half the expected market. Every strategic plan must backed up by a realistic operational and financial plan.

For example, a young entrepreneur, trained as a sales engineer at a large computer firm, decided to form his own company to design and assemble computer systems for the data management industry. Part of his strategic plan called for a joint venture with a major computer manufacturer, with the goal of building on the major manufacturer's trade name, warranties, and image to close sales on the new systems. Several Fortune 500 companies agreed to purchase the new systems, which spurred the budding entrepreneur to offer stock in his young company by an initial public offering (sale of stock on the stock market). Nearly $5 million was raised in the offering, which was used to establish research and development facilities, international sales staff, and a small manufacturing facility for some critical parts. What the entrepreneur failed to recognize was the difficulty of creating a full-scale coordinated management team to support this high-growth strategy. The new systems development program quickly came unglued, and in the meantime another highly recognized competitor entered the market place with a superior product. Orders were cancelled because of the slippage of delivery dates, and shortly thereafter a bankruptcy filing was made, which caused the joint venture to crumble.

· **Bankruptcy or Acquisition** of one of the partners can be two thorny problems unless dealt with adequately in the partnership agreement. A partner's bankruptcy may leave all the financial risks of a joint venture on the other partner's shoulders. Should one of the partners become bankrupt, file for protection under Chapter 11, or be acquired by another company, can the joint venture survive?

Less severe, but nevertheless often debilitating is an acquisition by another company that may not be amenable to the strategy or operations of the enterprise. In the legal documents some provision should be made for the interests of the joint venture to be acquired from one partner should an unfavorable acquisition occur.

For example, two major chemical companies had a longstanding relationship, and had been involved in joint ventures for many years. Their current joint venture was to develop, manufacture, and market a complex heat-resistant polymer for the plastics and aerospace industries. Prior to the finalization of research and development, one of the partners was acquired in a hostile takeover by a rival firm. The new owner was an archrival of the remaining joint venture partner, and the two CEOs could never "make music" together. Fortunately, the joint venture agreement gave an option to each of the original partners to buy out the other's interest should the other be acquired. The option was exercised immediately, and conflict never had the opportunity to erupt.

BUSINESS CULTURE ISSUES

Cultural problems refer to difficulties arising from style, informal rules, organizational values, and standards. If two companies have very different styles of management and decision making, a corporate culture clash can develop. This clash often occurs between large and small companies, companies from different parts of the world, and especially private–public partnerships. Paul Lawrence cautions venture managers to watch out for intergroup rivalry that can soon start feeding on itself.

Many American and European managers have difficulties in developing nations because their partners may have strong differences in social and ethical values. This problem can be further compounded when uneducated and unskilled workers are thrown together with foreign managers who have been acclimated to an educated, urbane workforce.

- **"Ultimate Objectives" Clashes** are likely to occur when two organizations having very different missions try to work together. Private–nonprofit ventures can provide an arena for this problem.

  For example, in a joint enterprise between a hi-tech manufacturer and a university to utilize a university-created technology for commercial use, the manufacturing department became livid about the university engineer's inability to meet agreed-upon time schedules, the lack of understanding of applications and manufacturing engineering, and what was perceived as highly academic dictating of final design and materials. The university engineers felt the manufacturing company was not interested in their design concept and wanted to require the manufacturing company to adhere to certain design specifications so as not to diminish the technology's operational performance and reliability. The resolution of the problem came from the manufacturer's appointment of a highly respected project manager with a PhD, who gained the respect of the academicians and still developed an acceptable, cost-effective commercialization process for the technology.

- **Territorial Prerogatives** often intervene as an issue when two natural competitors decide to form a venture in another marketplace but remain competitive in their original markets. A similar type of friction can arise when a captive joint venture (one that is designed only to supply its originators) wants to be more independent. Similarly, a constrained venture (where the partners maintain parallel production facilities that compete with the joint venture) can generate turmoil.

For example, two small northeast paint manufacturers, squeezed by competition from the three major competitors that controlled almost 80 percent of the market, decided to form a joint venture. Many small paint companies purchase their resins from outside manufacturers. To have a more economic source of raw materials, the two jointly purchased an existing manufacturing plant producing alkyloid resins for oil-based paints. They also argeed to share research data on the properties of these resins. The venture was good in theory, and would have worked if the partners came from different parts of the country. However, both had only regional market penetration. Their salesforces were constantly butting heads in the same distribution channels, which caused aggravations between the companies as they vied for a small share in the market. Finally, one of the partners was acquired by a medium-sized competitor looking for expansion. The larger acquirer also negotiated for rights to buy out the joint venture, and eventually expanded into a national market base. As part of the buyout agreement, the remaining small company received a favorable purchase rate to continue its supply of resins from the manufacturing plant.

· **The Problem of Synchronized Pacing** occurs because some companies are far faster paced, particularly those in production modes where the manufacturing culture is measured in terms of minutes and seconds, as opposed to a research and developoment culture where time is measured in years and development cycles. These two cultures can inadvertently cause a great deal of pain for each other.

For example, a well-respected chemical research group entered into a strategic alliance with a textile company to develop a new imitation silk for the fashion industry. When the enterprise was formed, the chemical engineers had the prototype fabric 100 percent perfected in the laboratory, and were confident a large-scale manufacturing process was relatively simple to create. The textile company was extremely excited about the potential of the cloth, and gave numerous samples to its salesforce to show to apparel companies at the New York trade show. Orders were placed, and spirits were high with what they thought was the sweet smell of success. But success was an illusion, as the textile company learned when their chemical research partner was unable to develop a large-scale manufacturing process with sufficient quality and cost efficiency. Moreover, these engineers were not used to the fast-paced nature of the ever-changing fashion industry, and did not respond well to the high pressure placed upon them by their textile partner. A year later, with much embarrassment for the textile partner and much frustration and cost for the chemical partner, the product was ready for the market.

· **Do It My Way** results from one partner dictating the rules and alienating the other partner from the decisionmaking.

For example, a large U.S. chemical manufacturer formed a joint venture with a French chemical company to make plastic resins in France. The U.S. company held the patents, and the two would jointly own the plant. Soon after the plant was in operation, complaints from customers came flooding in: The product was not according to specifications. The American company investigated and found its French partners had replaced some of the equipment with their own version. A team of Americans flew in, spotted the French equipment, had replacements on a plane immediately, and supervised the installation. Sixty days later, the complaints started again. The French, believing their way was better, had reinstalled their equipment. After countless hours of downtime and negotiations, the two partners agreed on a compromise piece of equipment.

CHEMISTRY ISSUES

"Chemistry" problems are encountered when the partners are just not in tune with each other. Sometimes the owner's capabilities are poorly matched. Other times, managers from disparate partners cannot work together. The potential for these problems can be diminished by the "incremental venture" that begins first with a cooperative agreement, such as a licensing agreement or a handshake to work together, and later closer alliance can emerge after the teams have tested each other through courtship. Some examples are:

· **Commitment Crisis.** Long-term development projects are especially prone to the "commitment crisis," particularly in the absence of pressing deadlines or when or or more of partners have other opportunities competing for time, money, personnel, and management attention.

Seldom do partners simply renege on their commitments. This problem often manifests itself when what was thought to be good technology was not as good as expected, or personnel were simply not qualified to deliver the owner's commitments. Most of these problems can be eliminated or reduced by due diligence and good planning before the venture starts.

For example, a building contracting company with financial and construction management skills formed a three-way alliance with an electrical contractor and a plumbing/heating contractor to bid against larger out-of-state general contractors who were making inroads in the local area. Ten months went by before a single joint bid was submitted because each of the contractors was too busy chasing individual contracts and keeping current jobs on schedule. Finally, they agreed to hire a project manager who was responsible for submitting bids, and who would subsequently supervise construction for any contracts landed by the venture. By making a financial commitment to the project manager's salary, the venture gained its first contract several months later.

· **The "Golden Rules."** When "He Who Has the Gold Rules" becomes the manner of operating a joint enterprise, conflict is sure to result, and failure likely to follow.

For example, a large corporation formed a joint venture with a small company. The small company's task was to engineer a specialty measuring device using laser technology, to be included in a large process control system. The small company, being undercapitalized, negotiated up-front development fees along with a purchase of a minority stock interest by the larger corporation in return for a minority ownership in the joint venture. After four months, the larger corporation, with overall management control of the joint venture, began dictating policy, personnel assignments, and manufacturing budgets without consulting the smaller company. When the smaller company dug in its heels and objected, the larger corporation retorted, "We have the largest risk and the overall responsibility for performance, therefore you are obliged to do as we demand." A wise and diplomatic chairman of the board of the small company held his angry president at bay, went to the chairman of the large corporation, and worked out a method to use the operational steering committee to greater advantage in engendering cooperation and commitment as a team, and gained agreements that as long as the small company and the joint venture were profitable, there would be no more unilateral dictates.

These strategic and structural issues are representative of a broad range of concerns facing business partnerships. If they cannot be resolved effectively, then the venture is probably ready for a "transformation." Some of the options for transformation are discussed in the next chapter.

14

When to Change the Terms

*Joint ventures and strategic alliances are simply a bridge be-
tween two businesses flowing on the tides of change. If the tides
flow in different directions, the bridge must adapt.*

The Author

TRANSFORMATION TIMING

A joint venture is simply a *process* used to achieve a strategic objective.
It is *not the objective* itself. To become locked into using the joint venture
structure when it no longer meets the strategic and operational needs of
the partners is a mistake. The original agreement should be written flexi-
bly enough to acknowledge that business interests do not remain stable
over time.

In the whaling era of the 1800s, joint ventures were scheduled to last
only for the term of the voyage, usually two to three years. Within 10 days
after returning to port, the owners were required by law to sell their cargo
and pay the captain and crew their salaries and any profit sharing. Then
the ship was sold, the partners paid, and the entity terminated.

Many real estate development joint ventures have termination dates
built in at inception, with terms ranging normally from seven to 10 years.
Mining joint ventures will often last as long as the mine has ore, at which
time the venture ends. Other joint ventures have lasted more than 25 years
and continue to this day as strong and healthy as ever.

The rule of thumb is, "Use the joint venture when it is the most effective means of accomplishing the objective. When another means is more appropriate, shift gears."

Buyouts and Liquidations

A number of journalists have commented on the "failure rate" in joint venturing. Very little scholarly analysis has been done on the failure rates of joint ventures, and apparently none done regarding strategic alliances. In the real estate, chemical, and mining industries, the success rates appear to be quite high.

In hi-tech, "seat-of-the-pants" estimates by companies like IBM have guessed at 30 percent to 50 percent failure rates for the riskier hi-tech ventures. However, a closer examination of those "terminated" ventures leads to some very different conclusions. About half of the terminated ventures were really not failures because they were bought out by one of the partners, reducing the "failure rate" in hi-tech to perhaps 15 percent to 25 percent. This percentage is actually quite good considering the risks. Peters and Waterman, authors of *In Search of Excellence,* write: "Most champions fail most of the time," but the key to "innovation success is a numbers game" in hi-tech development.[1] The only way to win is to toss the dice enough times. James Brian Quinn states: "Management must allow a sufficient number of projects with a long enough lead time for the characteristic 1:20 success ratio to have effect."[2]

A study done by Richard Thompson of the University of Massachusetts examined fifty "terminations" in the chemical industry over a 35-year period, and it yielded some very enlightening observations (see Table 14.1).

While this analysis cannot be predictive of any single joint venture, and it only relates to one industry, it is instructive to note that "failed" joint ventures were the result of external conditions or uncontrollable risks, whereas the "transformations" enabled the continuance of the operations in another form—certainly not a failure. When the ventures terminated, transformations outdistanced failures by two to one.

RESPONSES TO SHIFTS IN STRATEGIC ENVIRONMENT

Every joint enterprise exists in a "strategic environment," which presumably made the joint venture the best alternative when it was formed. Prior to the alliance's creation, various other alternatives should have been ex-

Table 14.1. Analysis of Joint Venture Terminations (Chemical Industry)

	Transformations
52%	Purchased by parent or other
8	Merged into parent or another joint venture
8	Broken up by antitrust (then sold or purchased by parent)
68%	Subtotal
	Failures
20%	Adverse market changes
8	Research efforts unsuccessful
2	Obsolete facilities
2	Bankruptcy of one parent
32%	Subtotal
100%	Total

Source: Richard Thompson[3]

plored, such as mergers, acquisitions, and internal expansion, to be sure the proper structural match was made to the strategic environment.

As the strategic environment changes or competitive pressures shift, the mission of the alliance may also shift to become more valuable to one of the sponsors and less to another. As Columbia University researcher Kathryn Harrigan states, quite eloquently:

> "Joint ventures are inherently unstable. The forces that promote cooperation are often fickle, even the success of a joint venture may encourage one owner to undertake *by itself* (and sometimes in competition with) the activities previously assigned to the venture . . . Because joint ventures are inherently unstable organizational forms, they are ideal for implementing transitional strategies, such as fade-out divestitures, organizational restructurings, and so on."[4]

Changes to the structure may be futile if it is not to one of the partner's strategic advantage to be part of an alliance. Try as the partners may, they might discover that no longer is the alliance the right structure for the strategic environment conditions. A multitude of conditions could change causing the partners to rethink the viability of the venture:

- **International Price/Political Changes.** Many venturers who were initially motivated to form international alliances will find when the host nation changes laws and monetary rates of exchange, the motive for formation will change drastically.

For example, a U.S. company formed a joint venture in Asia to manufacture plastics for luggage products marketed throughout the world. The Asian government required that a majority of any domestic company be owned and controlled by natives. One of the most attractive reasons for the joint venture was the underdeveloped Asian country's desire to grow a petrochemical industry. Price supports and tax advantages were provided to induce foreign investment and make the petrochemical products extremely competitive in the international marketplace. For six years, the venture was very lucrative. But major shifts occurred causing the demise of the venture. First, the Asian country went into an inflationary cycle that changed the value of its currency relative to other international rates of exchange. The inflationary cycle brought about major political changes, resulting in a withdrawal of price supports and tax advantages. Ultimately, when the ruling political party began nationalizing industries, the U.S. partner withdrew from what was fast becoming a crumbling joint venture environment.

- **Change in Technology.** Technological changes can provide superior competitive advantage, as long as the process remains on the cutting edge.

  For example, a joint venture developed a new methodology for coating metal with a substance having excellent anticorrosive properties. The venture was very successful, but eventually competitors learned that the process was not patentable. Each year competitors with superior distribution capabilities captured a larger and larger share of a market. Since the market was stable and not expanding, the joint venture continuingly lost market share, becoming less profitable; and eventually resulting in termination.

- **Competitors Entering Market.** Good business strategy is based on good competitive strategy. A formidable competitor can cause a realignment within the venture.

  For example, a computer company joined forces with a machinery company to design and manufacture a computer controlled machine to be used in the manufacture of specialized welding for medical devices. After several years, the venture was quite profitable. But as the market grew, other larger companies with extensive research and development capacity entered the market with a far more efficient designs at better prices, cutting the margins for the joint venture.

Eventually the joint venture partners decided to dissolve the venture because it could no longer remain competitive and profitable without a major infusion of money, which neither was willing to invest.

· **Market Changes.** Fundamental market changes cannot always be predicted. When they occur, all firms within an industry will see shifts in their own strategic underpinnings.

For example, three oil companies formed a joint venture to develop a synthetic fuel. After the venture was formed and research commenced in earnest, the Arab oil cartel lost its control of world oil prices (which no one predicted). As the bottom fell out of the pricing supports, synthetic fuels became unprofitable as the oil glut grew larger. The founders of the venture decided to curtail any further expenses by dissolving the venture.

· **Production Costs.** Production cost changes can have the same basic impact as changes in the market.

For example, a utility company and an engineering company formed a venture to dispose of waste products using a methodology patented by one of the engineering company's principals. The method of waste disposal was highly effective for detoxifying asbestos and its advantages remained strong until government regulations for waste disposal changed. These changes required major design changes to the machinery, which made the waste disposal costs highly expensive. A foreign technology was substantially different, making the foreign production process far more economical, resulting in a decision to terminate the domestic joint venture.

· **Strategic Realignments.** Within any industry, major and minor players are always jockeying for position.

For example, an industrial boiler and pump manufacturer created a joint venture with a small motor manufacturer to produce a product line of industrial pumps and circulators. After several years, the boiler and pump manufacturer was acquired by a European conglomerate that had a strong base in outfitting nuclear power plants. The new European owners wanted the joint venture to produce machinery for the nuclear industry. But the original motor manufacturing partner, faced with increased liability insurance, which was hard to obtain at the time, chose not to enter the nuclear market. Consequently, the European partner acquired the motor manufacturer, resulting in the joint venture being owned by a single conglomerate. The conglomerate then decided to disband the joint venture in favor of a supply line provided by its subsidiaries.

These changes were dramatic responses to dramatic strategic realignments. If, however, the strategic environment makes less radical course changes, then only minor changes to the structure and operational aspects of the venture may be in order.

RESPONSES TO INAPPROPRIATE OPERATIONAL CONDITIONS

Even if strategic conditions remain somewhat stable, the venture may suffer strains from operational conditions that cannot be corrected simply by mutual discussions and problemsolving. Some operational conditions may require a minor restructuring of the alliance, while other more serious problems may result in a more drastic change, such as termination or acquisition. Some of these possible situations are:

- **Change of Key Personnel.** Leadership and management are key elements to the success of any cooperative agreement. Without the right people committed to the enterprise, continued allegiance may be difficult at best.

  For example, a restaurant formed a joint venture with a theater arts department of a local college for a summer dinner theater in a small mountain resort. The group presented comedies and musicals. The restaurant provided a large dining area at no charge to the venture, along with the opportunity to provide food and drinks to the patrons; all food, beverage, labor, and overhead expenses would be borne by the restaurant. The theater arts group produced the performances, took all the box office admissions, and bore the costs of paying actors, royalties, and technical people. Advertising expenses were split 50–50 by the partners. The first season was such a success that the head of the theater arts department was spotted by a large city repertory company, and hired away. His replacement was not attuned to comedies and musicals, preferring heavier dramas and serious plays. The restauranteur exercised his option to take over the joint venture upon the exit of any key personnel, and in future years ran the dinner theater under the restaurant's ownership and management.

- **Lack of Commitment or Support.** Without commitment and support, no venture will survive. If the support or commitment is withdrawn, changes must be made.

  For example, two small manufacturing companies in the printing industry formed their joint venture. One company, a consulting and engineering group to the printing industry, had formulated a new type of color printing ink that was less susceptible to variations in shade or set-up error. The other partner, a regional distribution house, sold printing products, such as paper, inks, and solvents to large commercial printers. Operational leadership in the joint venture had been vested in the consulting and engineering company, although the expenses and profits were split 50–50. After several years of moderately successful operations, the owner of the consulting and engineering company, who had led the joint venture, died. Being a small company, it did not have the management depth to handle its normal business plus the joint venture. The regional distribution company was experiencing very strong internal growth, and had tapped its own management resources to the limit to handle their growth. Rather than let the venture trickle away, they approached a chemical manufacturer with strong management skills to become a third partner. The new partner accepted operational control and the pie was divided equally in three portions.

· **Conflicting Organizational Values.** What is important to a company today can often change dramatically if tomorrow other conditions change, thereby having an impact on the venture.

For example, a small chemical company with a very promising patented process for heat-resistant ceramic-based plastics formed its joint venture with a large manufacturer of machinery for the appliance industry to use hi-heat resistant plastics to replace certain metal products. The machinery manufacturer, located in the Northeast, was owned by a larger conglomerate, and the plastics company was privately owned by its original founder, a gentleman from the deep South. Shortly after the formation of the venture, several other companies owned by the conglomerate ran into severe financial difficulties, and headquarters exerted great pressure to make the joint venture produce a cash flow. Angry words began to flow at the weekly steering committee meetings when the larger partner showed reluctance to put more money into the venture to capture greater market share, which the smaller company had counted on to justify the substantial investment it had made in engineering and new machinery and equipment to commercialize the manufacturing process. Without stronger market share, the smaller company would be unable to amortize its investment. Without better cash flow, the larger conglomerated could not satisfy its high thresholds for return on investment. A stalemate was in the offing until a financial restructuring was proposed that gave the large corporation a larger cash flow in the short run, but enabled the smaller company to own a greater share of the equity of the venture in the long run.

- **Entrepreneurial Energy Mismatch.** The commencement of a joint venture resembles a business start-up and requires tremendous amounts of initial management energy.

  For example, when two large corporations began their joint venture they assigned very competent managers to the project who were competent in running existing corporate divisions. But these individuals lacked the experience, drive, and vision to start a new venture from scratch. Early on, costs were over-budget, projects were behind schedule, production delays were mounting, and morale was ebbing quickly. A entrepreneurial member of one of the board of directors of a parent company, who had started his own company 30 years before, was called in to analyze the problem as an outside consultant. Immediately, he spotted the problem and recommended a new top person with experience in either start-up or turn-around situations. The joint venture hired an individual who had a strong track record of taking over bankrupt companies and making them profitable quickly. High-performance results came within a few months. However, after a little more than a year, this person had been too abrasive for the more docile form of in-house corporate management, and he was replaced by a manager with better interpersonal skills.

- **Internal Financial Problems.** When one partner gets into financial difficulties, it automatically increases the risk to the joint venture and, therefore, to the other partner. In one three-way alliance, a small construction company, and engineering firm, and a heating system contractor united to bid and build a large apartment complex. The heating system contractor, who had been working on another large project that ran into serious financial difficulties, was owed over $100,000, and was unable to collect from the developer. Being too short of cash, the heating system company resorted to using inferior-grade materials on the apartment contract. After the complex had been finished for over a year, major defects began appearing in the piping, which eventually resulted in a lawsuit against the heating contractor as well as against the joint venture itself. The two other companies were forced to defend themselves in court for their partner's deficiencies.

- **Chemistry.** There is no guarantee that the important ingredient of organizational chemistry will last eternally.

For example, two very close friends—one the owner of a finance company, the other the owner of a personnel recruiting and consulting company—formed an alliance to provide parttime financial and personnel management resources to small, growing businesses. The joint venture's chemistry was excellent as long as the two partners devoted considerable time to the venture itself. However, when the finance-oriented partner had to devote considerably more time to managing a major growth period in his sponsoring company, the other partner was silently resentful of the devotion to duties outside of the joint venture and, by default, took operational control of the management of the joint venture, which made the finance partner feel resentful there was no longer a feeling of teamwork. Instead, now one partner was superior, the other subordinate. The result was the joint venture's subsequent failure to grow to its potential.

· **Production and Marketing Costs.** Even the best forecasters cannot predict the complexities created by nature's elements and politicians.

For example, an agricultural venture was formed between a consortium of small fishing companies and a fish processing plant. The objective of the venture was to have all the fishermen become the exclusive providers of fish to the processing plant at a guaranteed minimum rate, with the profits divided among all the partners at the end of the year in proportion to the amount of fish provided by each. The processing plant was guaranteed to meet its minimum operating costs from receipts of gross sales. The venture looked like a winner for the first six months, but several months of bitter winter weather combined with a change in the migratory patterns of the fish severely altered the supply of raw materials for the plant. On top of these problems, environmental laws were passed preventing the disposal of fish wastes at the local land fill, which was rapidly becoming full. Rather than provide for alternate disposal of the fish wastes, the governmental authorities simply closed the old refuse site, thus necessitating the trucking of materials out of state, which substantially increased production costs. Squeezed by the weather on one side, and the costs of production on the other, the members of the joint venture chose to abandon their agreement. The plant decided to close down operations until the state could change its rules, and the fishermen then went to a nearby port in another state to peddle their fish.

These examples cover a broad range. Some of the difficulties could have been minimized by a better strategy to begin with; other problems might have been avoided by a more carefully thought out agreement between the parties. But some problems were simply inherent in the nature of assuming future risks.

CONTINUATION

Some joint ventures have been so successful they are almost institutions in people's minds. Owens–Corning became its own separate corporation and continued to grow. Dow & Corning formed many joint ventures over the years between themselves and others over several decades. Gilbane Construction has been using joint ventures for years to increase its capabilities in cities where it did not previously have a presence. Stanley Bostich, one of the world's largest producers of industrial nailing machines, has had a joint venture with a Japanese counterpart for almost three decades. If conditions are right, a joint venture may last indefinitely, and indeed, one English insurance venture is reputed to be over two centuries old.

To make a joint venture work over a long period of time, it will probably require the partners to refocus the venture periodically. For instance, 25 years ago, an American manufacturing company formed a joint venture with a Japanese electric company. The American company manufactured synchronous electric motors, which their Japanese partner distributed and marketed throughout the Pacific basin. Over the intervening decades, the Japanese company had developed its own synchronous motors with new, more advanced technology, and the product supplied by the American company to the joint venture begin to diminish in importance, even though the "chemistry" was still right between the partners.

By the middle 1980s, however, both partners had independently developed motors, sensors, and computer systems to be used in the robotics industry. With the new products in hand, the two companies refocused the joint venture into the worldwide production, marketing, and servicing of industrial robots and automated production equipment.

MERGER

Joint ventures and strategic alliances have served as an excellent interim vehicle to test the strategic and operational "fit" of two companies before a merger occurs. Obviously, if the alliance is successful, the chances of a merger being successful are far more likely than if the partners never worked together at all. And if the alliance is too tense or fails, then relatively little was risked and the companies can continue on their own separate ways.

For example, Alpha and Omega hospitals were two small hospitals located near each other in a large eastern metropolitan area. In 1980 they formed a joint venture to create a health maintenance organization (HMO) using staff resources from each of the hospitals. After a rough start, a new administrator was brought in, the HMO finally began to work, and the two hospitals learned how to cooperate and coordinate together well.

Several years later, it became apparent the rising costs of health care could be better controlled by merging the two hospitals together, eliminating much administrative overhead, and making better functional use of the high-priced laboratory equipment necessary to sustain quality health care. The joint venture HMO had provided the administrative and medical staffs with a good opportunity to work together for several years. Each of the two hospital boards of directors voted to merge the two hospitals, making the HMO a subsidiary of the new unified hospital.

Other partners may find mergers enable the two partners to take advantage of economies of scale or vertical integration to build greater market dominance. Sometimes the merger will combine the two partners and the separate detached joint venture into one entity, if financial officers find the overhead to be cheaper as one.

ACQUISITION

Acquisitions are a more frequent occurence than mergers in the alliance business. There are three variations of acquisitions:

1. *One partner acquires the joint venture, converting it to a subsidiary.*
   For example, a real estate developer and general contractor formed a joint venture to build and operate an office complex in Minneapolis. The two partners anticipated building and operating several more office complexes in the suburbs during the next few years. However, the contractor landed several very large construction contracts from an expanding computer firm. The contracts required the purchase of a substantial amount of machinery and excavation equipment, along with cash reserves to handle bonding, subcontractors, and insurance binders. The contractor was short on cash, even with bank loans, and therefore decided to sell his interest in the office complex owned by the joint venture to raise the necessary capital. Fortunately for the contractor, the terms of the purchase by

the other joint venture partner were spelled out well in the agreement. The developer exercised his right to purchase the venture, and held the complex as a subsidiary of his development company.

2. *One partner acquires the other partner (and the joint venture by inclusion).* For example, a large European manufacturer of sealants and adhesives established a strategic alliance with an small American manufacturer with excellent marketing and development capabilities. The partnership was highly successful, and later converted into a joint venture, with a separate corporation established to build a U.S. manufacturing plant and to market through the existing U.S. company. Sales continued to grow, and the European company made an offer to purchase the smaller U.S. company, thereby merging the U.S. company together with the joint venture to create a wholly owned subsidiary.

3. *An outside party acquires the joint venture.* For example, three gas companies owning numerous gas wells in the Southwest formed a joint venture to build a pipeline to carry their gas to California. After completing the new pipeline, a large regional utility purchased the pipeline to link it to an even larger network. As part of the sales agreement, the original gas companies retained rights to supply gas to the new owner.

In another example, in 1982, Roger Penske, race car champion and organizer of several Indianapolis 500 race teams, formed a joint venture with Hertz to lease trucks, ultimately becoming the second largest truck leasing firm in the United States. Six years later, when a partnership financed largely by Ford Motor Company purchased Hertz, it triggered an option for Penske to purchase Hertz's 50 percent share of the venture. Penske chose to exercise the option, then sought out General Electric Capital's truck-leasing subsidiary as a new joint venture partner, thereby increasing the size of the joint venture an additional 35 percent, capturing an even greater market share.

LICENSING

Some cooperative ventures find that there really is not a need to work together closely. A friendly but arm's-length relationship is really all that is needed by many companies. Licensing can provide a safe and relatively low risk method of cooperation, requiring little capital investment. The licensing can also provide excellent royalty income (but without the upside advantage of high returns).

Some joint alliances and strategic alliances are converted to simple licensing agreements when one of the partner's strategic interests diverge from the purposes of the alliance or if anticipated markets stagnate. In these events, one partner may desire to purchase the rights to the product or technology.

For example, a small Canadian medical research group patented a machine to purify contaminated blood. They sold the world marketing rights to a large U.S. hospital supply house who, in turn, formed a joint venture with another hospital supply house in Europe. The U.S. firm retained the rights to market the product in North and South America, and the European company had rights in the Europe, Africa, and Asia. Approval was given by most governmental authorities in Europe and Asia, but competitors in the U.S. markets applied heavy pressure to block governmental approval. After five years of frustration, the American company gave up seeking approval, dissolved the venture, and sold its U.S. licensing rights to the European partner.

REASONS FOR TERMINATION

Termination of collaborative ventures can happen for a variety of reasons, including completion of a project, successful operations resulting in a merger of the partners, strategic realignments, and operational failure.

Business alliances are not usually intended to be permanent institutions; they are arrangements of convenience and opportunity. More often than not, the alliance's designers are anticipating a future transition placing their organization in a strategically stronger position. Some ventures are open-ended, with no ending point anticipated, and others are closed-ended, with a definite termination or review point.

Closed-Ended Ventures

Real estate joint ventures are normally closed-ended, and include a termination point in the agreement. For those real estate ventures formed by contractors only to bid and build (but not own), the joint venture is "project specific." Once the project is complete, profits are distributed; and the venture terminates.

If the venture was formed between a real estate developer, financial limited partners, and one or more contractors, the joint venture will have a clear termination point well into the future, usually in five, seven, or 10 years. This identified termination point triggers a sale of the property prior to termination, and all funds are liquidated: Mortgages are paid off, building management contracts expire, and any remaining profits are disbursed proportionately, as agreed at commencement of the venture, to the general and limited partners.

The reason for creating a termination point in a real estate deal is threefold: (1) financial investors can liquidify their funds at a pre-arranged point in the future, enabling liquidity and financial planning; (2) the longevity of the venture is long enough for the general partners to begin amortizing their mortgage and for the real estate to appreciate significantly to generate substantial profits for the investors; and (3) there is less likelihood of something tragic (i.e., death) happening to the general partners that would have a significantly adverse effect on the joint venture.

When a venture is closed-ended, the terms and conditions of the termination are clearly spelled out. Partners are often given the opportunity to have an independent audit of the books, and any formulas for division of profits are clearly specified. The clarity of the termination provisions severely limits any change of legal disputes at the end of the venture. Lawyers often spend considerable time with the founders of a joint venture at its inception to ensure clarity of the termination provisions.

Open-Ended Ventures

Conversely, open-ended joint ventures are less clear about termination provisions because the originators have no specific idea about when the alliance should terminate. Example of these abound, such as product development ventures or manufacturing and marketing agreements. When these ventures are formed, the conceivers seldom are able to anticipate the nature or timing of strategic realignments, failure to deliver on commitments, or insurmountable operational difficulties. But it is far better to think through these issues of termination in advance than to be deadlocked in a knot of litigation at a later date.

CONCLUSION

Business alliances are an excellent vehicle for gaining strategic advantage. They work best when the partners are capable of working cooperatively and when sharing risk and reward will yield financial gain and market share. When carefully structured and properly managed, cooperative ventures can substantially reduce risks, but careless planning and poor management can result in lackluster performance or termination. Joint ventures and strategic partnerships are seldom destined for eternity; they are vehicles that should be restructured and molded to the individual needs of the partners as future conditions change.

PART SIX

International Alliances

During the decade of the 1990s, the structure of business will change dramatically as businesses adapt to the dynamics of the global marketplace. Executives face the choice of either seizing the strategic advantage or being squeezed by aggressive competitors seeking to capture more market share. A corporation's future may require tighter and closer relationships formed by joining forces with a foreign ally to assure continued growth.

15

Building the Global Alliance

The decade of the 1990s is destined to be an era of unprecedented changes. Driven by consolidation of the global marketplace, accelerated by the dizzying pace of economic reforms in Western Europe (EC-92) and sociopolitical revolutions in Eastern Europe, and fired by the economic engines in the Pacific Rim, the next 10 years offer dramatic new opportunities for American enterprises entering the global market.

The 1980s frenzy directed toward corporate acquisition has masked the magnitude of a lopsided buying event: Japanese and European firms acquired three U.S. companies for every one that Americans acquired abroad. While U.S. CEOs were tied in knots defending their walls against the attacks of hostile-takeover artists, their foreign counterparts were building vast empires through massive capital expansions and their consequent control of global market share.

Clearly, corporate agnosticism is not a strategic option—it is a death sentence. And the commonly chosen, inwardly oriented responses selected by too many American business and political leaders, such as the verbal narcissism popularized by "Japan bashing," are ineffective placements of energy and responsibility.

The best conventional strategic options are either "*fight 'em*" or "*join 'em*." While fighting them may be the more heroic and natural reaction, and joining them risks loss of corporate control, a carefully controlled alliance can combine the most favorable elements of both choices.

REVOLUTION FROM REALIGNMENTS

The 1990s will be an era of massive organizational revolutions. If the last decade brought us the information revolution, the next decade will reorder our business structures. Giants of the past, to survive, will decentralize, become less hierarchical, and look and act more like small- and medium-sized companies, or go the way of the dinosaur. Some multinationals have recognized this fact and have already begun reorienting their corporate structures to encompass multiple ventures in multiple markets around the globe.

These realignments will cause extensive relocations of people and financial power. The advantage will go to the swift and flexible companies—small- and medium-sized businesses—and to the large multinationals whose strength is not encumbered by bureaucracy, ego, intransigence, or adherence to once powerful, but now ineffective, operational styles.

The strategic executive of the 1990s will not futilely fight these changes, but will opportunistically seize the advantage.

Opportunity or Danger?

Today's global market makes the cooperative venture an essential element to successful pursuit of foreign business. This course of action conserves capital and corporate energy, while it builds a more powerful force with which to face competitors on their home ground. A strong competitor who already enjoys a position in his own market can also become your fierce ally. Better to fight the competitive battle with an ally on your side than to face this same competitor in open combat. For example, Honeywell's long-standing alliance with Yamatake helps keep other Japanese competitors at bay.

Alliances may also diversify dependence on domestic markets by gaining an immediate position in foreign markets. According to Jerry Wasserman, vice president of Information Industries at Arthur D. Little: "Strategic alliances are no longer a business luxury, but have become a necessity to compete in the global marketplace. No one is self-sufficient any more."

Michael Bonsingore, president of Honeywell's International division, states: "As the global marketplace emerges as a powerful force, we will see more strategic alliances. American companies will have to become more comfortable with cooperative ventures as a way of doing business in the increasingly competitive environment of the future."

Ford Motor Company determined years ago that no auto company could remain competitive in the future on its own—if a company has global aspirations, it will need a partner, either through an acquisition or an alliance. Ford has used its alliance with Mazda, of which it owns 25 percent, to initiate joint sales in Japan and joint production in New Zealand, and Ford is considering joint production in Europe to ensure a more secure position for EC-92. Ford and Central Glass of Tokyo shook hands to build a production facility in the U.S. to supply glass to Japanese makers of autos in the U.S., making Ford, in effect, a supplier to its competitors.

Ventures with international partners can provide companies with access to excellent applications engineering and technology refinements, while securing an unwavering commitment to strategic growth.

The Future Isn't What It Used to Be

In the past, smaller companies could establish several sales agency agreements abroad, be content with managing the relationship, and watch sales grow. Developing foreign sales agents may be an excellent way to establish an initial beachhead overseas, but today it should be considered a short-term strategy, because many of these small agency agreements may not survive the tremendous competitive onslaught spawned by competitive realignments in overseas markets.

Two related forces—(1) the combined technology and information explosion and (2) the globalization of markets—are creating a revolution in the way both small and large companies are doing business. These forces have accelerated market changes, resulting in both greater instability and greater opportunity at the same time.

In the decade of the 1990s, it will be more important to customize products for more specific national, regional, or demographic market niches. Products will be more highly differentiated, of higher quality, and have shorter life cycles. We will see increased requirements for flexibility and tighter linkages between suppliers, manufacturers, market distribution systems, and the ultimate consumer—resulting in the forging of new partnerships in business to meet these demands.

U.S. companies are finding overseas investments far more lucrative than domestic business. Capital investment overseas is growing at twice the rate of domestic investment by U.S.-based multinationals, because their after-tax return on assets of foreign affiliates averages over 14 percent—in striking contrast to U.S. divisions, which average only a 2.5 percent return.

Multinational combines are emerging in the form of strategic alliances, joint ventures, mergers, and acquisitions—often with the active support of the public sector; a good example is Airbus, a consortium of German, French, British, and Spanish businesses initially subsidized by government investment which has now become one of the world's major competitors.

Ultimately, these new combines will have their sights set on lucrative U.S. markets, following in the steps of the Japanese. Nestlés, the Swiss food giant, nearly doubled its U.S. candy market share with its acquisition of RJR-Nabisco's candy divisions. Unilever, the Anglo-Dutch conglomerate, has made over $2 billion worth of acquisitions in the U.S., staking out the Number 3 position in the cosmetics market.

The Seductive Lure of a Start-Up Subsidiary

Pursuing the establishment of a start-up subsidiary can be a costly and time-consuming gambit requiring a developed product line and distribution systems properly matched to local market tastes. For years, foreign economic development officials have encouraged U.S. corporate executives to support the idea of establishing subsidiary companies, advocating the building of efficient new plants subsidized heavily by government loan guarantees and staffed by local workers whose pay is underwritten by job tax credits.

This seduction strategy is as alluring as the Sirens' Song in Homer's *Odyssey*, and equally fraught with risk. It makes sense only if a substantial amount of corporate revenue already comes from a specific overseas market. Intel, strong in the European computer and semiconductor market, has chosen to build a plant in Ireland. The reason: 25 percent of Intel's current revenues already originate from Europe, and it knows Europeans would rather buy from local manufacturers.

An Alliance or an Acquisition?

The tremendous proliferation of cooperative ventures in the past decade has occurred because alliances are quicker to form, more flexible to operate, and less risky; they require less cash, drain fewer resources from the sponsors, are relatively easily established, and allow stretching of financial, managerial, and technical resources.

For the same amount of time and money to make *one* acquisition, *several* cooperative ventures could be consummated in multiple markets.

Even industrial giants such aş AT&T and IBM have used the joint venture and strategic alliance extensively to enter the overseas marketplace.

If an alliance will not work, neither would have the acquisition. But the lesson can be learned more inexpensively with the alliance. If a joint venture fails, usually the cost is only 25 to 35 percent of the cost of a doomed acquisition. When Arco's joint venture with Sweden's Erricson was unsuccessful in penetrating the office-products market in the mid-1980s, the losses were so small the press hardly bothered to report it. Compare this with Exxon's disastrous office-products acquisition and integration strategy during the same period, which eventually cost over $1 billion in losses before abandonment.

Increasingly in the last few years, both large and small companies have chosen the middle of the spectrum—cooperative ventures such as distribution agreements, strategic alliances, and joint ventures—to provide both a presence overseas, and also to put a strong player on their team as they enter other global markets.

Consider the experience of Nypro, a $100-million U.S. plastics manufacturer. In 1975, Nypro went into France with a 100-percent acquisition. According to Gordon Lankton, Nypro's CEO:

"It wasn't long before all our French customers were letting us know they weren't about to do business with an American subcontractor. Furthermore, the French labor bureau began informing us that the rules were different in France. If a business downtown occurs, the French labor bureau calls the shots. Ultimately, we moved our operations out of France into Ireland, where we have a local 50/50 partner. The relationship has been extremely successful. We would never go back to France without a 50/50 French partner.

"Nypro has learned that there is a big world out there. It's a world we need to be a part of, but we can't do it alone. We only have $100 million in sales. If we could afford a staff of experienced international lawyers, financial analysts, and multilingual business executives, we might be able to do it alone. But I doubt we would want to."

Is Cooperation a Better Competitive Strategy?

Cooperation can be a highly effective form of competition, as General Electric has realized with its CFM aircraft engine joint venture with France's Snecma. CFM not only has orders worth billions of dollars for engines from European customers, but also holds major contracts with the U.S. military—the cooperative venture's competitive edge cuts advantageously both ways across the Atlantic.

Inherently, many foreign business cultures are more amenable to the cooperative venture than the acquisition. Better to have a positive trading relationship first, assess the business's real potential, and gain the confidence and understanding of current management, without the risk of a costly acquisition. Britain's Jaguar was far more receptive to General Motors' proposed alliance than to Ford's hostile takeover bid. Later the alliance can be transformed into either an acquisition or an increased investment share *if* signs are positive and both sides are willing.

Types of Cooperative Ventures

The last 10 years has brought an explosive increase in the number of international business collaborations. With it has come some confusion arising from a lack of understanding of terminology.

Strategic alliances are informal business relationships, usually consummated with a written contract, often with definable termination points, and do not result in the creation of a separate, independent business organization. Characteristics of strategic alliances are:

- Tight operating linkages, such as cross-training, product development coordination, long-term contracts based on quality rather than price, or cross-licensing or cross-marketing agreements
- Mutual vested interest in the other's future growth
- Long-term strategic orientation and top-rank support
- Frequency of contact at top and middle levels
- Reciprocal relationships sharing strengths, information, and mutual advantages
- Coordinative management styles organized around collaboration, not hierarchical power

Strategic partnerships are one level more involved than alliances, defined by having:

- Minority equity stakes (usually 15 to 35 percent) often with options or preemptive rights for more stock purchase
- Distribution agreements and trading relationships, especially those with features for mutual product development or cross-licensing, and OEM agreements

- Production and technology sharing agreements
- Informal joint ventures that legally establish a third independent entity but operationally do not form a separately managed organization, or
- Arrangements that legally bind companies together for an unlimited period of time and create supply and support relationships, joint marketing, exclusivity, protection, and long-term strategic involvement, such as franchise agreements

Joint ventures are more formal and sophisticated formalized alliances resulting in the creation of a new, separate business entity. Joint ventures are staffed and managed by a separate management team. The *acquisition joint venture* is a hybrid version whereby one company purchases a 50 percent interest in an existing subsidiary division of another company, which is then spun off as a separate joint venture corporation.

Additional characteristics of cooperative agreements may also involve interlocking directorates and simultaneous cooperation and competition, whereby companies retain their independence and autonomy, collaborating jointly in one market, but they may be fierce (yet ethical) competitors in another.

Strategic, structural, and operational principles are similar for alliances, partnerships, and joint ventures. However, the levels of intensity, coordination required, and resource commitments are greatest for joint ventures.

Triggering Conditions

When is the right time to begin moving into the global market? Typical conditions triggering the decision to form an alliance are:

- When a company is ready to penetrate a foreign market more fully, but lacks the management resources, capital, or full product line to start an overseas marketing company
- If overseas competitors are positioning themselves to capture a greater share of your market
- As a preemptive move to keep foreign competitors tied up on their home turf, so they cannot move into your domestic market
- To create a permanent distribution channel without expending exorbitant amounts of cash

- If foreign government policies prohibit control of their domestic corporations by a U.S. corporation, or if foreign regulations require local content, forcing a full or partial shift of production overseas to hold market share
- To establish an offshore production site to offset costs of shipping and exchange rate fluctuations, or to move closer to sources of material supply

THE STRATEGIC SPECTRUM

How should today's globally oriented company respond to a strategic threat or opportunity?

- First, it is generally better to fight the competitive battle overseas now, rather than facing the alternative: a competitive consortium on your domestic turf in five years.
- Second, timing is critical. Waiting too long to formulate strategy will let strategic advantages slip further away. Napoleon said he could always make up lost ground, but could never make up lost time.
- Third, the most effective strategy should be chosen from a spectrum of options (see Figure 15.1) based upon the company's most favorable risk/reward ratio.

Typically, larger U.S. companies have looked toward the more complex and more expensive options—acquisitions or building subsidiaries. However, acquisitions and subsidiaries are too often off-target, too slow to create, and too risky to operate in unknown foreign markets. A number of acquisitions or plants may be necessary to cover the breadth of the global market. And finding the right acquisition targets with the proper strategic and operational fit could take years—too long to wait in a rapidly emerging marketplace.

Smaller companies have normally opted for the other end of the spectrum: licensing and sales agents. These may be excellent *first* steps designed for *operational convenience*—to eliminate difficult-to-manage and expensive in-house sales forces or to recapture development costs. These generally require relatively minimal resources for implementation. For many smaller companies these are the first steps out of the domestic arena into the global market.

But these operationally driven overtures should be considered only as

Figure 15.1. The Strategic Spectrum

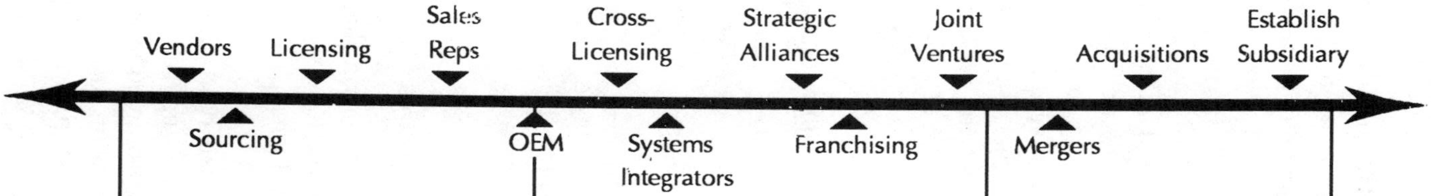

Spectrum axis (left to right): Vendors · Licensing · Sales Reps · OEM · Cross-Licensing · Systems Integrators · Strategic Alliances · Franchising · Joint Ventures · Mergers · Acquisitions · Establish Subsidiary · Sourcing

Complexity	Simple	Moderately Complex	Complex Organizations
Risk	Low	Moderate	High
Purpose	Operational/ Tactical	Primarily Strategically Oriented	Strategic/Financially Oriented
Style	Enterpreneurial Style	Mid-Sized Style	Corporate Style
Typical Company	Small Companies	Small & Large Companies Act Like Mid-Sized	Market Dominance Behavior
Market Behavior	Free Market Behavior Niche Marketing in Local Markets	Quick Market Response Niche Marketing in Global Markets	Mass Marketing Global Markets
Inter-relationships	One-way Operational & Vendor Relationships	Multidimensional Cooperative Strategic Relations	Superior-Subordinate Strategic Relations

short-term initiatives—the beginning of a process that will ultimately cul-
minate in a longer-term strategy to secure one's position against global
competition. In a relatively stable marketplace where competition is not
overly threatening, these arrangements often remain in place for years.
However, today's global market is not a stable competitive environment;
strategic conditions are in a dramatic state of realignment; the "rule-book"
is being rewritten. Standard licensing agreements and sales-agent relationships may leave smaller companies weak and vulnerable as competitors strengthen.

Once a U.S. company decides to enter the global market, it musk ask
critical questions about its own strengths and weaknesses, its competition, its resources available, its current depth of marketing networks, and
whether it will manufacture overseas. The development of a global strategy must consider:

· The competitive advantages and disadvantages of your company

· Your company's strengths, weaknessses, and resources

· The strategic spectrum of options

· The risks and rewards of each option

These factors must then be matched against the strategic spectrum of
global intervention options, ranging from the tactical to the strategic, and
from the simple to the complex. (See Figure 15.1.)

Evaluate Options Against Risks and Rewards

Rewards can be measured in a variety of ways, such as market share, cash
flow, or variety of product line, or organizational growth, to name a few.
Risks generally include political, monetary, technological, partner, and
market risks, among others (see page 77).

For many large companies in the 1980s, there had been an implicit
assumption that the best growth strategy was through mergers, acquisitions, and establishing subsidiaries. This scenario, promoted more by investment bankers than by careful strategic planners or sharp business
managers, imagined that the risk-reward relationship, when plotted
graphically (see Figure 15.2) would provide greater rewards the more
complex the deal, despite the increased risk.

The corporate strategist must consider other possible risk-reward scen-
arios. Clearly, the proper strategic objective is to choose the option yield-

Figure 15.2. Risk-Reward Analysis

In a theoretical environment, the risk-reward relationship might look like this:

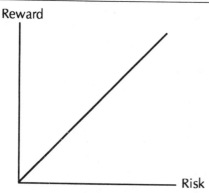

In this example, as complexity increases, so does the risk and the reward. However, most corporate strategies will not plot so perfectly, differing from company to company, from market to market, and from industry to industry.

ing the highest reward for the least risk, given the available resources. In Figure 15.3 a midspectrum cooperative strategy would be best. In Figure 15.4, a low-risk strategy would be best.

FINDING INTERNATIONAL PARTNERS

There is no guaranteed method for finding the "proper partner" in the overseas business community. Invariably, successful past relationships are the basis for the best alliances. If, however, a search for a partner is required, several methods have proven successful for many companies.

- **Industry Associations:** Often the foreign office of many industry organizations can provide valuable leads. However, do not rely on these organizations to play matchmaker. Industry newspapers are excellent sources of potential partners, combing the field of corporate activity for details, and mentioning names and the rationale for decisions. Industry conferences are worthwhile.

- **Customers and Suppliers:** Current business relations can provide a wealth of opportunities. Customers may have marketing and distribution systems for your products and services, but simply lack the resources that could be provided through a combined venture. Sup-

Figure 15.3. Risk-Reward Analysis
In this example, a midspectrum cooperative strategy would be best.

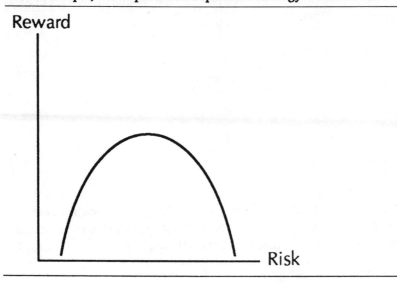

Figure 15.4. Risk-Reward Analysis
In this example a low-risk strategy might yield the highest rewards.

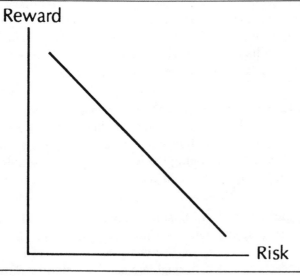

pliers may have new technologies and products in need of additional applications expertise and operational talents. Distributors can often recommend excellent companies with good business reputations.

- **Competitors:** An ethical competitor may make a superb ally in the overseas market. They may hold a market niche parallel to yours, consequently strengthening both your domestic and foreign position against attack by a larger competitor. Potential competitors generally make better prospects than current direct competitors.

- **"Shoulder Industries:"** Partners are often found in parallel industries related to, but not directly competitive with, your industry. These alliances create horizontal or vertical integration possibilities, as well as applications for emerging technologies.

- **Professional Advisors:** Merchant and investment bankers, consultants, accountants, and attorneys in overseas offices are usually good sources for leads. They pride themselves on being in the know. However, be sure they are steering your company in its best interests, not theirs. The opportunities for high fees can often cloud their vision.

- **Foreign Trade Missions:** Trade missions and commercial consulates in the United States can be an excellent source of leads. Most are located in New York City. Some countries have additional locations in such cities as Los Angeles, San Francisco, and Washington, D.C.

- **U.S. Department of Commerce:** This federal agency's monthly magazine *Business America* has a column devoted solely to overseas companies seeking partners for licensing, distribution agreements, and joint ventures. DOC has commercial officers stationed in overseas embassies to assist in developing trade between foreign companies and U.S. corporations. Within DOC is the International Trade Administration (ITA), which can play an important role to a company beginning the process of entering the global market. The ITA's Foreign Commercial Service program offers several services including:

  1) **Agent/Distributor Service**, which lists and helps find potential joint venture partners

  2) **Trade Opportunities Program,** which has on-line computer services to match companies to potential partners

  3) **Commercial News USA,** which reaches 100,000 businesses overseas

  4) **Matchmaker Trade Delegation** to seek overseas partners

  5) **Trade Shows** sponsored by DOC overseas to promote products and unearth potential partners

6) **Mailing Lists** of potential agents, licensees, and joint venture partners

7) **Foreign Mission Commercial Officers** to help with the "due diligence" process to ensure an ethical partner through a World Traders Data Report

8) **Trade Opportunities Program,** which provides an on-line computer program updated daily with joint venture leads

It should be noted that the Department of Commerce's primary mission in the 1990s is to promote U.S. exports to improve the balance of payments. Because of this export orientation, DOC officials will bend over backwards if they believe a prospective alliance will result in exports rather than imports. Business managers should bear this in mind when seeking assistance. For example, if a manufacturing company is seeking an ally to market its product in Asia, DOC will respond with greater assistance than if the manufacturing company was seeking a low-cost sourcing subassembly manufacturer.

CHARACTERISTICS OF A WELL-STRUCTURED INTERNATIONAL ALLIANCE

Regardless of the industry, a well-conceived cooperative venture with an overseas partner will have common characteristics. Elimination of any one or more of these factors will reduce the likelihood of a successful venture:

· **Strategic Synergy:** Always look for complementary strengths—strategic synergy—in a potential partner. To be successful, the two partners should have more strength when combined than they would have independently. Mathematically stated: "1 + 1 = 3." Mutual advantage must exist, and if it does not, the venture will eventually unwind. Beware of "niche collision," where multiple ventures with other companies produce confusion and overlap about priorities, proprietary information, and product offerings.

· **Positioning Opportunity:** An alliance should create an excellent opportunity to place your company in a leadership position—to sell new products and services, or to secure access to technology, components, or raw materials. Similarly, your partner should be uniquely positioned with the know-how and reputation to help you take advantage of that opportunity. Watch out for partners lacking the motivation and desire for leadership positions in the marketplace. Their energy and strategic vision will be insufficient for a long-term relationship to develop.

· **Less Risk:** Lowering risk is an essential ingredient in forming an alliance. Product introduction costs can be exorbitant. Manufacturing and development costs can sap the financial strength of even the largest corporation. With a partner, the likelihood of success must be significantly higher. If the chance of success is only marginally higher, and the risk only slightly less, an alliance may not be worth the additional complexity it requires.

· **Win-Win:** All members must apportion the operations, risks, and rewards fairly among the members. Fair apportionment prevents internal dissension that can corrode, and eventually destroy, the venture. The dynamics of the global marketplace are like shifting sands beneath a stormy sea. Risks and rewards, like the tides, are ever-changing. As when sailing a boat, partners must maintain a flexible course, modifying the terms of their agreement, like trimming sails to meet the wind and tides, readjusting again when the strategic or operational environment changes. Partners must be willing to address new risks, be committed to flexibility and creativity, and be ready to transform the structure of the alliance.

· **Style of Operations:** Companies with similar goals, rewards, methods of operations, and corporate cultures tend to make better partners. A history of past working relations is beneficial, enabling management to build trust and communication on an existing foundation. Differences in national styles and methods of handling problems can become thorny if managers are not selected for their multicultural understanding or are not properly cross-trained.

· **Support at Top Echelons:** Companies tend to reflect the attitudes of their presidents. Without top-level support, middle managers devote energies to other priorities that they believe will lead to their promotion. There must be a corporate "meeting of the minds" at the CEO level to ensure that the proper attitude filters to the lower managers. To maintain an international alliance, CEOs must expect to visit their counterparts overseas at least once a year. Similarly, they must expect to receive a visit from their counterparts annually. Without this interaction, a signal is sent to all subordinates that there is inadequate support, coordination, commitment, and communications.

With these characteristics, an international alliance has a reasonable chance of success. While there are no guarantees, remember one key rule:

The higher the level of ambiguity, the higher the probability of failure. Alliances are the stepchild of uncertain risks and opportunities. Uncertainty breeds ambiguity, and ambiguity is the seed of business failures.

Do everything possible to reduce the risk of the unexpected interfering with success.

CULTURAL DIFFERENCES

One major area that distinguishes international ventures from monocultural alliances is the potential difficulty in bringing together people from dissimilar frames of reference. The principles discussed in the section on management (Chapters 10–12) are even more important for international ventures.

The style of doing business can confound managers not accustomed to foreign managers' decision-making patterns, which may be autocratic in third-world countries, democratic in socialistic countries, or seemingly secretive in Asian cultures. Managers must be familiar with the corporate values and hierarchy of relationships of their partners.

Similarly, the way employee relations are handled can create frictions if managers transgress the cultural traditions and norms of their host country. In many third-world countries, lower-level employees have very little status, often related to their low educational levels. Yet in Europe, the higher status of employees is legislated as well as being derived from higher expectations and education. Venture managers must be sensitive about how to handle foreign employees or risk low morale, conflict with partner managers, or employee strikes.

Market conditions are also a reflection of cultural differences. Customer preferences can vary dramatically from one country to the next. The same packaging may succeed in one location, and fail dismally in another. Distribution networks and competitive practices will vary from country to country.

MATTERS OF SOVEREIGNTY

Cooperative ventures must conform to the rules and regulations of the host country. For formal joint ventures, the selection of country of origin should be made very carefully, because of the legal and tax implications.

Governmental regulations must be carefully reviewed to determine whether there are any limitations on the percentage of ownership allowed, whether export controls may be in place, and whether there are antitrust rules that may limit the scope of business or pending environmental rules that may restrict future endeavors. Labor regulations must be checked to determine the status of employees and any potential contractual relationships that might be incurred.

Other legal issues, such as contract law, partner liabilities, patents, exclusivity, and confidentiality, should be carefully examined for potential exposure.

The economic and monetary system of each country will also have important impacts on the structure of the alliance. Free market/capitalist countries will behave far differently from socialist or transitioning communist countries. Countries signing the tax-treaty agreement will treat profits and dividends in a more uniform manner than nonmember countries. The advice of an accounting firm with international foundations is essential.

NEGOTIATING THE INTERNATIONAL DEAL

Unlike the traditional American style of jumping right into a deal, European and Asian allies consider the negotiations stage a crucial time to learn what to expect of their prospective partner. Negotiating a deal will probably take three times longer in the overseas environment because prospective partners will want to learn, in detail, motives, resources, weaknesses, past experiences, expectations, skills, operational requirements, and methods of communications.

Negotiations should initially be conducted high rank to high rank, to ensure proper commitment and support. Clarity of objectives is essential. Any ambiguity will only cause concern and delays.

Successful allies generally refrain from using a single negotiator and opt instead for a negotiating team, thus building the foundation for future teamwork. Try bringing along the key operational managers responsible for implementing decisions; their early commitment will be essential later. These managers will be a good barometer of whether the right "chemistry" exists beyond the CEO level. Those middle managers from the trenches will highlight problems and obstacles before they occur. Whereas the CEO will be focusing on the strategic and financial "fit" in the venture, the operational managers will be measuring operational "fit"—timing, cost controls, communications, engineering, allocation of personnel, and day-to-day problem solving. A cooperataive venture will never work unless you have the support of middle management. Use a negotiating team well versed and educated in the foreign culture of the potential partner.

Do not let lawyers act as the key negotiators. This is the role of management. Lawyers should advise. Foreigners are fearful of the U.S. legal system's propensity for litigation over problem solving, and even the hint of an appearance of a lawyer too early in negotiations can sour a deal. Remember, alliances never fail because of the quality of their legal agreements—a good legal agreement protects against downside risks in the event of a failure.

Parity among foriegn partners will be desirable, because, regardless of their stake, they will be far more likely to consider all partners equals than traditionally more domineering Americans. Foreign partners are likely to take time to build consensus and to gain commitment—"arm-wrestling over a bottle of wine"—as the French call it. According to Gordon Lankton, CEO of Nypro, and orchestrator of several alliances with companies in both Asia and Europe:

"Marriage is the oldest type of partnership in the world. Every good marriage has evolved into a real 50/50 partnership. Likewise with business partnerships.

"I never want to be a 49-percent partner. . . every 49-percent partner goes to the table as a second-class citizen. . . . Who wants to sit at a table concentrating on issues and developing strategic plans, all the while knowing that he or she really doesn't count as much as the other person? . . . It spells doom for the partnership from day one. . . . Who wants to go to a board meeting that will clearly not be a free and open relationship between equals? Not me. I want everyone present to have the same voice.

"Global strategic partnerships develop out of 50/50 partnerships. As in marriage, the contributions of the partners will not be identical, but they should be equal in importance. One may provide the potential for opening new markets, while the other may provide technology. The secret to success is that both partners recognize their need to contribute equally. Both will strive to do more and to carry more than their 50 percent of the load. This is what pushes the partnership forward."

If negotiations about control become adversarial, the alliance will probably be doomed before it starts. Alliances relying heavily upon dominance for control lack the fundamental strategic synergy and operational chemistry for long-term success.

ART OF INTERNATIONAL ALLIANCE MANAGEMENT

Ultimately any cooperative venture's success lies not upon its legal agreements, but upon the success of day-to-day operations. Yet most companies approach venture management "seat-of-the-pants" style: they encounter problems and learn the hard way. Always remember that no matter how inspired the alliance, ultimately it is people who make or break the deal. Research and experience have established several key factors critical to international alliance management.

- **Clarity of Purpose:** It is not enough to have high levels of trust, energy, vision, and communications. Ventures with specific, concrete objectives, timetables, lines of responsibility, and measurable results are best suited for potential success. Avoid partnerships that cannot clearly delineate results, milestones, methods, and resource commitments.
- **Coordinative Skills** are critical. Because alliances cannot be "commanded" but must work together, managers need excellent person-to-person skills to compensate for cultural and organizational differences between partners. Managers should be selected based upon the presence of excellent "integrative" skills—the ability to effectively manage the diverse perspectives of a wide variety of specialists.
- **Frequent Communications** are essential. Because of distance and time zone differences, working hours may be dramatically different between partner sites. Many companies communicate by computer and fax to speed delivery of information where telephone communication is difficult to arrange. One successful alliance manager recommends responding to every message within 24 hours. Even if the only realistic response can be an acknowledgment of the memo, he recommends telling the ally when to expect a complete answer.
- **Personnel Selection** is vital. Appoint one senior manager to be responsible for the alliance, even if the alliance is loosely structured. This person must be assigned the alliance management function as a primary responsibility, and report frequently and directly to the CEO. Major decision making must be quick, clear, and involve the alliance manager.

- **Management Support** from the sponsors in the form of resource allocation and executive commitment will make or break most ventures. A key factor is the presence of a strong, high-ranking "champion" (usually at the senior VP level) to manage the partner relationship within each of the sponsoring companies.

- **Cultural Sensitivity** is essential for the understanding of linguistic differences, national idiosyncrasies, operational decision making, and business values. Venture management selection and key staff and liaison functions must take into account the much greater need for understanding of cultural differences and how they can have a major impact on morale, decision making, and partner relations. While there is disagreement on whether venture managers should be expatriates or multilingual, most successful international alliances provide ample corporate cross-training of top- and middle-level managers. Fuji-Xerox has many Japanese engineers serving at its New York headquarters. Honeywell-Yamatake regards the frequent visits of alliance managers between Minneapolis and Japan as a necessity for effective alliance management.

- **"Win-Win" Commitments** by both parties must underpin all successful alliances, reinforced by a spirit of trust, cooperation, and integrity. Be adaptable. As the venture matures, sponsoring companies must be willing to address new risks, be committed to creativity, and be ready to transform the structure of the alliance in conformance to new strategic and operational conditions. Without this frequent re-formation of the venture, the alliance may be relatively short-lived.

  Partial commitment can be disastrous, as A. T. Cross's John Lawler warns: "Once you get over the trust issue, you've got to open up and fill the bond of trust. You can't go in halfheartedly. You can't inch along when you should be taking leaps and bounds."

In America, operations management does not have the same luster-effect as does strategic maneuvering, financial leveraging, and deal making. However, most foreign corporations place high values on these operational skills. Any CEO who closes the deal with a ceremonial handshake, turns everything over to a general manager, and then hopes for the best will soon meet disappointment.

Without a work force educated in the foreign culture, failure will result. Cultural differences can frustrate and confound the uninitiated, but "*Vive la différence!*" Like sexual differences in marriage, contrasting styles in alliances can be used inspirationally and productively, or, to the contrary, destructively.

PITFALLS TO AVOID

Seldom is failure the result of the quality of the legal agreements. During the negotiations phase, avoid placing too much emphasis on legal technicalities, ownership formulas, and decision-making processes, and paying too little attention to operations planning, clarity of goals, personnel selection, resource allocations, teamwork, reporting systems, cost controls, and desired results. Always organize and manage for mutual success, regardless of the legal agreements.

Managers incapable of working in a collaborative environment will always produce disappointing results. Avoid "double management," with joint auditors, joint legal and financial advisors, joint chairmen, and especially dual managers; these are an unnecessary and costly waste. Fujitsu–TRW ran into this problem, which resulted in an entangling bureaucracy. Ultimately Fujitsu fashioned a wholly owned subsidiary with simple reporting systems.

16

Strategies to Penetrate World Markets

Strategists for companies in the global market focus on the "triad strategy," which acknowledges the vital importance of having a strong presence in the Pacific Rim region, North America, and Europe. These markets provide over 80 percent of the world market for goods and services.

THE RISE OF EUROPE

Each week the business media run banner headlines exhorting American companies to gain a beachhead in Europe, as if 1992 were the new date set for the Normandy invasion. Envision boatloads of businesspeople, armed with attaché cases, flanked by their bankers, accountants, and lawyers, landing on the shores of a unifying Europe, ready for making deals in a market of 320 million people—a market larger than the entire United States.

But the realities are different. The invasion is, for the most part, a dream, and the opportunities remain largely unexploited.

Meanwhile, Europeans are embracing unification with an almost religious fervor. Undaunted by an entangled history of provincialism and cumbersome bureaucracies, EC-92 has uncannily cut through centuries of red tape and formed a European consensus that would make Metternich envious.

Just as Japan became a financial giant in the 1970s, and the "tigers" of the Pacific Rim (Hong Kong, Singapore, Korea, and Taiwan) have emerged in the 1980s, so will the Europeans in the 1990s. The new Economic Community is their proving ground. With the active support of the public sector, these new combines ultimately have their sights set on lucrative U.S. markets, readying to invade American shores with money, buyout offers, and innovative products.

Lowering Trade Barriers Strengthens European Competitors

Invariably, the lowering of trade and regulatory barriers, along with the establishment of a single European currency will have profound strategic implications throughout the world. Long constrained by governmental restrictions, new, more powerful, and highly innovative combines—strategic alliances, joint ventures, acquisitions, and mergers—are being established in Europe to gain competitive position.

In the field of finance, Germany's largest public sector bank, Westdeutsche Landesbanke is forming a 50-50 joint venture with Britain's largest multinational bank, Standard Chartered, to create a new merchant bank joining WestLB's corporate finance division with Standard's investment banking division. The banks designed the cooperative venture to enhance their business strategy to gain market share. Airbus, the German, French, British, and Spanish consortium, has now become one of Boeing's major competitors. Air France and Lufthansa have joined forces in cargo handling, pilot training, aircraft acquisitions, and marketing, and are seeking to include Iberia and JAL in this global network. Nestlés nearly doubled its U.S. candy market share through acquisitions. Unilever spent over $2 billion for acquisitions, to become third in the U.S. cosmetics market.

U.S. companies must recognize the necessity of keeping foreign competitors on their toes on their home turf. By being strategically aggressive in Europe now, U.S. firms will force European competitors to spend their time and resources in their native markets. If the European markets are conceded, Americans will then fight the next battle for market share in North America.

The typical U.S. corporate response to these competitive challenges has been to conquer through acquisition. But U.S. acquisition frenzy has been focused internally within our own shores, not overseas. And moreover, other, perhaps more effective, strategic options should be considered. Finding the right acquisition targets with the proper strategic and operational "fit" could take two to five years—too late in a marketplace emerging with the rapidity of Europe.

Obstacles to European Acquisitions

Businesses fortified with acquisition experience in the U.S. are often frustrated by the lack of opportunities in Europe. Britain has attracted the most acquisition attention with its concentration of only one-fifth of the EC's population and over 50 percent of its publicly listed companies, with no language barrier. But, English companies have historically looked toward America for their expansion. Few have seen continental Europe as their fundamental market base, leaving them without developed networks in the overall EC marketplace.

On the Continent, most potential targets are smaller in size, closely held, and often family owned—not great acquisition fodder for the hungry investment banker. Several other critical impediments exist to deter acquisitions:

- **Cash** is the normal consideration used for continental acquisitions, because unique share structures often make stock swaps impractical.

- **Valuation** is central to every acquisition; an analysis of the balance sheet, cash flow, and margins will normally yield a commonly agreed upon valuation range in both the U.S. and UK. However, accounting procedures vary tremendously from country to country on the Continent, and valuations often require extensive investigation.

- **Trust** is vital to negotiating a successful acquisition and retaining top-quality management afterwards. Both hostile and foreign takeovers, while more accepted in Britain, are not in vogue on the Continent. A better approach is to build trust through cooperative ventures, then later make an acquisition offer after establishing relationships.

- **Information Sources** on businesses are lacking in many continental countries. While public companies in Great Britain, France, Germany, and Italy are relatively well documented, the European versions of Standard & Poor Directories, D & B Reports, and 10K forms are simply not available in most of the other EC countries. According to the English merchant banking firm of Hill Samuel, "Information is of inconsistent quality, accounts are sometimes years out of date, directories often not verified, and corporate information filings incomplete or poorly maintained."

Furthermore, while Europe is becoming a *united economy*, it will remain a *fragmented market* with a wide diversity of cultural traditions. This factor may necessitate several acquisitions for companies seeking to cover the breadth of the EC market.

Euro-branding is still an emerging new concept. While there are a few brands recognized universally throughout Europe, such as Coca-Cola, Levi's, Rolex, and Dior, most of Europe's tastes are highly fragmented along national lines. For example, instant coffee may sell in England, but would be totally rejected in France. Top-loading washing machines may sell well in one country, but the neighboring country may insist on front loaders. And, while one would never expect Mexican food to sell well in Northern Europe, the Norwegians love it.

Without a thorough understanding of the EC markets, an acquisition strategy should be considered very risky.

For example, Vickers Office Furniture of the UK sought synergy when it acquired a Swiss-German office-chair manufacturer. However, the Swiss-German designs did not marry well with their existing Anglo-French designs, and consequently the integrated marketing functions failed.

In the last five years, Europe has become the biggest destination for exported U.S. manufactured goods, with sales increasing 60 percent. In fact, the U.S. has no trade deficit with Europe. Exporting directly into Europe has limitations because restrictive tariffs place many products at a competitive pricing disadvantage if they do not meet the 45 percent local content regulation.

Keeping Abreast of EC-92

Each week the EC-92 Commission in Brussels issues new policy directives for economic unification. Digesting this constantly evolving material and promulgating it in the form of booklets and newsletters to U.S. businesses is being handled by:

U.S. Department of Commerce
International Trade Administration
Room 2106
Washington, DC 20230
and
American Chamber of Commerce
EC Affairs Office
Avenue des Arts Boite 50, B-1040
Brussels, Belgium

Write to them for up-to-date materials.

Eastern Europe

The dramatic changes in Western Europe are paralleled by equally exciting developments in Eastern Europe. In particular, the countries of Poland, Czechoslovakia, and Hungary are very attractive because of the low
labor costs and highly skilled work force.

While great opportunity awaits in Eastern Europe, none of these countries have experienced capitalism in the last 45 years. Consequently, certain basic elements of business are often missing—there may be no
marketing or selling skills, no accounting systems, no contract law, and
inadequate means of ordering parts and supplies, among other problems.

Most companies entering Eastern Europe are using Western Europe as
their base of operations because of proximity and cultural similarity. The
EC-92 directorate has moved to make Eastern European countries adjunct
members. Already East Germany, through its merger with West Germany,
has joined EC-92. Once Poland, Czechoslovakia, and Hungary achieve full
EC-92 status, the European Community will become the world's single
largest economy.

SOVIET UNION

The Soviet Union is in the greatest state of change of any country in the
world. Along with these changes come the twin sisters of opportunity and
risk. Aside from having one of the largest populations on earth, and hence
a large potential market, the Soviet Union also has excellent natural resources such as oil, gas, timber, and minerals. Their need for telecommunications, transportation, distribution systems, and consumer goods is
enormous.

But those experienced in dealing with the Soviet system always express great caution. For one thing, a company operating in the USSR will
require a partner to navigate the convoluted legal and economic system,
which makes the U.S. tax code look simple by comparison.

In addition, the joint venture partner will probably be a government
ministry—never an easy ally. Who you know, as well as the influence of
the ministry within the Soviet bureaucracy, is more important for cutting
through endless streams of red tape than any other factor. Try to choose a
powerful partner who can cut through the bureaucratic paperwork and
deliver resources, including personnel and materials, otherwise the deal
will be mired for years, draining energy and capital.

When negotiating a Soviet deal, remember, *everything is negotiable.*

This includes literally everything. The Soviets will write a special law, special tax deals, special cost structures, and special duty agreements for each individual deal. In no other country can a business custom-tailor its business conditions like this. For these deals, it is advisable to have an experienced lawyer on your team to help navigate through the complexities of the Soviet legal system and who can also propose special legal arrangements.

One must assume nothing about simple things in the Soviet Union, such as where the supply of materials or product is coming from and at what price? One's expectations must take into consideration that nothing works with the logic of a capitalist country. Everything is slow to happen. One manager responsible for Polaroid's Soviet joint venture humorously recommends sending Americans on an Outward Bound experience before being stationed in the Soviet Union.

Because nothing can be done in the Soviet Union unless there is a special law allowing it, a "Nyet Mentality" has arisen. Natasha Wolniansky, an experienced Soviet-American deal maker, tells the anecdote about the "nyet way."

"The motto of every Soviet citizen is the 'the safest answer is no answer.' The moment Soviets take a side, resolve a matter, answer a question 'yes' or 'no'—they automatically cut their chances of being right (or safe) by 50%.

"If a Soviet bureaucrat makes a mistake and falls from grace, there is usually no coming back. This is why Soviets are so loathe to take responsibility or sign a contract. A Russian joke lists the five rules of survival:

"Don't think!
If you thought it, don't say it!
If you say it, don't write it down!
If you wrote it down, don't sign it!
If you signed it, deny it!"

Expropriating profits from a Soviet business is a thorny problem because the ruble has not been convertible into dollars. While the ruble policy will eventually change, other problems loom, such as corruption, lack of an accounting system acceptable to western standards, few skilled managers, a primitive telephone system, and a distribution and supply system that is virtually nonexistent.

The Soviet economy is a disaster, but every problem has its opportunities, and for the right business with the right partner, that opportunity may be enormous.

JAPANESE-AMERICAN ALLIANCES

The opportunity for Japanese-American alliances is growing. These alliances can be constructed for development of products and markets in North America, Asia, or Europe. The Japanese are building plants everywhere in America; their presence in the United States is so large they will become one of the nation's largest exporters by the mid-1990s. In the auto industry alone, midwestern states have provided billions of dollars of subsidies to Japanese auto companies to construct plants to compete with American firms—both manufacturers and suppliers. By 1990 there will be 300 Japanese parts suppliers for these auto manufacturers in the U.S.

Clearly, our view of the Japanese must change from the 1950s, when we saw them as vanquished foes, from the 1960s, when we saw them as a Third World country, and from the 1970s, as imitators of our technology. Today the Japanese are world-class competitors with something valuable to offer. John Lawler, head of international marketing for A. T. Cross Writing Instruments, which has had an alliance in Japan since 1970, says: "Japanese investment in the U.S. is a healthy thing, it brings in new ideas and new operating processes. The hype by politicians and journalists neglects these factors. This is a breath of fresh air shaking up the way we do business—helping us understand and invest in international business."

Mr. Lawler's position is realistic. Honeywell's International president Michael Bonsingore, comments on their 60-year alliance with Yamatake: "Looking back over the past, we are both stronger, more profitable, and more competitive as a result of our cooperation. Honeywell could not claim a worldwide position without having a strong presence in Japan."

Japanese Strategy for the 1990s

As an insular nation, Japan in the 1990s resembles England 200 years ago when she sought to establish dominance in trade throughout the world. As England did then, the Japanese today recognize the need to avoid isolation—hence the need to push aggressively into foreign markets.

Today, Japanese multinationals have very high aspirations: to be leaders in every major market in the world. Fundamental to this goal is *market share*. Controlling market share is to the Japanese multinational corporation what controlling the skies is to the air force or controlling sea lanes is to the navy—it is their fundamental mission, their key to success.

Japanese Alliances—What Has Changed?

When the first Japanese–American alliances were formed in the 1960s, most were market-oriented, to provide access through intricate Japanese distribution channels. At that time, joint ventures were required because Japanese national law limited the amount of stock owned by a foreign company to a 50-percent share.

These marriages were formed mainly for tactical or operational reasons—to gain market entry, to take advantage of low labor costs, and primarily to serve a local Japanese marketplace. Many ventures did not survive that period, mainly because, in the long run, they failed to satisfy the strategic needs of the Japanese partner or because operational conditions changed.

The long-term venture between Asahi Chemical and Dow Chemical broke up when economic conditions in Japan changed and the partners could not adapt. Asahi supplied the venture with low-cost raw materials. However, after more than a decade of successful operations, the cost of materials increased in Japan, and Asahi could not sell at a price competitive with other world sources. Dow wanted to maximize its profits by lowering material costs bought from an outside supplier, and Asahi wanted to increase its own sales. The partners could not agree, and ultimately the venture was terminated by Asahi's purchasing Dow's portion of the alliance for $185 million.

In 1973 the Japanese government lifted its regulations on foreign ownership. As Japanese companies became more interested in strategic exports to the U.S. market, few U.S. companies refocused their relationships. The resulting strains and conflicts caused many partnership arrangements to fail. Despite these failures, a number of very successful ventures still flourish from that earlier era. They provide the basis for what is needed to create a successful venture in today's global market.

The Successful Alliances

All the alliances remaining from the first generation have three main characteristics:

- First, they have been *flexible* enough to transform themselves to harmonize with the enormous changes in the world marketplace and in Japan itself.

- Second, these alliances have been built on a *close relationship* between CEOs who made a continuing series of adjustments, thereby steering the transformation from the top echelons.

- Third, while these alliances may have been initiated originally for operational convenience, they were all able to take on a *strategic focus* that excited their Japanese partners and, more significantly, enhanced the success of the venture.

The failures of that era came from fundamental problems—not knowing the market, not understanding the partner's motivations, or not adapting to changing business conditions.

The Driving Forces

Future alliances with the Japanese must be, first and foremost, strategically motivated. The typical Japanese pattern begins with establishing an *initial market presence*, followed by gaining a *maximum market share*, then pushing for *profitability five years out*.

The Japanese are also looking for partners to provide technology access and systems integration. Unlike the circumstances of a decade or two past, however, the Japanese are not just seeking a means to copy technolgoy, they now offer their own advanced technological abilities.

For example, Electronic Designs Inc., a $25-million Massachusetts company and a buyer of Sharp memory chips for the military market for several years, is involved in a five-year joint development project with Sharp's U.S. Microelectronics Technology division. EDI will place a design team in Sharp's North American facility to study advanced microchip technology to expand its line of chips for military applications. Both Sharp and EDI will share ownership of the new technologies, and Sharp will continue to manufacture the chips.

Japanese partners seek companies to tighten supply, production, and marketing linkages, to ensure better inventory control, higher quality production, better customer service, and more customized products for specialized application marketing niches.

Ford's alliance with Tokyo's Central Glass will be operated by Central. Ford will supply flat glass, which will then be formed at the joint venture facility, replicating the technology used in Japan. The CEO will be Japanese, but the remaining management will be composed of Ford and Central officials. Ford currently sells to Mazda's production facilities in the U.S. and Central sells to Nissan in Japan. Ford believes a Japanese partner, who knows how to deal with Japanese companies and has a good track record, will increase its likelihood of success.

For a Japanese-American alliance to work, both parties must truly believe that the pursuit of strategic objectives is too risky to undertake independently and their ability to succeed will result only through mutual cooperation. Both partners must have a strong vested interest and be ready and willing to jump into a leadership position in the marketplace.

Unique Opportunities

A Japanese alliance offers several benefits: a unique window into the global marketplace, new and improved production skills, excellent human resource talent, and access to capital for growth that may not be found by going alone. But more significantly, today's alliance with the Japanese offers access to their technology and applied engineering expertise, which were not present in the marketing-oriented ventures of the 1960s and 1970s.

Alliances also provide a unique opportunity to capitalize on differences in national cost structures and fluctuations in foreign exchange. Ford and Mazda jointly own Autorama, a sales organization that sells Ford-branded vehicles in Japan. Each year over 70,000 American-made Fords, along with Ford-labelled cars produced by Mazda, are sold through this distribution channel comprised of over 300 outlets. The dual supply of cars from both Japan and America ensures dealers the best values regardless of fluctuations in the dollar or the yen.

For those who put fear of cultural differences aside and have a strong desire to be world competitors, the Japanese have resources and skills that often make them excellent allies in the world market, particularly when an advantageous deal is struck. Before considering an alliance, it is critical to decide what is important. As a General Motors manager commented: "If you enter an alliance with the Japanese as a quick money making venture, you'll be in for a big shock; this is just not important to the Japanese—they don't care about making profits for at least five years— all they want is market share. Japanese companies are not looking for a quick fix."

The Japanese are, by tradition, excellent alliance builders, possessing a grand history of partnerships, joint ventures, research consortia, operating linkages, and cooperative affiliations in a myriad of forms. Because of their history of tight working relationships, interlocking directorates, and long-term supply contracts, the Japanese tend to be more satisfied with alliances than Americans.

A Tradition of Collaboration

Americans perceive the Japanese as having an advantage with their tight business linkages, by which strategic and tactical maneuvering becomes easy. Often this coordination is well orchestrated, like a fine piece of music. One CEO told the story about his experience with a venture in Japan's chemical industry:

> "In Japan, there was never excess production capacity. When it was our partner's turn to expand, we did. There was nothing written down, it wasn't in the books, there was nothing official, it was just decided it was our turn. It kept the suppliers happy, it made things economically viable. No wonder Just-In-Time-Inventory works—the Japanese are so coordinated, unlike the unstructured competition in this country where we all expanded at the same time and created a glut on the market, dropping prices, ruining margins, and creating headaches for everyone in the industry."

Japanese business culture is rich with formal and informal business alliances, which may explain the results of a recent survey that indicated three out of four Japanese were enthusiastic about alliances, whereas less than one in five Americans were positive.

The Japanese have both formal (*Keiretsu*) and informal (*Shudan*) alliances. The Keiretsu hold formal legal status and are essentially vertically oriented structures dealing with complex products such as autos and electronics. They lack centralized management, and rely on informal coordination for decision making. The head of the Keiretsu guides his affiliates (but affiliates are not subsidiaries), who supply parts, financing, marketing, etc. These are organized much as the shipping industry ventures in America in the first half of the 19th century.

The Shudan are broad-based, informal groups, established in trading, industry, finance, and real estate, such as Mitsui, Mitsubishi, and Sumitomo. Often involving cross-ownership of shares and interlocking directorates, these strategic alliances demonstrate mutual involvement in each other's business, with informal coordination of policy and strategy, but without control by either company.

These two structures result in tight working relationships at top echelons, where mutual benefit is understood, and control takes the form of coordination, without subservience. Assuming a wide variety of relationships, the Keiretsu and Shudan are an integral part of most Japanese companies with whom an American business will form an alliance. They provide a rich opportunity for U.S. companies to gain access to additional resources and working relationships. They should be investigated as part of the due-diligence process during negotiations.

For those companies that have taken the time to cultivate a close relationship with their Asian counterparts, the results can be quite rewarding.

Can the Japanese Be Trusted?

The question of integrity is always raised regarding Japanese ventures. While the Japanese trust the U.S. more than any other country, Japan ranks only eleventh among countries Americans trust, and both Japanese and Americans trust each other less than five years ago, according to a recent Gallup poll. Why do we not trust the Japanese? Cross Pen's John Lawler suggests:

> "All too often the Japanese partner is not invited over here to know our families, see our homes, to understand our values as we would do with an American partner. Japanese seem quiet and withdrawn, they aren't made to feel welcome, we treat them differently. At Cross Pens, we treat our Japanese partners as family—our management is close to its employees and we treat the people from Japan like that too."

Americans underrate the Japanese acumen, to a large degree because we don't understand them. This leads to fear and lack of trust. The question of culture is supremely significant, and both sides must come to terms or the venture will fail. Clarify suspicions up-front. According to George Rabstenjek, CEO of Harbridge House, a Boston consulting firm, "The Japanese definition of honorable and trustworthy is not the same as in our culture. But within their culture, honor and trust is paramount."

It is essential to understand that the Japanese can be trusted if a relationship is established, and that the terms of that relationship clearly require honoring noncompete agreements, and other terms that ensure trust.

Stable Relationships Essential

Relationships between top executives in Japan are a fundamental factor in the success of Japanese business, and are equally important in understanding the operation of an alliance.

Even the largest Japanese firms often find more comfort dealing with smaller, more stable, family-run companies. Sony's joint venture with Tecktronix has existed since 1964. One of the key elements to its endurance has been the stable relationship between the top echelons, particularly between the founding entrepreneurs of both firms. From Sony's perspective, joint ventures will fail unless the partners are picked carefully and both make a long-term commitment.

The Japanese want a stable interest controlling the U.S. side of the partnership. There must be a good personality mix as well as a strategic fit. Honeywell's Bonsingore says, "The number one factor in achieving success with the Japanese is establishing good personal relationships. The most copious legal document is not worth the paper it is printed on without trust and understanding between the partners."

Veterans of numerous joint ventures with foreign partners frequently refer to this as "chemistry," which forms a structural bond between partners. When one joint venture was floundering, a quick investigation revealed that the U.S. CEO had not been in Japan and had not spoken with his Japanese counterpart in two years. No top staff people had been assigned to work with the alliance. Always be sure CEOs know each other face to face.

Many publicly owned companies may be too volatile to withstand a cooperative venture. U.S. CEOs are often too anxious about stock analysts and hostile takeovers, leaving them frustrated, insecure, unhappy, worried about being knocked off, and consequently less able to deal with such important issues as strategic alliances. In addition, our high personnel turnover rates at the middle levels make it difficult to build operational relationships.

These stability factors are compounded by what is perceived by the Japanese to be inconsistent American quality standards. Furthermore, the Japanese are extremely concerned about our nearsightedness. They see American firms as too obsessed by short-term profits to care about market share.

How to Protect the Crown Jewels

One of the largest concerns among American companies is whether the Japanese can be trusted with our technology. These fears are reinforced because the Japanese are adept at combining ideas, capturing market niches, gaining the low-cost production position, then becoming a competitor par excellence.

Often cited are the examples of the Savin-Ricoh and the Bell & Howell–Canon alliances where the American partners claimed the Japanese milked the partnership for technology and then turned around to become a rugged competitor in the U.S. market.

While there is some truth to these accusations, Americans have often been complacent and naive about showing the Japanese their technology. The Japanese are serious about their objectives and are very tough negotiators, and they expect their partners to be just as tough.

Seasoned veterans say that most problems with Japanese use of American technology have stemmed from naiveté concerning Japanese intentions and unstable relationships, compounded by poor understanding of the Japanese business culture, particularly the intricacies of Japanese patent law. But the Japanese adhere fastidiously to their commitments. In his dealings with the Japanese since 1963, ADL's Jerry Wasserman observes that he had never seen them violate an agreement: "But their ethics are different. They take technology then improve it, then take advantage of it. Most of the problems come from cultural and legal differences in how the Japanese view ethics, patents, negotiations, legal documents, and information interchange."

If you are concerned about the future use of technology, get a commitment, either verbally or in writing. Once the Japanese make a commitment, they will adhere to it. Stanley/Bostich's John Poccia, who manages their 25-year-old alliance with Japan's Max, put the issue in sharp perspective when he said, "I've found when the Japanese say something is 'perfectly clear,' then I can trust their word exactly. A commitment by the Japanese is a commitment. 'Yes' only means 'I understand,' it does not mean 'I agree.' Similarly, 'that will be difficult' is a polite way of saying 'no.' You must verify things you think you've agreed to in order to get everything very clear. If there is no agreement, then nothing is agreed upon; which means there is carte blanche for anything to happen."

3-M's alliance with the Japanese provides licensing to enable the joint venture to adapt its technologies to satisfy the local requirements and demands in Japan. Douglas Hanson, head of 3-M's International Division has no fear about the Japanese stealing technology, stating, "In my own experience, they have been extremely ethical. As partners we involve them in our strategic planning decisions. We have an outstanding relationship."

It is not essential to provide full access to all technology. In Boeing's alliance with Mitsubishi, the Japanese partner is prohibited from some meetings and has limited access to certain technologies.

Be clear from the outset what information is to be shared. Use noncompete agreements limiting products or geography. Do not feel compelled to use the very latest, most advanced technology for the joint venture; if necessary, hold back this second generation technology for strategic leverage in the future, but be sure such an action does not violate your agreement.

Managing Cultural Differences

The Japanese come from a uniquely different culture, language, and political environment. These differences can frustrate and confound the uninitiated. As one experienced consultant states: "We tend to be impatient, they tend to be inscrutable. We tend to 'play it by ear,' they work out operational details."

Japanese management techniques are also notably different. According to John Gillespie of Clarke Consulting, who works with American corporations venturing with the Japanese: "The Japanese make decisions and resolve conflicts very differently from Americans—it is the reason so many Japanese–U.S. partnerships have a poor track record—the two sides enter with very different assumptions and operating styles of corporate culture—their operating procedures are so different, their means of compensation, hiring and firing, their views of strategy."

Americans think of a goal as a clear object for achievement, whereas the Japanese think of a goal as a direction. Top managers seldom give orders; they listen, act as arbiter, guide, then orders are given reflecting the consensus after guidance. This process is an essential element in building teamwork. 3-M's Douglas Hanson advises, "Be patient. Before making a decision, check its implications with key Japanese managers. Tell them 'Here's what I'm thinking of doing. How will they see this? How will they react? Will there be support for this?'"

Stanley/Bostich's John Poccia is pleased with his experience with the Japanese management style: "We haven't had to wait too long for answers, and their consensus style has given us very thorough answers."

Contrasting styles can be used inspirationally and productively—*Vive la différence!*—or destructively.

CONCLUSION

Mutual advantage is the name of the alliance game. Foreign business executives are very astute; they will look for, and will take, advantage. American CEOs must do likewise. And mutual advantages will be forever changing as strategic and operational conditions change.

Don't look to an alliance primarily for a quick cash infusion or as a substitute for expensive product development, and then wonder why the venture was not strategically advantageous five years later when the partner pulls out.

Alliances keep rolling over, taking new forms, making transitions to reflect new global situations. The measure of success will not be the alliance's longevity, nor its quarterly earnings report, but its long-term strategic value.

Notes

CHAPTER 1

1. Peter Drucker, "The Shape of Industry to Come," *Industry Week*, Jan. 11, 1982, pp. 55–59.
2. Frank Heffron, "Friendly Ties," John Marcom, writer, *Wall Street Journal*, Nov. 8, 1985, p. 1.
3. Carlo DeBenedetti, "Olivetti's Strategy: Alliances for Progress," Beth Karlin writer, *Electronic Business*, Oct. 1, 1985, p. 114.
4. Howard V. Perlmutter, "Friendly Ties," op. cit. p. 1.
5. Thomas E. McGinty, *Project Organization and Finance*, Cleveland Cliffs Iron Company, 1981, p. 8.
6. Frederick G. Withington, "Failed Marriages," Laurie P. Cohen, writer, *Wall Street Journal*, Sept. 10, 1984, p. 1.
7. Frederick Wang, "Failed Marriages," op. cit. p. 18.
8. W. James McNerney, Jr., "Friendly Ties," op. cit. p 15.

CHAPTER 2

1. Phillip Chadwick Foster Smith, *The Empress of China*, Philadelphia Maritime Museum, 1984, p. 13.
2. Alexander Giacco, "Making Joint Ventures Work," *Chemical Week*, Aug. 17, 1983, p. 34.
3. Richard Hayes, "Strategic Partners," Norm Alster, writer, *Electronic Business*, May 15, 1986, p. 54.
4. Deming Sherman, "Legerdemain," Peter Kadzis, writer, *Providence Business News*, Dec. 15, 1986, p. 9.

CHAPTER 3

1. Barre Mitchell, Gary Alexander, Barry Conrad, "The Polymer Composite Sheet," *TAPPI Journal*, Feb. 1987, pp. 47–51.

2. Paul J. Rizzo, "Friendly Ties," op. cit. p. 1.

3. David Jemison, Sim Sitkin, "Acquisitions, the Process can be a Problem," *Harvard Business Review*, March/April 1986, p. 113.

CHAPTER 4

1. Robert J. Conrads, Amir Mahini, Editorial, *Wall Street Journal*, Jan. 16, 1984, p. 22.

2. Herbert Granath, "Friendly Ties," op. cit. p. 115.

3. William Norris, "Strategic Partners," op. cit. p. 50.

CHAPTER 5

1. Philip L. Zwick, "Making Joint Ventures Work," op. cit. p. 32.

CHAPTER 6

1. McGinty, op. cit. p. 17.

CHAPTER 7

1. Donald J. Trump, *Trump, the Art of the Deal*, Warner, 1987, p. 127.

2. Rudolf Schwenger, "Strategic Partners," op. cit. p. 52.

3. Humphrey Neil, *The Art of Contrary Thinking*, Caxton Press, 1971.

4. Irving Janis, *The Victims of Group Think*, Houghton Mifflin, 1972, pp. 209–214.

5. J. William Scruggs, "Strategic Partners," op. cit. p. 52.

6. *IBM Business Conduct Guidelines*, IBM Corporation, 1983, p. 15.

CHAPTER 8

1. Norris, op. cit. p. 54.

2. Heffron, op. cit. p. 1.

3. J. Peter Killing, "How to make a Global Joint Venture Work," *Harvard Business Review*, May/June 1982, p. 122.

4. Edwin M. Martin, Jr., *Corporate Partnering*, Practicing Law Institute, 1986, p. 15.

CHAPTER 9

1. Alfred Prommer, "Strategic Partners," op. cit. p. 54.

2. Martin, op. cit. p. 48.

3. James Hlavacek, Brian Dovey, & John Biondo, "Tie Small Business Technology to Marketing Power," *Harvard Business Review*, Jan./Feb. 1977, p. 115.

CHAPTER 11

1. Katherine Rudie Harrigan, *Managing Joint Venture Success*, Lexington Books, 1986, p. 168.

2. Martin, op. cit. p. 16.

3. Thomas J. Peters & Robert H. Waterman, Jr., *In Search of Excellence*, Warner Books, 1982, p. 207.

4. Ibid., p. 208.

5. Ibid., p. 208.

6. Killing, op. cit. p. 122.

7. Ibid., p. 126.

8. Paul R. Lawrence, Jay W. Lorsch, *Organization and Environment*, Harvard Business School, 1967. Paul R. Lawrence & Jay W. Lorsch, "New Management Job: The Integrator," *Harvard Business Review*, Nov.–Dec. 1967, pp. 85–93. Lorsch and Allen, *Managing Diversity and Interdependence*, Harvard, 1973.

9. Jay Galbraith, *Designing Complex Organizations*, Addison-Wesley, 1973, p. 49.

10. Drucker, op. cit., pp. 55–59.

11. Norm Alister, "Strategic Partners," op. cit., p. 50.

12. Scruggs, op. cit., p. 52.

13. Galbraith, op. cit., p. 55.

14. Richard Clawson, "Controlling the Manufacturing Start-up," *Harvard Business Review*, May/June 1985, p. 14.

15. Ibid., p. 20.

16. Galbraith, op. cit., pp. 97–98.

17. Edward Roberts, "Strategic Partners," op. cit., p. 52.

18. Killing, op. cit., p. 124.

19. Harrigan, op. cit., p. 189.

20. Killing, op. cit., p. 124.

21. Whittier, op. cit., p. 52.

22. Alister, op. cit., p. 54.

23. Killing, op. cit., p. 126.

CHAPTER 14

1. Peters & Waterman, op. cit., p. 209.

2. James Brian Quinn, "Technological Innovation, Entrepreneurship, & Strategy," *Sloan Management Review*, Spring, 1979, p. 25.

3. Richard J. Thompson, "Competitive Effects of Joint Ventures in the Chemical Industry," Dissertation, University of Massachusetts, Dec. 1970.

4. Harrigan, op. cit., pp. 46–47.

Appendices

A. Sample Strategic Alliance Agreement for Large Marketing Company and Small Manufacturing Company

B. Sample Joint Venture Partnership Agreement for Real Estate Development

C. Sample Joint Venture Corporation Agreement for International Manufacturing

D. Sample Confidentiality and Nondisclosure Agreement

E. Sample Noncompetition

F. Joint Venture Case Study: Tri-Wall Corporation

Please note: These documents are samples only. Each joint venture or strategic alliance should develop specific documents tailored to its own needs with the assistance of competent legal counsel.

APPENDIX A. SAMPLE STRATEGIC PARTNERSHIP AGREEMENT

STRATEGIC ALLIANCE
FOR THE PURPOSE OF
LITTLE-CO TO DEVELOP TECHNICAL PRODUCTS
TO BE SOLD EXCLUSIVELY TO BIG-CORP
FOR INTERNATIONAL DISTRIBUTION

Contents

Exhibits

This is a MANUFACTURING AND MARKETING AGREEMENT made as of June 1, 1990 between: BIG-CORP, INC., a Texas corporation, (hereinafter referred to as "BIG-CORP") and LITTLE-CO COMPANY, a Delaware corporation (herein after referred to as "LITTLE-CO" or "Seller") for the purchase and subsequent sale by BIG-CORP from LITTLE-CO of Products described in Exhibit A.

The parties agree as follows:

1.0 SPIRIT OF AGREEMENT

BIG-CORP and LITTLE-CO recognize that the optimum performance of this Agreement requires a cooperative working environment established upon good communications and a good faith working relationship between both parties. It is within this cooperative spirit that BIG-CORP and LITTLE-CO agree to interact in the performance of this Agreement.

By recognizing that the technology used in the Product has been developed by LITTLE-CO and has not been thoroughly tested in a mass production environment, BIG-CORP will provide whatever technical liaison to LITTLE-CO to assist in perfecting the manufacturing processes required for the execution of this agreement.

2.0 INFORMATION TRANSFERS

BIG-CORP and LITTLE-CO intend to exchange information essential for the accomplishment of this Agreement. Such information may include, but is not limited to, product and quality specifications, pricing and cost data, on order and inventory data, build and delivery schedules, BIG-CORP customer order data and any other information essential to the objectives of this Agreement. It is expressly agreed that any and all information provided by LITTLE-CO to BIG-CORP shall not be confidential or proprietary information of LITTLE-CO and in no event shall disclosure of LITTLE-CO information establish a confidential relationship of any kind between BIG-CORP and LITTLE-CO.

2.1 Non-Confidential Information: All disclosures of information by BIG-CORP to LITTLE-CO shall be made by or under the supervision of the designated Project Coordinator for LITTLE-CO. All disclosures of information by BIG-CORP will be deemed to be non-confidential, unless specifically designated at the time of disclosure as confidential information of BIG-CORP.

2.2 *Confidential Information:* In the event that confidential information of BIG-CORP is disclosed in writing, said writing will state the date of disclosure, that the information contained therein is confidential and that it is being disclosed pursuant to this Agreement, and will contain an appropriate legend such as "BIG-CORP Confidential". All disclosures of information by LITTLE-CO are agreed as described above to be non-confidential.

2.3 *Exceptions:* These obligations will not apply to any information that:

1. Is already in the possession of LITTLE-CO or any of its Subsidiaries without obligation of confidence;

2. Is independently developed by LITTLE-CO or any of its Subsidiaries;

3. Is or becomes publicly available without breach of this Agreement;

4. Is rightfully received by LITTLE-CO from a third party;

5. Is released for disclosure by BIG-CORP with its written consent; or

6. Is inherently disclosed in the use, lease, sale, or other distribution of any production (excluding documentation) or service by or for LITTLE-CO or any of its Subsidiaries.

3.0 ADMINISTRATION

3.1 *Project Coordinators:* Each party will promptly designate a Project Coordinator under this Agreement, and will promptly notify the other in writing of its Project Coordinator.

The Project Coordinator is responsible for representing the parties in all business and technical matters relating to the performance of work under this Agreement, including but not limited to:

1. Weekly Project Coordination meetings.

2. Semi-annual performance reviews;

3. All issues, meetings, consultations, modification of terms and conditions, technical appendices, administrative actions and procedures relating to overall workscope, termination, product specifications, price, quality, testing and performance, packaging specifications, training, and the production scheduling and delivery of Products or services;

4. Handling all disclosure, receipt and return of BIG-CORP confidential information (business and technical) and handling of non-confidential information.

5. Coordinating and communicating as required with their respective technical staff on the status/changes of business and technical related matters.

3.2 *Order Of Precedence:* In providing products and services under this Agreement, LITTLE-CO shall comply with the provisions specified in this Agreement and BIG-CORP purchase orders.

In the event of inconsistency or ambiguity, LITTLE-CO's Project Coordinator shall notify BIG-CORP's Project Coordinator as soon as these inconsistencies are discovered.

3.3 *Program Management:* Upon 24 hour notification BIG-CORP shall have the right to send BIG-CORP employees into LITTLE-CO's facility at all reasonable times for the purpose of normal contract administration liaison to inspect the progress and quality of the work being performed hereunder or to inspect and obtain any information relating to the performance of this Agreement.

4.0 STATEMENT OF WORK

4.1 *Manufacture of BIG-CORP Products:* LITTLE-CO will procure parts, fabricate, and manufacture for BIG-CORP Products and Spare Parts to Product Specification which is attached hereto as Exhibit A. LITTLE-CO agrees to sell only to BIG-CORP and deliver all Products and Services listed and priced in Exhibit C. Mutual agreement by BIG-CORP and LITTLE-CO is required prior to making any changes to Exhibits A and C.

4.2 *Quality Requirements:* The consistent delivery of high quality defect free Products and Spare Parts to BIG-CORP's customers is essential in the performance of this Agreement. Quality acceptance testing and inspection procedures to be performed by LITTLE-CO for all BIG-CORP's Products and Spare Parts purchased hereunder are attached as Exhibit B and included in this Agreement. Written agreement by BIG-CORP and LITTLE-CO is required prior to making any changes to Exhibit B. Quality acceptance testing and inspection will take place at LITTLE-CO's facility prior to delivery of BIG-CORP Products and Spare Parts to BIG-CORP's customers. LITTLE-CO will maintain sufficient quality records for audit as requested by BIG-CORP in Exhibit B.

4.3 *Delivery of Products and Services:* Timely delivery of all BIG-CORP Products, Spare Parts and Repair Services by LITTLE-CO to BIG-CORP's customers is essential in the performance of this Agreement. LITTLE-CO's delivery obligation is defined as the satisfactory receipt of undamaged products and services by BIG-CORP's customers on the date specified by BIG-CORP. At least 4 weeks in advance, BIG-CORP will provide to LITTLE-CO a monthly BIG-CORP Product delivery schedule stating specific delivery dates and the number of BIG-CORP Products to be delivered. BIG-CORP will provide to LITTLE-CO sufficient BIG-CORP customer order information (customer name, address, order number, etc.) to allow LITTLE-CO to ship and deliver properly.

4.3.1 *Delivery Delay Notice:* In the event that LITTLE-CO is unable for any reason to make all or any portion of any delivery of Products on the scheduled delivery date, LITTLE-CO will notify BIG-CORP at least five (5) business days prior to the scheduled delivery date as to the date LITTLE-CO believes delivery can be made. Such notice shall not relieve LITTLE-CO of any obligations under this Agreement.

4.3.2 *Continuity Of Supply For BIG-CORP Products:* LITTLE-CO agrees to maintain a sufficient "on-order" parts and finished goods inventory to assure the continuous supply and delivery of Products as scheduled by BIG-CORP. The amount of on-order parts and inventory shall be reasonable; and at any time the combined quantity of "parts on order, plus in-inventory plus in-process or completed product volumes shall meet the Delivery schedule in Exhibit F plus 5%. BIG-CORP authorized LITTLE-CO to procure parts based upon Exhibit F projections. LITTLE-CO will exercise prudent materials management judgment to make rational purchasing and inventory decisions and implement only those actions which are consistent with the objectives of this Agreement. BIG-CORP agrees to reimburse LITTLE-CO the actual excess parts inventory carrying cost, in the event that in any quarter BIG-CORP's purchase orders are less than Exhibit F projections by less than 5%.

4.4 *Spare Parts and Repair Services:* For a period of five (5) years after delivery of the last BIG-CORP Product, LITTLE-CO agrees to sell only to BIG-CORP Spare Parts and Repair Services. The prices and delivery requirements for Spare Parts and Repair Services are specified in Exhibit C. Upon delivery of the last BIG-CORP Product,

the parties agree to negotiate reasonable prices and delivery schedules for Spare Parts and Repair Services purchased by BIG-CORP
during the first year of the five (5) year period following the end of
the production run.

4.4.1 *Spare Parts:* LITTLE-CO agrees to ship all Spare Parts
within two (2) business days after notification by BIG-CORP.

4.4.2 *Repair Services:*

(a) *Customer Under-Repair Contract Prior to Warranty
Expiration:* LITTLE-CO agrees to repair solely for BIG-
CORP all BIG-CORP Products and Spare Parts for BIG-
CORP customers prior to the expiration of the original
warranty period.

(b) *Customer Under-Repair Contract After Warranty Expiration:* BIG-CORP will sell Repair Contracts and give
LITTLE-CO the percentage of the sales price as specified
in Appendix C.

(c) *Customer Without Repair Contract and Expired Warranty:* LITTLE-CO agrees to repair solely for BIG-CORP, on
a fixed cost repair basis, all BIG-CORP Products and Spare
Parts for BIG-CORP customers that have not purchased a
maintenance repair contract from BIG-CORP after the expiration of the original warranty period.

4.5 *Records and Reporting:* LITTLE-CO agrees to maintain sufficient
and accurate records in the performance of this Agreement, including quality data, design change activity, repair service activity and
customer delivery information. Upon request by BIG-CORP, LITTLE-
CO agrees to provide to BIG-CORP accurate and timely status reports
and any other necessary information required by BIG-CORP in the
performance of this Agreement.

5.0 MARKETING AND SALES

5.1 *Sales Distribution:* BIG-CORP intends to distribute LITTLE-CO
products throughout its international sales distribution system.
LITTLE-CO will make available one sales representative on an as-
needed basis (up to full time if necessary). Any travel and out-of-
pocket expenses will be reimbursed in full by BIG-CORP.

5.2 *Support Training:* The LITTLE-CO sales representative will be
knowledgable in all aspects of LITTLE-CO products and provide a

two day training program for presentation to BIG-CORP sales representatives. A schedule of dates and locations will be provided 60 days in advance by BIG-CORP.

5.3 *Product Literature:* BIG-CORP will be responsible for development and production of all product literature. LITTLE-CO will provide technical drawings, performance data, or currently available (off-the-shelf) literature as requested by BIG-CORP.

5.4 *Advertising:* All advertising costs will be borne in full by BIG-CORP.

6.0 *PRICES, PAYMENT, ORDERING PROCEDURE*

6.1 *Product, Spare Parts and Repair Service Prices:* Attached as Exhibit C, are the prices for all Products and Repair Services to be purchased by BIG-CORP from LITTLE-CO. All prices are F.O.B LITTLE-CO's plant, exclusive of all excise, sales, use, or similar taxes. The parties agree that the BIG-CORP Product, Spare Part and Repair Service prices specified in Exhibit C are firm through June 1, 1995 unless agreed to in writing by the parties. After this date the parties agree to review the repair service cost data every ninety (90) days and to negotiate reasonable Repair Service prices based upon actual historical repair cost data.

6.2 *Price Changes:* LITTLE-CO and BIG-CORP agree that price decreases for all BIG-CORP Products is desired during the term of this Agreement. Therefore, LITTLE-CO and BIG-CORP agree to take all reasonable actions to obtain reduced pricing in order to capture larger market share. Such actions include, but are not limited to product design changes, improved productivity, and lower vendor prices. No changes to prices shall become effective until mutually agreed to by BIG-CORP and LITTLE-CO by updating Exhibit C. If LITTLE-CO decreases the wholesale price to BIG-CORP, BIG-CORP in turn will make a proportionate decrease in the retail price.

6.3 *Payment Term:* For BIG-CORP Products and Spare Parts, LITTLE-CO agrees to invoice BIG-CORP after shipment on a weekly basis. Fixed price repair services will be invoiced after shipment by LITTLE-CO. Payment terms are net fifteen (15) days after receipt of an acceptable invoice by BIG-CORP's Accounts Payable Department.

6.4 *Ordering Procedures:* On a quarterly basis BIG-CORP agrees to provide LITTLE-CO with a written projection of BIG-CORP's delivery schedule for BIG-CORP Products for the following twelve (12) month period. The rolling twelve (12) month delivery projection shall be attached as Exhibit F and updated on a quarterly basis. Exhibit F shall authorize LITTLE-CO to procure purchased parts for Products as described in Section 4. It is understood that such twelve month delivery schedule projections are to only be used to procure *purchased parts* and are not to be construed by LITTLE-CO as firm commitments by BIG-CORP to fabricate, assemble, test and ship BIG-CORP products. LITTLE-CO agrees that the BIG-CORP Start-To-Build Schedule described in Section 7 together with the receipt of a BIG-CORP purchase order is the only authorization for LITTLE-CO to start fabrication, assembly and test of BIG-CORP Products.

6.5 *Order Cancellation:* BIG-CORP purchase orders issued under this Agreement may be cancelled by BIG-CORP upon written notice by BIG-CORP. Within sixty days after upon receipt of such cancellation notice, LITTLE-CO shall stop the production run and take all reasonable action to minimize BIG-CORP's financial liability in the event of such cancellation. Such actions may include, but are not limited to, notifying LITTLE-CO's suppliers to cancel all related open purchase orders, negotiating supplier cancellation charges, returning existing part and material inventories to suppliers for credit and halting all internal fabrication and assembly activities.

In such event, BIG-CORP shall pay LITTLE-CO for all completed BIG-CORP products and Spare Parts as authorized by this Agreement at the prices specified in Exhibit C and reimburse LITTLE-CO the reasonable cost of purchased and/or fabricated parts procured pursuant to this Agreement that LITTLE-CO cannot use in its sole judgment for other purposes.

7.0 *PRODUCTION SCHEDULING*

Five months prior to the required delivery BIG-CORP will provide to LITTLE-CO, on a monthly basis, a firm Start-To-Build Schedule stating the volume and mix of BIG-CORP Products and Spare Parts that LITTLE-CO is authorized to start fabrication, assembling, and testing for delivery to BIG-CORP. BIG-CORP agrees to purchase from LITTLE-CO the cumulative volume and mix of BIG-CORP Products and Spare Parts stated in all monthly Start-To-Build Schedules.

7.1 *Production Schedule Increase:* LITTLE-CO agrees to accept and manufacture increased BIG-CORP Product volumes specified in the monthly BIG-CORP Start-To-Build Schedule providing: 1) purchased parts are available, 2) such schedule does not exceed the previous month's Start-To-Build Schedule by more than 20%, and 3) does not exceed LITTLE-CO's manufacturing and tests38capacity.

8.0 *LOANED TEST EQUIPMENT*

BIG-CORP will loan to LITTLE-CO the test equipment specified in Exhibit D. All loaned test equipment is subject to the terms and conditions of the "BIG-CORP Equipment Loan Agreement" attached hereto as Exhibit D and included in this Agreement.

9.0 *ADDITIONAL PRODUCT RIGHTS*

9.1 *Labeling:* LITTLE-CO agrees to affix to all Products BIG-CORP nameplates which include the BIG-CORP trademark/logo, serial numbers, type or model numbers, or any such designation and patent information. BIG-CORP shall supply these plates.

9.2 *Product Design Changes:* Throughout this Agreement, BIG-CORP shall retain engineering control over the design, design changes, and have the authority to alter LITTLE-CO's manufacturing process in the event that the Products do not perform as specified in Exhibit A. In the event of such changes, LITTLE-CO will evaluate the workscope change and the parties agree to negotiate reasonable price changes if required.

9.2.1 *BIG-CORP Design Changes:* BIG-CORP may request changes in BIG-CORP Product design upon written notice to LITTLE-CO. Such changes may result in an increase/decrease in price and/or a different delivery schedule. Within twenty (20) days after receipt of such notice, LITTLE-CO will advise BIG-CORP in writing the cost of implementing such change(s) and the date(s) the change(s) can be included into production. No such changes shall be made until both parties agree either orally or in writing. All oral agreements shall be confirmed within ten (10) days in writing.

9.2.2 *LITTLE-CO Design Changes:* BIG-CORP encourages LITTLE-CO to submit for BIG-CORP's approval design changes that will improve the Product's function, performance, reliability, schedule, safety, maintainability or reduce costs. Such change request will be provided to BIG-CORP in writing by LITTLE-CO and include a description of the change request, the anticipated benefits and the effect on pricing and delivery. All design change requests submitted by LITTLE-CO, including those changes not implemented by BIG-CORP, shall become the sole property of BIG-CORP. No such changes shall be implemented until authorized in writing by BIG-CORP.

9.3 *Licenses and Patents:* BIG-CORP acknowledges that the patent rights to the product technology belong exclusively and solely to LITTLE-CO. So long as this Agreement or its extentions or modifications remain in effect, LITTLE-CO grants to BIG-CORP an exclusive unlimited license to sell LITTLE-CO's technology as incorporated in the Product Specifications (Exhibit A). Should any of the following conditions occur, LITTLE-CO grants an exclusive license to BIG-CORP in return for royalty payments as specified in the Standby Licensing agreement.

(1) LITTLE-CO is unable to manufacture sufficient quantity of the Product to meet BIG-CORP's production schedule.

(2) LITTLE-CO terminates this agreement under the provisions of Section 12.

(3) LITTLE-CO files for Bankruptcy.

(4) 25% or more of LITTLE-CO's stock is acquired by any of BIG-CORP's competitors.

10.0 PRODUCT WARRANTY

Under normal use and service, LITTLE-CO warrants that all BIG-CORP Product, Spare Parts, and Repair Services delivered under this Agreement will be free from defects in materials and workmanship for a period of 90 days from the date of shipment from LITTLE-CO. Without charge to BIG-CORP or BIG-CORP's customers, LITTLE-CO will promptly repair or replace the BIG-CORP Product or any parts (normal wear and tear and expendibles excluded) which are determined to be defective within the warranty period.

11.0 PACKAGING AND SHIPPING

11.1 *Packaging:* LITTLE-CO shall package for shipment to BIG-CORP's customers all BIG-CORP Products and Spare Parts delivered hereunder in accordance with the attached packaging specifications attached as Exhibit E.

11.2 *Shipping, Delivery and Freight Charges:* Shipment of all BIG-CORP Products, Spare Parts and Repair Services ordered under this Agreement will be shipped by surface transportation, F.O.B. destination (BIG-CORP customer's dock), freight charges prepaid by LITTLE-CO (LITTLE-CO will select the carrier).

12.0 EXTENSION AND TERMINATION

12.1 *Extension:* Upon expiration of the initial term, BIG-CORP shall have the option to renew this Agreement for an unlimited number of consecutive twelve (12) month periods.

12.2 *Termination*

12.2.1 *Consent:* This agreement may be terminated at any time by the mutual consent of both LITTLE-CO and BIG-CORP.

12.2.2 *By BIG-CORP Without Cause:* This Agreement may be terminated without cause by BIG-CORP upon written notice delivered by BIG-CORP to LITTLE-CO ninety (90) days in advance of the termination. In such event, BIG-CORP has no liability for termination other than those stated in Section 6.5 (order cancellation) providing all remaining BIG-CORP obligations pursuant to this Agreement have been executed. All rights to the technology shall then revert wholly to LITTLE-CO.

12.2.3 *By LITTLE-CO Without Cause:* This Agreement shall not be terminated without cause by LITTLE-CO before June 1, 1995. After which this Agreement may be terminated by LITTLE-CO without cause upon one hundred eighty (180) days written notice delivered by LITTLE-CO to BIG-CORP provided all scheduled start-to-build BIG-CORP Products and Spare Parts not to exceed the 180 day period have been delivered as specified by BIG-CORP. Such termination shall activate the Standby Licensing Agreement, Exhibit G.

12.2.4 *By Default:* This Agreement may be terminated by either party upon default by the other party, provided that written notice of such termination is delivered to the other party within ninety (90) days of the date of default. Default shall mean any material breach of this Agreement by either party that is not corrected within thirty (30) days after written notice from the other party of such breach.

12.2.5 *Post-Termination Obligations:* Termination of this Agreement shall not in any way interfere with the provisions of this Agreement which survive such termination or with the obligations of the parties to pay all monies payable as of the date of such termination or which become payable for BIG-CORP Products, Spare Parts or Repair Services ordered and delivered after termination of this Agreement which survive such termination.

12.3 *Force Majeure:* If the performance of this Agreement or of any obligation hereunder is prevented, restricted or interfered with by reason of fire or other casualty or accident; strikes or labor disputes; inability to procure raw materials, power or supplies; war or other violence; any law, order, or requirement of any governmental agency or any other act or condition whatsoever beyond the reasonable control of the parties hereto, the party so affected, upon giving notice to the other party, shall be excused from such performance to the extent of such prevention, restriction or interferences; provided that the party so affected shall use reasonable efforts under the circumstances to avoid or remove such causes of non-performance and shall continue performance hereunder with the utmost dispatch whenever such causes are removed; and provided further, that no such occurrence shall extend the term of this Agreement beyond that specified in Section 12.1.

13.0 *TAXES*

Items purchased by BIG-CORP from LITTLE-CO hereunder are meant ultimately and primarily for resale to BIG-CORP's customers. BIG-CORP will supply LITTLE-CO with a resale certificate for such items purchased.

14.0 *INVENTION AND PATENT PROVISIONS*

14.1 *Invention and Disclosure:* "Invention" shall mean any idea, design, concept, technique, invention, discovery or improvement, whether or not patentable, made, solely or jointly by LITTLE-CO and/or LITTLE-CO employees, or jointly by LITTLE-CO and/or LITTLE-CO employees with one or more employees of BIG-CORP during the terms of this Agreement and in the performance of services hereunder, provided, that either the conception or reduction to practice occurs during the term of this Agreement and in the performance of services hereunder. LITTLE-CO shall promptly make a complete written disclosure to BIG-CORP of each Invention, specifically pointing out the features or concepts which LITTLE-CO believes to be new or different.

14.2 *Patent Rights and Licenses:* Inventions made jointly by LITTLE-CO and/or LITTLE-CO's employees with one or more employees of BIG-CORP shall be jointly owned, title to all patents issued thereon shall be joint, all expenses incurred in obtaining and maintaining such patents shall be jointly shared (except as provided hereinafter), and each party shall have the right to license third parties by mutual consent. All licenses granted to BIG-CORP shall be worldwide and irrevocable and shall include the right to grant sublicenses to its Subsidiaries.

15.0 *INDEMNIFICATION*

BIG-CORP hereby agrees that it will at all times during the period of use of LITTLE-CO manufactured BIG-CORP products, at the expense of BIG-CORP, defend all actions, litigation or claims made or filed against LITTLE-CO, agents or Subsidiaries brought for infringement of any patent because of the use, lease or sale of any BIG-CORP Product manufactured in accordance with the provisions of the Agreement, provided that LITTLE-CO shall have notified BIG-CORP, in writing, of such actions, litigations, and claims against it, its agents or subsidiaries.

16.0 *MISCELLANEOUS PROVISIONS*

16.1 *Disclosure of Agreement:* For a period of three years from the date of this Agreement, neither of the parties shall disclose the existence of the terms and conditions of this Agreement without the prior written consent of the other party unless such disclosure is required by law.

16.2 *Liability:* Neither party, except to the extent evidenced by this Agreement, shall assume any of the liabilities of the other party.

IN WITNESS WHEREOF, the parties here to execute this Agreement by their duly authorized representatives as of the day and year written above.

_____   _____

BIG-CORP, INC.   LITTLE-CO COMPANY

Exhibits

A. PRODUCT SPECIFICATIONS

B. QUALITY ASSURANCE PLAN

C. PRODUCT, DELIVERY, REPAIR SERVICE, SCHEDULE, AND PRICES

D. EQUIPMENT LOAN AGREEMENT

E. PACKAGING SPECIFICATIONS

F. 12-MONTH DELIVERY SCHEDULE

G. STANDBY LICENSING AGREEMENT

APPENDIX B. SAMPLE JOINT VENTURE PARTNERSHIP AGREEMENT

JOINT VENTURE PARTNERSHIP FOR THE PURPOSE OF DEVELOPING REAL ESTATE

Table of Contents

Agreement of Joint Venture General Partnership

AGREEMENT dated as the 29th day of February 1989, by and between Seaside Development, (SEASIDE) Incorporated, a Delaware Corporation, and Mountain View (MOUNTAINVIEW) Company, a California Limited Partnership, (individually referred to as a "Partner" and collectively as the "Partners."

WITNESSETH

WHEREAS the parties wish to fully state their rights, obligations, and duties as general partners of the Joint Venture General Partnership,

NOW, THEREFORE, based upon the mutual covenants contained in this agreement, the parties agree as follows:

1.0 *FORMATION:*

The parties agree to form the General Partnership in accordance with the Uniform Partnership Act of the State of Florida.

2.0 *NAME:*

The name of the partnership shall be Brookside Ventures.

3.0 *PURPOSE:*

The purpose of the partnership is to acquire, develop, and own real estate located on Bellevue Avenue in the City of Springfield (the "Property") and to construct upon the site and subsequently operate a commercial office building (the "Project").

4.0 *AUTHORIZED ACTIVITIES:*

In furtherance of its purpose, but subject to the provisions of this Agreement, the Partnership is hereby authorized to:

4.1 *Acquisitions:* Acquire, by purchase or lease, any real or personal property which may be necessary to the accomplishment of the purposes of the Partnership.

4.2 *Improvements:* Construct, renovate, operate, maintain, finance, and improve the Project, and to own, sell, lease, mortgage, or otherwise transact (without limitation), all real and/or personal property necessary to accomplishing the purposes of the Partnership.

4.3 *Borrowing:* Borrow money by mortgage, pledge, or lien, in furtherance of the purpose of the Partnership.

4.4 *Repayment of Debt:* Prepay, repay, refinance, or modify, in whole or in part, any mortgages or debt instruments affecting the property.

4.5 *Contracts:* Enter into any contracts necessary to the accomplishment of the purposes of the Partnership, including the Real Estate Purchase and Sales Agreement dated January 1989 between the seller and the Partnership.

5.0 *PLACE OF BUSINESS:*

The principal place of business of the Partnership shall be located in Springfield, or any future location agreed to by the partners.

6.0 *TERM:*

The Partnership shall commence upon the date of this agreement, and shall continue until December 31, 1998, unless terminated in accordance with paragraph 17 of this Agreement.

7.0 *MANAGEMENT:*

Normal operations of the Partnership shall be managed in accordance with the following:

7.1 *Operational Steering Committee:* Each of the Partners will select two (2) individuals to serve on the Operational Steering Committee (the "Committee"). The Committee will make all business decisions of the Partnership, including, but not limited to:

(a) preparation of development plans

(b) conduct of contractor negotiations

(c) application for all governmental permits

(d) selection and retention of architects, engineers, and construction managers.

(e) overseeing all marketing and daily management of the Project once complete.

7.2 *Committee Decisionmaking:* Day-to-day operations of the Partnership shall be authorized by a majority of the committee members. Four members shall constitute a quorum. The following decisions shall require the unanimous authorization of all the committee:

(a) the sale, exchange, lease, mortgage, pledge, or other transfer of all or substantially all of the Property, other than the lease of the Property in the ordinary course of business.

(b) the borrowing of any funds or the incurring of any debt in excess of $ _____ by the Partnership.

(c) the payment of compensation to a Partner.

7.3 *Breaking Decisionmaking Deadlocks:* In the event the Committee is unable to reach agreement regarding particular decisions, the following procedures will come into force:

(a) first, each of the partners shall appoint a third, temporary representative to the committee for the purpose of breaking the deadlock. This third person shall be a senior person, trusted by the appointing partner, and skilled in negotiations and problem solving. All the rules of the decisionmaking shall remain the same. This "enhanced" committee shall have thirty days to resolve the deadlock.

(b) second, in the event the enhanced committee is unable to reach agreement, the matter shall be submitted to mediation under the Rules of Commercial Mediation of the American Arbitration Association. The appointed mediator shall have expertise in commercial real estate development.

(c) third, in the event the enhanced committee is unable to reach agreement with the help of a mediator, the matter shall be submitted to binding arbitration of the American Arbitration Association, irrespective of the limitation in those rules on the size of the claim that may be submitted for expedited arbitration.

8.0 *OTHER PARTNERSHIP INTERESTS:*

Any Partner may engage in any other business ventures with any other partners of every nature and description, including the ownership, operation, management, and development of real estate, and neither the General Partnership, nor any Partner, shall have any rights in and to such independent ventures or the income or profits derived therefrom.

9.0 *COMPENSATION TO THE PARTNERS:*

The Partners shall receive no compensation for services rendered to the Partnership unless otherwise agreed by all of the members of the Operational Steering Committee. Any Partner or business entity controlled by a Partner may enter into an agreement to provide goods or services to the Partnership, so long as the terms are approved by all of the members of the Operating Committee. It is expressly agreed and understood, however, that the Partnership will enter into a Management Agreement with Seaside Development providing for the operation of the Property as a parking lot until the construction of the Project has commenced.

10. *CAPITAL INVESTMENT AND LOAN PROCEDURES*

10.1. *Capital Investment Accounts:* The Partnership shall maintain on its books a Capital Investment Account for each Partner. The Capital Account for the Partner shall *increase* each time a Partner contributes either: 1) cash or 2) allocations of Partnership income to the Partner, or 3) the fair market value of property (properly appraised and net of liabilities). Any non-cash contributions by a Partner must be deemed acceptable by all members of the Operational Committee.

The Partner's Capital Account shall *decrease* each time a Partner receives: 1) a cash distribution from the Partnership, or 2) property in lieu of cash (by the amount of the fair market value of property, properly appraised and net of liabilities), or 3) allocation of Partnership losses, or 4) allocation of Partnership expenditures (not normally deductable in computing Partnership income and not properly chargeable to the capital account).

10.2. *Account Balances:* A Partner shall have a *negative* account balance when the balance is less than zero. A partner shall have a *positive* account balance when the balance is greater than zero.

10.3. *Account Restrictions:* A Partner shall not be entitled to interest on its Capital Account, to withdraw any part of its Capital Investment, or to receive any distribution from the Partnership, except as specifically provided in this Agreement.

10.4. *Future Financial Obligations:* A Partner shall not have a further financial obligation to the Partnership based solely upon the existance of a negative account balance. However, other financial considerations of the Partnership may require further investment by a Partner having of a negative account balance. A Partner may agree with the Partnership to restore all or limited portion of any Negative Capital Account, or may contribute a Promissory Note payable within 60 days of demand and bearing a variable rate of interest not less than the Prime Rate in order to confirm such Partner's Agreement to make additional contributions to the Partnership.

10.5. *Loans by Partners:* Loans by any Partner to the Partnership shall not be considered contributions to the capital of the Partnership, and shall not be reflected in the Partner's Capital Investment Accounts. Any Partner loans shall be subordinated to all loans and mortgages by independent financial institutions. Any loans may receive interest, but at a rate determined by the Operational Committee and no higher than 1 percentage point over the Prime Rate published in the Wall Street Journal.

10.6 *Liability for Repayment of Capital Investment:* The Partnership itself shall have sole responsibility for repayment of each of the Partners capital investment contributions. None of the Partners shall be responsible to the other partners for such repayment.

10.7 *Transfer of Partner Interests:* In the event a Partner sells, transfers, or otherwise exchanges his interests in the partership with another business entity, the Capital Account interests shall be carried over to the transferree Partner.

10.8 *Unequal/Unexpected IRS Impact:* Should one Partner or both Partners receive an unexpected and/or disproportionate adjustment or allocation due to Internal Revenue Service rulings or regulations which causes or increases a Negative Capital Account for the Partner(s), then the Partner(s) shall be allocated, pro-rata, items of income and gain for the taxable year in an amount and manner sufficient to eliminate or equalize the Partner(s)' Negative Capital Account(s) as quickly and fairly as possible.

11. *PARTNERS' CAPITAL INVESTMENT AND LOANS*

11.1 *CAPITAL INVESTMENT:* The Partners shall each contribute $100,000 (one hundred thousand dollars) as its initial capital contribution to the partnership. No interest shall be paid on Partnership Capital Investment, and no Partner shall be entitled to withdraw any part of its capital contribution except as provided by this Agreement.

11.2 *LOANS:* Each of the partners loans $250,000, at variable prime rate, with only interest due for the first five years, then amortizing over a period of 10 years, and due upon liquidation of the partnership. Such loan documents are attached as exhibits to this agreement. The Partners acknowledge these loans to be subordinated to any loans by independent financial institutions.

12.0 *ALLOCATION OF PROFIT AND LOSS:*

The term "net profits" and "net losses" means the taxable income or loss of the Partnership determined for federal income tax purposes in in conformance with generally accepted accounting procedures.

12.1 *Operational Profits and Losses:* Unless revised as provided in this Agreement, the net profits and net losses from normal business operations shall be allocated as follows:

Seaside Development:	50%
Mountain View Company:	50%
	100%

12.2 *Profits upon Sale:* Net profits from sale or other distribution of all or substantially all of the Property shall be allocated first to the Partners with Negative Capital Accounts, until these Accounts are brought to zero. Thereafter, net profits shall be allocated pro-rata in proportion to the ratio of paragraph 12.1 above.

12.2.1 *Losses upon Sale:* Net losses from the sale or other distribution of all or substantially all of the Property shall be allocated first to the partners with Positive Capital Accounts, until these Accounts are brought to zero. Thereafter, net losses shall be allocated pro-rata in proportion to the ratio of paragraph 12.1 above.

13. *DISTRIBUTION PROVISIONS:*

At least annually, and upon sale of the Property, the Partnership shall distribute profits, losses, and gains in the following manner:

13.1 *Annual Cash Flow:* After paying regular operational expenses, and retaining a reasonable reserve for future expenses, the Partnership shall distribute any remaining funds, pro-rata, to the Partners, at least annually.

13.2 *Capital Gains:* Upon Sale of the Property, the gross proceeds shall be paid in the following sequence: first to pay for all partnership indebtedness to outside creditors, providing a reasonable reserve for miscellaneous additional Partnership expenses; then second to Partners for their outstanding loans; and then third any remaining cash funds shall be distributed in accordance with paragraph 12 (b) or (c) above.

14.0 *FUTURE FUNDS REQUIREMENTS:*

The Partners recognize the income produced by the Property may be insufficient to pay development and operational costs.

14.1 *Call for Additional Funds:* In the event the Operational Committee determines the Partnership requires funds in excess of the initial capital contributions set forth above, the Partners agree to transfer the required funds to the Partnership in the proportion set forth in paragraph 12(a) within 90 days of the call for funds. The Operational Committee, in accordance with acceptable tax rulings and financial cash flow projections, shall determine if such additional funds shall be considered as a loan or as additional capital investment.

14.2 *Failure to Provide Additional Funds:* In the event a Partner does not make timely payments upon call for additional funds, such Partner shall be deemed in default, and the Defaulting Partner may elect to:

(a) find a Substitute Partner acceptable to the Remaining Partner;

or

(b) find an acceptable Co-partner who will assume all or a portion of the Defaulting Partner's indebtedness to the Partnership. In this event, the proportions of paragraph 12.1 will be modified to reflect the new arrangement, and the vote of the Defaulting Partner on the Operational Committee will be divided pro-rata between the new Co-Partners.

If neither a) nor b) occurs within 90 days, the Remaining Partner may elect:

(c) to declare the entire interest in the Partnership and its Properties to be transferred to the other Remaining Partner, or to another party selected by the Remaining Partner who shall assume the Defaulting Partner's obligations to the Partnership and who shall succeed to the interest of such Defaulting Partner and become a Substitute Partner, whereupon the Defaulting Partner shall be released from further liability to the Partnership;

or

(d) to declare the entire unpaid balance of the capital or loan commitment of the Defaulting Partner as due and payable, without any further demand or call by the Partnership, and thereupon commence legal proceedings against the Defaulting Partner to collect the entire unpaid balance of its capital or loan commitment to the Partnership, plus interst on the unpaid balance at a rate of 12% per annum, and any collection expenses.

15.0 *FINANCIAL ACCOUNTING:*

The Partnership shall maintain an auditable accounting system in accordance with generally accepted accounting practices. The accounting firm shall be Anderson, Arthur, and Price, unless otherwise determined by the Operating Committee. The accounting firm shall provide timely annual statements to the Partners. The Partnership shall hire a person to handle day-to-day accounting and bookkeeping. The fiscal year of the Partnership shall be the calendar year, and the books of the Partnership shall be available at all times for inspection and audit by any Partner at the Partnership's place of business during business hours. The "Tax Matters Partner" shall be Mountain View Company regarding all duties set forth in the Internal Revenue Service Code.

16.0 *TRANSFER AND WITHDRAWAL OF PARTNERSHIP INTEREST:*

Except as provided in this paragraph below, no Partner may sell, assign, or encumber its interest in the Partnership or otherwise withdraw from the Partnership without the prior written consent of the all the other Partners.

16.1 *Withdrawal:* A Partner may withdraw from the Partnership by giving 90 days written notice to the Remaining Partner, which shall automatically provide the Remaining Partner with a 90 day option to purchase the Withdrawing Partner's interests at a purchase price determined as follows:

(a) The purchase price shall be the Withdrawing Partner's prorata share as set forth in paragraph 12.1 of the fair market value of all Partnership assets, minus Partnership liabilities and the aggregate balance to the Partner's Capital Accounts. To this amount shall be added the Withdrawing Partner's Capital Account.

(b) The Partners shall chose a qualified independent appraiser who shall determine the fair market value as of the last day of the month following receipt of request for appraisal. In the event the Partners cannot mutually agree upon an appraiser, each Partner shall name his own appraiser, and the two selected appraisers shall name a third appraiser. The fair market value shall be the average of the appraiser's determinations.

(c) The purchase price shall be payable at a closing within the 90 day period, in cash or by delivery of a promissory note(s) bearing an interest rate of at least 10% per annum, compounded annually, and shall be payable one year following the notice of withdrawal date.

(d) If the property is sold after the notice of withdrawal date, but prior to the promissory note due date, then payment shall be due upon the closing of the sale of the Property.

16.2 *Transfer:* Should the Remaining Partner chose not to purchase the interests of the Withdrawing Partner within 30 days of withdrawal notice, the Withdrawing Partner may request a Substitute Partner to which all rights would be transferred. The Remaining Partner shall have veto rights over acceptance of a Substitute Partner.

16.3 *Dissolution:* In the event the Remaining Partners do not acquire the interests of the Withdrawing Partner and do not accept a Substitute Partner, the Partners shall be deemed to have consented to the dissolution and liquidation of the Partnership.

17.0 *TERMINATION PROVISIONS:*

The Partnership shall be terminated only by the occurance of any of the following events:

17.1 *Term Expiration:* the expiration of the term specified in paragraph 6.

or

17.2 *Bankruptcy:* the bankruptcy, insolvency, or assignment for the benefit of creditors by one of the Partners.

or

17.3 *Sale of Property:* the sale or other disposition or condemnation of all or substantially all of the Property.

or

17.4 *Partner Consent:* the consent of all the Partners.

Upon termination, the Partners shall execute and file all documents necessary.

18.0 *MISCELLANEOUS PROVISIONS*

18.1 *Indemnification:* No Partner or member of the Operating Committee shall be liable in damages to any of the Partners for any loss or damage incurred by reason of act or omission performed or omitted in good faith on behalf of the Partnership and in a manner reasonably believed to be within the scope of the authority granted by this Agreement and in the best interests of the Partnership. The Partnership shall indemnify and save harmless the Partners or members of the Operating Committee from any loss or damage, provided however, the Partner or member of the Operating Committee was not guilty of misconduct, fraud, or bad faith with respect to act or omission.

18.2 *Investment Representation:* Each Partner represents that it is acquiring its intest for its own account, and not with intention for distribution or resale.

18.3 *Amendment:* This Agreement contains the complete agreement of the Partners and may be amended only in writing by unanimous consent of the Partners.

18.4 *Governing Law and Severability:* All provisions of this agreement shall be subject to the provisions of the law for the State of Delaware. If any provisions of this agreement are found invalid or unenforceable, the remainder of the agreement shall not be affected.

18.5 *Notices:* All notices, requests, consents, and statements shall be deemed properly given if deliverd by certified mail within the United States, return receipt requested, and addressed as follows:

MOUNTAIN VIEW:

SEASIDE:

18.6 *Heirs and Successors:* This Agreement shall be binding upon and shall inure to the benefit of the respective heirs, successors, and assigns of the parties hereto.

18.7 *Compliance with State Laws:* Each partner hereby agrees to execute all documents as may be required by the laws of the various state in which the Partnership does business to conform with the

IN WITNESS WHEREOF, the parties hereto set their hands as of the day and year written above:

_____   _____

MOUNTAIN VIEW   SEASIDE

(abridged format courtesy of the Law Firm of Tillinghast, Collins, and Graham)

APPENDIX C. SAMPLE JOINT VENTURE CORPORATION AGREEMENT

INTERNATIONALLY OWNED JOINT VENTURE CORPORATION FOR THE PURPOSE OF ESTABLISHING A BUILDING PRODUCTS COMPANY IN THE UNITED KINGDOM

Table of Contents

Exhibits

AGREEMENT made this ____ day of ____,1988 by and between AMER-ICO SYSTEMS, INC., a corporation duly organized under the laws of the State of Illinois, U.S.A. (hereinafter "Americo") and BRITISH SAXON Limited, a corporation duly organized under the laws of the England (hereinafter "British Saxon").

WHEREAS, Americo is engaged in the business of the manufacture and sale of exterior roofing finish systems both in the United States and internationally, and

WHEREAS, British Saxon is engaged in the business of fabrication and installation of building products in England, and

WHEREAS, Americo and British Saxon desire to enter into an Agreement for the formation of a jointly owned corporation under the laws of the United Kingdom to manufacture, fabricate, sell and install exterior roofing in England.

NOW, THEREFORE, in consideration of the mutual covenants and promises contained herein, the parties agree as follows:

1.0 *DEFINITIONS.*

The following terms shall have the meanings ascribed to them herein whenever they are used in this Agreement unless otherwise clearly indicated by the context.

1.1 *"Articles of Incorporation"* shall mean the articles of incorporation of the Joint Venture Company (JVC).

1.2 *"JVC"* shall mean the Joint Venture Company to be formed pursuant to Article 4 of this Agreement.

1.3 *"Products"* shall mean the products identified in Exhibit "A" attached hereto which are to be processed, fabricated, manufactured and sold by the JVC. Additional products may be added to Exhibit "A" by mutual agreement of the parties.

1.4 *"Propriety Information"* of a party shall mean such technical, engineering, economic, marketing, financial or other information as may be developed by or owned by a party and generally treated as confidential by that party but is not necessarily registerable under pertinent American trademark, patent or copyright law.

1.5. *"Related Agreements"* shall mean such other agreements and documents as are reasonably necessary in order to achieve the purposes of this Agreement referred to in Article 13.

1.6 *"Effective Date"* shall mean the date when this Agreement shall become effective in its entirety in accordance with Article 21 hereof.

1.7 *"Territory"* shall be that territory described and set forth in Exhibit "B," appended hereto and incorporated herein.

2.0 PURPOSE OF THE AGREEMENT

The purpose of this Agreement is to provide for the establishment, ownership, and operation of a Joint Venture Corporation to fabricate and erect Americo and conventional roofing products.

3.0 PURPOSE OF THE JOINT VENTURE CORPORATION

3.1 *General:* The purpose of the JVC will be to manufacture, assemble, and sell systems, and such other products as the parties may agree on, all as set forth in Exhibit "A" annexed hereto and made a part hereof.

3.2 *Services & Products Provided:* Americo Systems, Inc. or its subsidiaries will provide on an "as is needed basis" technical training and field service support. Americo Systems, UK, Ltd. and British Saxon, Ltd. will provide sales support for the JVC. British Saxon, Ltd. will provide, when necessary to JVC, such manufacturing space and personnel as may be necessary to manufacture the systems. The JVC will pay for such space and personnel at the prevailing rental and wage rates. In addition, British Saxon will provide at prevailing rates engineering, architectural erection, and transportation/travel for these personnel.

4.0 THE JOINT VENTURE CORPORATION

4.1 *Establishment:* Promptly after the effective date of this Agreement, Americo and British Saxon shall cooperate to establish the JVC in accordance with the laws of the United Kingdom. The JVC will be named "British Saxon-Americo" or other name as may be agreed if that name shall prove unacceptable to the Registrar of Companies.

4.2 *Memorandum and Articles of Association* shall be as agreed to by and between the parties and shall conform with English legal requirements and the terms and conditions of this Agreement. The Memorandum and Articles of Association shall be binding upon the parties to this Agreement. If any discrepancy is found between this Agreement and the Memorandum and Articles of Association, the terms of this Agreement shall prevail and the parties shall amend the Memorandum and Articles of Association in accordance with this Agreement.

4.3 *Duration:* The duration of the JVC shall be perpetual subject to the provisions of the Articles of Incorporation and of this Agreement.

4.4 *Enforcement:* As soon as reasonably possible after the establishment of the JVC, the parties shall cause the JVC to execute this Agreement whereby the terms and conditions of this Agreement shall become enforceable by and against the JVC as if it were an original signatory hereto.

5.0 CAPITAL SUBSCRIPTION

5.1 *Capital:* At the time of the organization and registration of the JVC, the JVC shall have an authorized capital of $000,000.00. Capital stock shall be divided into 00000000 common shares of the voting stock of JVC. Each share of capital stock shall have no par value.

5.2 *Shares:* At the time of organization and registration of the JVC, the JVC shall issue 0000000 shares being equal proportions of "A" and "B" shares.

  i. Americo shall subscribe for 0000 "A"shares;

  ii. British Saxon shall subscribe for 0000 "B"shares.

5.3 *Subscription:* The shares which shall be issued under Article 5.2 hereof shall be subscribed to within 60 days of the signing of this agreement as prescribed by the laws of the United Kingdom.

5.4 *Proportion of Ownership:* Unless the parties otherwise agree in writing, it is intended that the ownership of the stocks of the corporation shall be in equal shares: Americo Systems, Inc. 50%, British Saxon, Ltd. 50%.

6.0 SHARE CERTIFICATES

6.1 *Form:* The share certificates which are to be issued by the JVC shall be in non-bearer form.

6.2 *Transfer Limitation:* During the terms of this Agreement, each share certificate issued hereunder shall bear the following legend:

"Transfer of the shares of stock represented by this certificate is subject to a Joint Venture Agreement between Americo and British Saxon signed __(date)__"

7.0 PREEMPTIVE RIGHTS

7.1 *New Issue Rights:* Shareholders of the JVC shall have preemptive rights with respect to any new issue of shares of the JVC.

7.2 *Termination:* Should British Saxon sell 25% or more of its stock to a competitor of Americo, Americo shall have the right to terminate its license to the JVC and exercise any termination options pursuant to Article 18.3.

8.0 TRANSFER OF SHARES

8.1 *Offering:* If either party hereto desires to sell or transfer all or any part of its shares in the JVC, such party ("selling party") shall offer all such shares by written notice first to the other party (offeree party) specifying price, terms and conditions of sale. The offeree party may accept this offer with regard to all of the offered shares or may designate one or more persons or legal entities ("designee") who are entitled to purchase all of the offered shares in lieu of the offeree party. If the offeree party or designee does not accept all of the offered shares within 60 days from the date of such notice (acceptance), then the selling party shall thereafter be free to dispose of all of its shares within a period of three months ("free sale period") after the expiration of said acceptance period; provided, however, that the selling party shall not sell such shares to any third party at (a) a lower price than the price which such shares were offered to the offeree party and/or its designee and (b) on other terms or conditions more favorable than those offered to the offeree party or its designee. If all of the shares are not sold or transferred to third parties upon the terms established herein and within the free sale period, then they shall automatically become subject once more to the terms of this article as if they had never before been offered for sale; provided, however, if either party is required to sell or transfer any portion of its shares of the JVC pursuant to any order of a court or other governmental agency that party shall be free to sell or transfer such portion of its shares free of the restrictions.

8.2 *Sale:* Notwithstanding 8.1 above, each party may without restriction sell or transfer its shares in the JVC to a wholly owned subsidiary or holding company as defined by the Companies Act of 1985 provided that such a party shall:

(i) purchase or otherwise recover ownership of all the said shares whenever its subsidiary ceases to exist and

(ii) the subsidiary shall be bound by all provisions of this agreement and the related agreements to the same extent as the party who transferred the shares.

8.3 *Agreement to Terms and Conditions:* If either party hereto shall sell or otherwise transfer all or any part of its shares to an affiliate or to a third party, such selling party shall cause the party acquiring such shares as a condition of such acquisition to furnish a written undertaking to the other parties and the JVC agreeing to observe and be bound by all terms and conditions of this Agreement.

8.4 *Rights to Disapprove:* Each party agrees to notify the other in writing of the identity of any entity to which the selling party proposes to sell any of the shares of the JVC in accordance with this Article at least 60 days before the proposed sale is made. Each party hereto reserves the right to disapprove the sale, assignment or transfer of shares of the JVC under any of the following circumstances:

(a) such third party is engaged in a business or activity which is in direct competition with the JVC, the disapproving party or its affiliate,

or

(b) such third party does not have sufficient financial standing to be able to guarantee on its own credit the proportionate amount of the outstanding guaranteed debts, if any, of the JVC,

or

(c) such third party is otherwise engaged in a business or activity which conflicts with the products fabricated, manufactured and sold by the JVC.

8.5 *Involuntary Transfer:* No party shall pledge or hypothecate the shares of the JVC or otherwise use such shares as collateral or for any other purpose which could result in an involuntary transfer or assignment of such shares to third parties unless consent to such pledge or hypothecation is given by the other parties.

9.0 *GENERAL MEETING OF SHAREHOLDERS*

The Board of Directors, in accordance with the requirements of the Companies Act of 1985, shall decide the time and place for convening and the matters to be transacted in all general meetings of shareholders. The notice of all general meetings of shareholders shall be given to each shareholder in the manner prescribed by the Memorandum and Articles of Association.

10.0 BOARD OF DIRECTORS

10.1 *Number of Directors:* Americo and British Saxon shall exercise their respective voting rights so as to procure:

(a) The Board of Directors of the JVC shall consist of five members. Two shall be nominated by Americo; two shall be nominated by British Saxon. Each party shall procure the nomination and election of parties nominated by the other party provided that such nominee is not prohibited from appointment under the Companies Act of 1985. The fifth member shall be the Chairman.

(b) The Chairman of the Board of Directors shall be nominated alternatively by the "A" and "B" shareholders for twelve month periods. The Chairman for the first twelve months shall be nominated by British Saxon. Each party shall procure the appointment of the other's nominee. The Chairman shall not have a casting vote. The "A" shareholders and "B" shareholders shall each nominate two members of the Board of Directors set forth herein. Each member of the Board shall have one vote.

(c) If either British Saxon or Americo wishes to change any of its nominated directors with or without cause, the other party will vote accordingly provided, however, that if such dismissal gives rise to a claim for damages, the party proposing such dismissal shall indemnify and hold the JVC and the other party harmless for any and all damages and other expenses that may arise from such action.

10.2 *Duties of Chairman:* The Chairman shall preside over all meetings of shareholders and Board of Directors meetings.

10.3 *Meetings* of the Board of Directors shall ordinarily be called at the request of the Chairman when deemed necessary or advisable or when any director so requests. The notice of Board of Director's meeting shall be given to each director in accordance with the Articles of Association.

11.0 FISCAL YEAR AND BOOKS OF ACCOUNT

11.1 *Commencement:* The fiscal year of the JVC shall commence on January 1st of each year and end on December 31 of the same year, provided, however, that the first fiscal year of the JVC shall commence as of the date of organization of the JVC pursuant to Article 4.1 hereof and end on the following December 31st.

11.2 *Bookkeeping:* The JVC shall keep accurate books of account and financial and related records in accordance with the requirements of English law and with generally accepted accounting principles, standards and procedures consistently.

11.3 *Audit:* At the end of each annual fiscal year of the JVC, the books of account and records of the JVC shall be audited at the expense of the JVC by the independent auditor. The independent auditor shall prepare for and supply to British Saxon and Americo certified balance sheets, profit and loss statements and other financial reports suitable for use by each of the parties hereto in connection with its financial and tax reports.

11.4 *Auditor:* The JVC shall have one independent auditor. The auditor for the first year shall be the firm of Scrooge & Marley.

11.5 *Dividends:* shall be paid within two months after the declaration of dividends as resolved at the general meeting of shareholders unless otherwise agreed by the parties.

12.0 *FINANCING*

12.1 *Advances:* If the JVC requires funds in excess of the paid-in capital, such funds shall be financed by advices made to the JVC by Americo and British Saxon in equal amounts as needed to a initial maximum amount of $000,000.00.

The JVC will carry these amounts as obligations on its books of account. Repayments need not be made towards this amount during the first year of operation; however, no distribution of profits shall be made to any of the parties until these advances have been repaid.

12.2 *Additional Funds:* Each party shall assist the JVC in obtaining funds through credit. To the extent the JVC requires funds in excess of those funds obtained by the means described in Article 12.1 above, each party shall assume responsibility as guarantor in proportion to its share of equity interest in the JVC.

12.3 *Documentation:* The parties agree that no officer, director or other employee of the JVC shall execute an agreement, negotiable instrument, minutes or any other document on behalf of the JVC which document is incomplete in terms of amount or due dates of obligations or in any other material respect unless expressly authorized by the Board of Directors.

13.0 RELATED AGREEMENTS

13.1 *Licenses and Trademarks:* Americo and/or its affiliates shall grant to the JVC such licenses as may be necessary, including trademarks and designs for the JVC to manufacture, market and distribute products within its territory.

13.2 *Quality Standards:* The JVC shall take all necessary measures to insure that both Americo's trademarks, designs and tradenames are used only with respect to products meeting the quality standards of Americo for all such products.

14.0 CONFIDENTIALITY OF INFORMATION

14.1 *Precautions:* Each party hereto agrees to keep secret and confidential all proprietary information and other information obtained from the other party hereto or the JVC which is designated or may be considered as confidential by other party or the JVC as the case may be. The parties agree to take all necessary precautions in a manner acceptable to the party furnishing the proprietary information or confidential information to keep secret such information and to restrict its uses.

14.2 *Compliance:* The JVC shall take all necessary steps to insure that its directors, officers, employees, agents and subcontractors will comply in all respects with this Article 14 and with the specifications and directives regarding the application, construction and erection of JVC products.

14.3 *Return of Information:* At the expiration of the JVC, each party shall hand back to the other, all documentation, data, etc. containing the other's confidential or proprietary information and undertake not to make use of it. Information which is general knowledge (as of the date of the agreement) or which was known to the other party before the agreement or becomes so known during the agreement without breach of the confidentiality undertaken in the agreement shall be excluded from the definition of "confidential information".

15.0 NONCOMPETITION

During the term of this Agreement, neither party shall, within the territory, engage in a business nor enter into any business relationship with any other entity or person any of which will directly compete with or has material adverse effect on the business of the JVC, except those businesses the parties presently are engaged in or as they may otherwise agree.

16.0 *PAYMENT OF DEBTS AND TAXES*

If any shareholder of the JVC does pay any debt including unpaid tax obligations of the JVC then the shareholder making such payment is entitled to be indemnified by any and all other shareholders of the JVC to the extent that those other shareholders have not borne a proportion of the debt equal to their proportionate share of equity ownership in the JVC. Ownership percentages are to be measured as of the date the JVC became liable for the obligation. The shareholders shall use their best efforts to cause the JVC to reimburse the shareholders for any amounts paid by the shareholders on behalf of the JVC.

17.0 *COMPENSATION OF OFFICERS AND EMPLOYEES*

17.1 *Board Approval:* The officers of the JVC shall receive compensation in accordance with terms approved by the Board of Directors.

17.2 *Annual Review:* Salaries, bonuses and other benefits of the officers and employees of the JVC, if any, shall be reviewed annually by the parties in consultation with the Directors of the JVC and will be based upon performance and earnings of the JVC.

17.3 *Managing Director* will be hired by the JVC not later than December 31, 1988. The Managing Director shall be selected by mutual agreement of Americo and British Saxon and his or her salary and expenses will be the responsibility of the Joint Venture.

18.0 *TERM AND TERMINATION*

18.1 *Commencement:* The term of this Agreement shall begin as of the effective date and shall continue in force for an indefinite term thereafter until the JVC shall be dissolved or otherwise cease.

18.2 *Termination:* This Agreement is terminable by either party if any enactment of law or regulation either state, federal or municipal, in the reasonable opinion of the party:

(i) makes performance of this agreement and/or any related agreements impossible or unreasonably expensive or unreasonably difficult for the party,

or

(ii) alters the rights and obligations of the parties,

and/or

(iii) interferes with the benefits contemplated by this Agreement and/or related agreements

In addition to the foregoing, this Agreement is terminable under any of the following conditions:

(a) by either party if the other party shall commit a breach of any of its obligations under this Agreement which shall not be remedied within 60 days from the giving of written notice requiring said breach to be remedied;

(b) by either party if the other shall become incapable for a period of 90 days for performing any of its said obligations under this Agreement because of force majeure as defined in Article 21.4 hereof;

(c) by either party if either party or its creditors or any other eligible party shall file for the other party's liquidation, bankruptcy, reorganization, or dissolution or if the other party is unable to pay any debts as they become due, has explicitly or implicitly suspended payment of any debts as they become due (except debts contested in good faith) or if the creditors of the other party have taken over its management or if the relevant financial institutions have suspended the other party's ability to borrow, or if any material of significant part of the other party's undertaking, property or assets shall be placed in the hands of a receiver or other trustee for the benefit of creditors;

(d) by either party if the warranties or representations made to the party pursuant to this Agreement and/or Related Agreements are found to be false or misleading, or if any of the covenants made therein for the benefit of the party are not complied with, and such non-compliance is not remedied within sixty (60) days of receipt of written notice from the party not in default;

(e) by either party if any Related Agreement is terminated for any reason other than expiration.

18.3 *Options upon Termination:* If this Agreement is terminated pursuant to (b), (d) or (e) of Article 18.2 above, the party not subject to such clauses shall have the option upon written notice to the other party within 30 days after termination:

(i) to purchase all of the shares of the other party within 60 days of the completion of the appraisal by an independent auditor at the cost of the JVC, or

(ii) to sell all of its shares to the other party at fair market value as determined by an independent auditor, or

(iii)   to proceed to the dissolution of the JVC.

A fair market value of shares for purposes of this Article shall be not less than the proportion of the net worth of the JVC represented by such shares. A contract for the sale and purchase of shares shall be deemed to have been entered into upon the dispatch of written notice to the other party of the election of the terminating party to exercise the option under(i).

18.4 *Arbitration:* If this Agreement is terminated pursuant to the provisions of Article 18, the parties agree to submit disputes arising under this Section to arbitration in accordance with the provisions of the Arbitration Act.

18.5 *Force Majeure:* This Agreement may also be terminated pursuant to Article 21.4. (force majeure). In such case, the parties shall proceed to the dissolution of the JVC unless they agree to a sale of the shares to one party or a third party.

18.6 *Trademarks:* If this Agreement is terminated for any reason whatsoever, the JVC and/or British Saxon shall not use any trademark or tradename of "Americo".

19.0 *REPRESENTATIONS AND WARRANTIES*

19.1 *General:* Americo and British Saxon each represent and warrant that:

(a)   it is a corporation, duly organized, validly existing and in good standing of the laws of the competent jurisdiction.

(b)   it has all necessary corporate power and authority to enter into this Agreement and to perform all of the obligations to be performed by and hereunder.

(c) this Agreement constitutes valid, legally binding obligations of each party enforceable against each party in accordance with its terms.

(d)   this Agreement and the consummation of the transactions contemplated hereby have been duly authorized, approved by and on behalf of the party to enter into this Agreement and to perform all of the obligations to be performed by and hereunder.

(e) this Agreement constitutes valid, legally binding obligations of each party enforceable against each party in accordance with its terms.

(f)   this Agreement and the consumation of the transactions contemplated hereby have been duly approved by all requisite corporate action.

(g)   the execution and delivery of this Agreement and the consummation of the transactions contemplated hereby in the fulfillment of and compliance with the terms and conditions hereof do not:

(i)   violate any judicial or administrative order, award, judgment or decree applicable to the party, or

(ii)   conflict with the terms, conditions, or provisions of the Articles of Incorporation or by-laws of the party.

19.2   *Hold Harmless:* Each party agrees to hold the ot' er party harmless and to indemnify the other party against any and a.. ..abilities, losses, costs, damages, attorney's fees, finder's fees, commissions or expenses which the other party may sustain by reason of the breach of any of the warranties set forth in this Article.

20.0 *NOTICE*

Notices required or permitted to be given hereunder shall be in writing, shall be valid and sufficient if dispatched by registered mail, postage pre-paid, delivered personally or sent by telex or cable, confirmed by letter sent the same day to the other party.

If to Americo:

If to British Saxon:

21.0 *MISCELLANEOUS PROVISIONS*

21.1   *Governing Law:* This Agreement shall be governed by the substantive and procedural laws of England.

21.2   *Force Majeure:* A party hereto shall not be liable to the other party for any loss, injury, delay, damages, expenses or costs suffered or incurred by that other party arising from any cause including (but without limitation) strikes, riots, storms, fires, explosions, Acts of God, war, action of any government, or any her cause beyond the reasonable control ("force majeure") of the party who would otherwise be liable. Failure or delay of either party hereto in performance of any of its obligations under this Agreement due to one or more of the foregoing causes shall not be considered a breacn of this Agreement. The party suffering such force majeure shall notify the other party in writing within 14 days after the occurrence of such force majeure and shall to the extent reasonable and lawful use his best efforts to remove or remedy such causes.

21.3 *Attorney Fees:* Each party shall bear its own attorney's fees and other expenses incurred to execute this Agreement.

21.4 *JVC Fees:* All fees related to incorporation of the JVC including but not limited to attorney's fees and fees paid to governmental bodies shall be borne by the JVC and paid out of its initial capital.

21.5 *Entire Agreement:* This Agreement embodies the entire agreement of the parties with respect to the subject matter hereof and supersedes and cancels any and all prior understandings or agreements verbal or otherwise, in relation hereto which may exist between the parties. No oral explanation or oral information by either of the parties hereto shall alter the meaning or interpretation of this Agreement. No amendment or change hereof or addition hereto shall be effective or binding on either of the parties hereto unless reduced to writing and executed by the respective, duly authorized representatives of each of the parties hereto.

21.6 *Severability:* In the event any term or provisions of this Agreement shall for any reason be invalid, illegal or unenforceable in any respect, either party adversely affected hereby shall have the right either to terminate this Agreement by giving at least 30 days prior notice to the other party or to declare by such notice that such invalidity, illegality or unenforceability shall not affect any other term provisions hereof.

IN WITNESS WHEREOF, the parties hereto have caused this Agreement to be executed by the respective officers thereunto duly authorized as of the date first herein above written.

_____   _____

AMERICO SYSTEMS, INC.   BRITISH SAXON, LTD.

EXHIBIT A: ADDITIONAL PRODUCTS

EXHIBIT B: TERRITORY

EXHIBIT C: ARTICLES OF INCORPORATION

(Abridged format courtesy of the law firm of Breslin, Sweeney & Earle)

APPENDIX D. SAMPLE CONFIDENTIALITY AND NONDISCLOSURE AGREEMENT

SAMPLE CONFIDENTIALITY AND NONDISCLOSURE AGREEMENT

This Agreement is made between _____ (the DISCLOSING Party), a corporation headquartered at _____ and _____ as an individual and in his/her representative capacity of _____ (the RECIPIENT party), a corporation headquartered at _____, having the full authority to so bind the RECIPIENT party to this contract.

WHEREAS the DISCLOSING party agrees to reveal Confidential and proprietary technical information, and

WHEREAS the nature of the technology is sufficiently sensitive as to require the RECIPIENT party to agree, in advance, not to disclose the technology to others without the expressed permission of the DISCLOSING party,

NOW, THEREFORE, the parties agree to the mutual covenants contained herein as follows:

1.0 *CONFIDENTIAL INFORMATION:*

The Confidential Information disclosed relates to: _____

_____

2.0 *CONTROL:*

This Confidential Information has been disclosed to: _____ and may be further disclosed to: _____ after they sign this Agreement. No other persons, firms, or corporations may be informed of this information without the expressed permission of the DISCLOSING party and the signing of this Agreement, and no copies of any written/printed material may be made without the DISCLOSING party's consent.

3.0 *DERIVATIVE WORKS:*

In the event that the DISCLOSING party and the RECIPIENT party agree to engage in future business activities, as a Joint Venture or otherwise, the source data and any further inventions derived from the source data shall be the property of the DISCLOSING party, unless otherwise agreed by the parties.

4.0 *TERM OF AGREEMENT:*

This Agreement shall remain in effect until the earlier of:

(a) Filing of Patent, Copyright, or similar documentation with the U.S. Patent Office

(b) Public Disclosure of the technology,

(c) _____ years from the date of the signing of this Agreement

5.0 *EXCLUSIONS:*

The parties hereto agree that the information shall not be deemed Confidential and the RECIPIENT party shall have no obligation with respect to any such information which:

(a) is already known to the RECIPIENT party, or

(b) is or becomes publicly known through no wrongful act of the RECIPIENT party, or

(c) is rightfully received from a third party without similar restriction and without breach of this Agreement, or

(d) is independently developed by the RECIPIENT party without breech of this Agreement, or

(e) is approved for release by written authorization of the DISCLOSING party, or

(f) is disclosed pursuant to the requirement of a Governmental agency.

6.0 *IDENTIFICATION:*

All Confidential material will be stamped on the front page clearly identifying to the RECIPIENT party that material which the DISCLOSING party deems Confidential or proprietary.

7.0 *LIABILITY:*

The parties agree that the RECIPIENT party shall not be liable for:

(a) inadvertant disclosure provided that:

(i) it uses the same degree of care in safeguarding such Confidential information as it uses for its own Confidential information of like importance, and

(ii) upon discovery of such inadvertant disclosure, it shall endeavor to prevent further inadvertant disclosure, and

(iii) such inadvertant disclosure, upon becoming known to the RECIPIENT party, is reported promptly to the DISCLOSING party,

(b) unauthorized disclosure or use by unauthorized persons who are or who have been in its employ, unless it fails to safeguard such information with the same degree of care as it uses for its own Confidential information of like importance.

8.0 *OWNERSHIP:*

All written data delivered by the DISCLOSING party to the RECIPIENT party pursuant to this Agreement shall be and remain the property of the DISCLOSING party, and, should a Joint Venture, or other similar business association not be consummated, all such written data shall be promptly returned to the DISCLOSING party upon written request, or destroyed at the DISCLOSING party's option.

9.0 *LIMITATION:*

Nothing contained in the Agreement shall be construed as granting or conferring any rights or license under any patent or copyright or any right to claim compensation or royalty for any invention, discovery, or improvement made, conceived, or acquired prior to or after the date of this Agreement.

IN WITNESS WHEREOF, the parties hereto have executed this Agreement this _____ day of _____ 19 _____.

_____   _____
DISCLOSING PARTY   RECIPIENT PARTY

APPENDIX E. SAMPLE NONCOMPETITION AGREEMENT

SAMPLE NONCOMPETITION AGREEMENT

This Agreement is made between SPHERE Technology, Inc. (SPHERE), headquartered in _____ and GLOBAL Marketing Resources, Inc. (GLOBAL), headquartered in _____.

WHEREAS SPHERE is engaged in the design, development, and manufacture of various computer products, and

WHEREAS GLOBAL is involved in the marketing and selling worldwide of various computer technologies, and

WHEREAS SPHERE and GLOBAL have entered into a JOINT VENTURE AGREEMENT dated _____ whereby SPHERE will manufacture computer products and GLOBAL will serve as marketing and sales agent for products developed by SPHERE, and

WHEREAS SPHERE and GLOBAL have previously executed a CONFIDENTIALITY & NON-DISCLOSURE AGREEMENT dated _____, and desire to enter into this Agreement to protect the business interests of the parties, and

WHEREAS the parties are willing to execute this Agreement and be bound by its provisions,

NOW, THEREFORE, the parties agree to the mutual covenants contained herein as follows:

1.0 *DEFINITIONS:*

1.1 *Confidential Information* is any information disclosed or obtained by GLOBAL from SPHERE as a result of or relating to its relationship to SPHERE as defined by the Confidentiality Agreement.

1.2 *Proprietary Techniques:* If at any time during the course of GLOBAL's involvement with SPHERE, GLOBAL conceives, develops, participates in the development of, or causes to be developed any products, programs, methods, techniques, inventions, improvements or any other processes or formulae, whether or not patentable, relating to the business or products of SPHERE, such proprietary techniques shall remain or become the exclusive property of SPHERE and shall be deemed Proprietary Information included in the Confidentiality Agreement. GLOBAL waives any and all rights and royalties to any such Proprietary Techniques.

1.3 *Term of Service:* GLOBAL's terms and conditions of service shall be as set forth in the Joint Venture Agreement.

2.0 *DISCLOSURE*

During the term of GLOBAL's service as marketing and sales agent, GLOBAL shall not, without prior written consent of SPHERE, copy or cause to be copied any document or other material or disclose, directly or indirectly, any Confidential or Proprietary Information except in the ordinary course of business, and in accordance with the terms and conditions of the Confidentiality Agreement.

3.0 *COMPETITION*

3.1 *Limitations:* During the term of GLOBAL's service as sales and marketing agent, and for one year thereafter, GLOBAL and its management shall not, without SPHERE's prior written consent:

> (a) Be an officer, director, partner, sole proprietor, agent, employee, or holder of securities (except the holder of 5% or less of securities listed on the New York or American Stock Exchanges) or principal of, or consultant to, or independent contractor with any business that is in competition with SPHERE in any geographic region in which SPHERE regularly conducts its business, or

> (b) engage in any research, development, production, manufacturing, consulting, marketing, or any other activity relating to any and all products the same as or similar in function or performance to those under research, in development, developed, produced, manufactured, or marketed by SPHERE.

3.2 *Discontinued Products and Services:* Should SPHERE discontinue the manufacture of any of its products or withdraw or limit any if its services contrary to the written advice and desire of GLOBAL, then GLOBAL shall be released from the terms and conditions of this agreement for that specific product or service, and may establish whatever business relationships are required to fulfill any of GLOBAL's existing or potential customer requirements.

4.0 *SOLICITATION OF EMPLOYEES*

During the term of GLOBAL's service, and for one year thereafter, GLOBAL shall not, without SPHERE's prior written consent, solicit or discuss with any person who is or was an employee of SPHERE's the employment by any business or other entity (other than an accredited academic or research institution), that conducts research, develops technologies, or manufactures or markets any products or techniques or provides services similar to those developed, produced, manufactured, or provided by SPHERE, or be an employer, directly or indirectly, of a SPHERE employee.

5.0 SOLICITATION OF CUSTOMERS

During the term of GLOBAL's service, and for one year thereafter, GLOBAL shall not, without SPHERE's prior written consent, solicit or accept from any corporation, company, or person, or affiliate of such entities, who was a client or customer of SPHERE's at any time prior to the signing of this Agreement, any business with respect to any and all of SPHERE's products and services.

6.0 EQUITABLE REMEDIES

GLOBAL acknowledges that because of the nature of the business of SPHERE, a breach of any of the provisions of this Agreement will cause irreparable injury to SPHERE for which monetary damages will not provide an adequate remedy, and GLOBAL agrees that SPHERE shall have the right to have any provisions of this Agreement enforced by any court with proper jurisdiction.

IN WITNESS WHEREOF, the parties hereto have executed this Agreement this _____day of _____19_____.

_____   _____

for SPHERE   For GLOBAL

APPENDIX F. JOINT VENTURE
CASE STUDY

TRI-WALL CORPORATION

Contents

by Bernard Roth, former Vice President of Marketing
and Strategic Planning

1.1 *SITUATION*

1.0 *Date:* 1961

1.2 *Product:* Corrugated Fiberboard Boxes

1.3 *Location:* One plant in Upstate New York

1.4 *Strategic Advantage:* Patents on a proprietary triple-wall corrugated construction for boxes with light weight, high stacking strength, weather resistance, high shock absorbency. Very suitable for heavy industrial export packaging. Excellent replacement for wooden crates.

1.5 *Product Mix:* ⅓ production devoted to proprietary corrugated product; ⅔ production devoted to normal corrugated boxes

1.6 *Profitability:* Loss or marginal business on normal boxes; high profit on "Triple-Wall" product, company is only marginally profitable, but has great promise. No debt, but little net worth.

1.7 *Sales:* $3 million, concentrated in Eastern United States

1.8 *Basic Manufacturing Process:* A paper mill manufactures rolls of paper, which are sent to a "corrugator" which creates the layers of corrugation in very large sheets. Then the sheets are brought to a "sheet" plant (sometimes integrated with the corrugator, and sometimes in another location), where the sheets are scored, printed, slotted, cut, and glued or stapled into completed boxes.

2.0 *STRATEGIC FACTORS*

2.1 Opportunities for Worldwide Expansion:

2.1.1 *Solid patents, legally strong overseas patent filings, and value-added marketing techniques.*

2.1.2 Product that competitors cannot make if Tri-Wall had a fire or a union strike.

2.1.3 Proprietary set of marketing/sales methods that can be "transferred" to other industrial regions characterized by either heavy exports and imported wood for packaging, or by long distance freight hauling by road or by rail. Manufacturing tech-

371

niques can be transferred to a conventional corrugating plant with some minor technical modifications.

2.1.4 Fortune 500 customers who want the product to serve their new trading areas, with local foreign counterparts could be induced to use because: "*Kodak, DuPont, GE, IBM, GM, Ford, etc. used the Tri-Wall product.*"

2.1.5 While many major U.S. competitors are consolidating into larger business units, this form of consolidation is proceeding more slowly overseas, with a five-year lag over U.S. consolidation. Tri-Wall has a history to show overseas partners.

2.2 Barriers to Expansion

2.2.1 No depth in middle management for either domestic or overseas expansion.

2.2.2 Little knowledge of commercial law, administrative practices in target regions—UK, Europe, Japan, Australia, Eastern Mediterranean, Canada or South America. (Eventually South America was rejected because manufacturing exports, GNP per capita, etc. were deemed too low to offer a reasonable risk/reward ratio.)

2.2.3 *Large competing corrugators are:*

(a) already integrated with paper mills

(b) "fixated" on tonnage through their plant (objective: operating efficiency instead of profit).

(c) consolidating and price cutting (which makes smaller, conventional corrugators unprofitable and run at a loss unless there is an attached paper mill).

(d) management is monolithic, many layers, and slow to make decisions.

2.2.4 Starting up a new Tri-Wall plant from scratch would cost about $3 million. Tri-Wall's $300K net worth would require high financial leveraging, which, at the time, would involve very high risk until enough sales volume (60% capacity) was attained to reach break-even. New corrugator plants take one year to build, although equipment to augment an existing plant was readily available on short notice.

3.0 STRATEGIC PLAN—North America

Expand Strategic Alliances until Tri-Wall is ready to add its own plants in West, Mid-West, and Canada. Tri-Wall wants to find major paper suppliers willing to modify their existing corrugating plants and make Tri-Wall's product:

3.1 *Mid-West (1962):* Find a paper supplier to make complete finished boxes for Tri-Wall's Mid-West sales force. At appropriate volume time, Tri-Wall would build a sheet plant to score, print, and join boxes in the Mid-West, and only take corrugated sheet from the paper company. Eventually Tri-Wall would add full corrugating capacity to the sheet plant. Added advantage to Tri-Wall was the use of enough paper annually to negotiate a better price than published prices. International Paper is the chosen partner, and the alliance is consummated on a handshake and a short memo, but no formal legal documents.

International Paper gets:
· the added paper tonnage to achieve better efficiency
· a small converting profit

Tri-Wall gets:
· a source of finished product in Mid-West market with no immediate capital expense
· a better price on paper because it now uses higher volumes

Tri-Wall eventually builds its sheet plant, which is supplied with corrugated paper by both International Paper in the Mid-West and by Tri-Wall's home plant in upstate New York. A year before the expected time to add corrugator capabilities to the sheet plant, Tri-Wall decides to order construction and equipment just before a major boost in inflation would have increased costs 10%.

3.2 *California (1965):* Tri-Wall leases an abandoned sheeting plant in California, partially equips it with proprietary technology for printing and joining boxes, at a cost of $250K, takes in sheets scored and cut to width and length at International Paper's plant in San Jose, and converts into boxes.

International Paper gets:
· the added paper tonnage
· a small converting profit
· a lease for a plant that had been written off due to ruinous competition

Tri-Wall gets:

- a building with a nominal lease payment which could eventually be applied to a future purchase price
- a source of sheet 3,000 miles closer to the West Coast markets
- a sales force expansion to the West Coast (Tri-Wall does market research to insure enough business for West Coast plant, and eventual conversion to full corrugator plant.)

The alliance works under the terms of a loose arrangement, with a transfer price mechanism for sheet based on published prices of paper.

3.3 *Canada:* While very close physically and politically to U.S., many aspects are different. Tri-Wall's Canadian distributor in Ontario, adding sales offices in Quebec, Ontario, and Vancouver, is best opportunity for alliance.

As tariff walls come down, more imports were transported by rail between the U.S. and Canada. Tri-Wall participates with its Canadian distributor who also owns a plant with manual box finishing equipment (low set-up costs) capable of smaller runs of 20–30 boxes, which are excellent for samples, small orders, and special custom configurations. Tri-Wall eventually buys out the manufacturer/distributor when he wishes to retire, continuing his varied packaging business.

3.4 *License:* International Paper, who has participated in the U.S. strategic alliance, asks for a license to sell Tri-Wall's boxes, which Tri-Wall is loathe to grant, even with a royalty.

However, patent law requires granting of the license. Tri-Wall offers sales training (which is declined), gives a limited geography, states potential sales prospects, and provides a license to sell for one year, at the end of which Tri-Wall and IP will mutually assess results. None of the target accounts are penetrated by International Paper in the twelve-month period. After dropping the license, Tri-Wall's sales force is introduced to the target accounts and eventually converts seven out of ten key accounts to Tri-Wall customers.

Thereafter, as a defensive measure (Tri-Wall has large competitors infringing on its patents), the International Paper sales force introduces Tri-Wall to potential Tri-Wall applications, and IP salesmen receive sales credit from IP for the "tonnage."

4.0 *STRATEGIC PLAN—Overseas*

4.1 *Strategy:* Find strategic joint venture partners in areas prioritized by market size—Europe, UK, Japan, Australia, Israel. Flexible timing, and the ideal sequence is desired but not critical.

Note: UK would be easier because of lower language and administrative barriers, but UK is a much smaller market than Europe (the Common Market had just begun, and UK is still "outside"). Best location in Europe is Alsace, because it is logistically centralized. Best tax laws are in Switzerland, but it is outside the Common Market, and work permits are highly restricted for expatriates.

4.2 *Finding Partners:*

4.2.1 *Attributes of Partner:*

(a) Should have a corrugating plant with space to add augmented equipment

(b) Capacity on the corrugating production line to take the Tri-Wall product

(c) Family-owned for ease in decision making. Owners should be entrepreneurial, to enable them to see Tri-Wall vision without layers of bureaucratic decision making

(d) High quality output essential

(e) Marketing force in place (if possible)

4.2.2 *Methods of Finding Partners:* In Europe, Tri-Wall finds "targets" during a market research project performed by a small international consulting firm. Tri-Wall's Vice President of Strategic Planning partakes in about 10% of the field work. Library research is augmented with prospect data on volume, competing product costs, and acceptance in a variety of countries and industries within Europe. The objectives are to find target manufacturers and distributors in each country then have an initial visit to determine mutuality of interest, "chemistry" between CEOs, and local manufacturing costs and constraints between the newly formed Common Market countries.

Similar studies are done in-house by TW International, a holding company set up after the second joint venture to manage all international operations. The VP of Strategic Planning performs the study for Israel, and others in the firm for Japan and Australia, using the same pattern set up for UK and Europe.

4.2.3 *Benefits to Offer Sales Prospects:* To speed acceptance by prospects, and to convert prospects to large orders more rapidly, Tri-Wall offers technical people abroad to:
· Inspect trial shipments arriving by ship or air
· Follow shipments to their destination and
· Report on the shipment's condition after the package arrived

4.2.4 *Deal Structure:* Start a new Joint Venture Marketing Company with 50–50 ownership, which would target the designated region, staffed "lean and mean" with marketing/sales personnel, financial record keeping and administrative people. Tri-Wall would invest roughly as much in establishing and supporting the sales organization as the manufacturer would invest in machinery and equipment to bring their plant to Tri-Wall specs.

While Tri-Wall's cash is expended and irretrievable if the venture fails, the European manufacturer has the added equipment and new manufacturing know-how from Tri-Wall. Tri-Wall's patents are licensed to the marketing company, with rights to sub-license all manufacturing to its partner.

The transfer price of boxes between partner's manufacturing company and the Joint Venture Manufacturing company was pegged at 1% over manufactured cost (defined as labor—with productivity standards based on Tri-Wall's U.S. standards—materials at published/invoiced prices, overhead at a specified ratio to labor costs as found in the manufacturing partner's normal mix). Audit work would be performed by a "Big Eight" branch jointly agreed to, and the audit firm would mediate any transfer cost disputes. The manufacturing partner has right to decline incremental production if he could prove that he could make more profit on his own products overall. Life of the agreement is for fifteen years, with extensions of ten years by mutual consent.

The Board of Directors of the Joint Venture Company would be 50–50, and profits will be split 50–50. The Joint Venture partners will guarantee the debt of the new company up to an agreed amount, or at a ratio to sales. The Manufacturing Partner will be trained in Tri-Wall's product manufacture and quality control. Any innovations created by the Joint Venture Company will be jointly owned by both partners, and either partner and the Joint Venture Company will be free to use the technology. New patents on similar products would be licensed to the Joint Venture company by Tri-Wall. Tri-Wall will be responsible for recruiting, hiring, managing, and training sales application engineers for the Joint Venture Company. Deadlocks would be solved by patience and consensus.

Basic territory is to be UK or Europe or Australia. Tri-Wall

(U.S.) has power to approve or deny expansion to any joint venture to outside defined territory. For example: a plant in Russia can be owned by U.S. or by the European Joint Venture, at Tri-Wall's (U.S.) pleasure. Similarly, the Japanese Joint Venture can only expand into China, Taiwan, etc. with U.S. approval.

The entire Letter of Intention/Strategic Outline fits on two pages!! (Before legal attention).

5.0 STRATEGIES AS IMPLEMENTED

5.1 Europe

5.1.1 Alsace is the first attempted target in 1963, because of strategic location and the fact that the "target" firm already made a triple-wall corrugated product (not as good as Tri-Wall's, but better than U.S. imitations). The Alsace plant management likes the concept of the Joint Venture, because they have lower risk than an average partner, as less equipment is needed, and they are acclimated to handling large boxes.

However, the attempt fails to be consummated in wedlock for non-business reasons. (The cooperation given to France in 1962 by the CIA negated an agreement with the Chairman of the Alsace group, who was a friend of De Gaulle, and to whom, at that point, all Americans were persona non grata).

5.1.2 Tri-Wall's second European target, this time in Holland, is upset with U.S. competitive practices in recent acquisitions in Holland and will not talk to any American firm.

5.1.3 Tri-Wall turns its eyes towards the UK, where Tri-Wall already has a distributor eager to cut the time and cost of ocean freight. The distributor makes introductions to thee firms.

The first firm is too big and monolithic in decision making (not family owned). The second is interested in four-color printing rather than high strength. The third firm "took."

5.1.4 By 1965, two years after the UK agreement, the original "target" in Holland calls Tri-Wall. They like how Tri-Wall has operated across the Channel. Feeling pressure from their U.S. competitors, Holland company requests a meeting. Having done its "homework" on local customs and taboos, Tri-Wall speedily inks a deal in the same pattern as was originally conceived.

5.2 *Middle East and Orient*

5.2.1 *Israel (1966):* Focus is placed on Israel because of Tri-Wall's inability to sell a good idea to U.S. citrus interests. Tri-Wall's U.S. operations have been trying to sell a bulk handling citrus box to Sunkist for two years without success. Its Texas and Florida sales engineers have demonstrated the excellent economics to citrus growers and shippers, but no sale!

During a vacation to Israel in 1966, the V.P. of Strategic Planning visits one corrugator which is owned by two friendly U.S. companies, which make introductions to the Israeli firm. However Tri-Wall receives a cold shoulder from the Israeli plant operators because the product is "Not Invented Here!"

A short discussion with the Investment Ministry finds a newly established corrugator in Haifa whose manager quickly gets "fired" up for a joint venture. His enthusiasm also gets him fired, as his company waffles at the proposition and he quits.

Tri-Wall looks at freight and time logistics, concluding that a sheeting plant in Israel can be supplied with corrugated paper stock from either the UK or Holland partners. Tri-Wall does a market study in Israel on industrial (not citrus) exports and sees viability.

Tri-Wall decides to build the sheet plant in 1967 and hires the Israeli who had earlier quit his job to run it, and gets started. Within seven months the venture is in the black. The Israelis quickly penetrate their citrus market and begin shipping citrus products to the U.S., which finally catches the attention of Sunkist, Blue Goose, et al in the U.S. to use the Tri-Wall product.

Eventually the Haifa firm comes to Tri-Wall for a Joint Venture, which supplies locally produced corrugated sheet to the plant. The Joint Venture's business also sells its product to Greece, Lebanon, Iran, Kenya, and South Africa.

5.2.2 In 1968 Tri-Wall consummates a similar joint venture in Japan, then six months passes before another one emerges in Australia. Each one becomes easier. While the initial "target" doesn't take in each case, patience and more than one target in a region eventually brings success, reinforced by the references provided by already established successful partnerships.

6.0 *TECHNIQUES, BENEFITS, GLITCHES*

6.1 *Techniques*

6.1.1 Always promise less than you can deliver—in sales, profits, manpower to teach. (The reality: had Tri-Wall expressed its real expectations—which were quite high—it would not have been credible.)

6.1.2 Overseas, sell through Value Analysis—at higher margins than Robinson–Patman Act permits in U.S. (treat every customer with the same prices), because Tri-Wall priced through Value Analysis, its margins were quite high.

6.1.3 Use local talent in each country, sending outsiders in to hire, train, coach, and then return home. Tri-Wall had one full-time American overseas.

6.1.4 Avoid major capital expenses. Tri-Wall avoided a paper mill, which was a financial transaction with too much leverage and risk.

6.1.5 Develop informal marketing methods from the U.S. into formal systems overseas, then import the best ideas back to the U.S. and on into other regions.

6.1.6 Use trips abroad for all applications engineers for two-way applications technology transfer, and also as a non-financial incentive. Encourage them to take their spouses along.

6.2 *Benefits*

6.2.1 The synergy afforded by monitoring trial shipments around the globe with swift photos and reports back to the originator meant accelerated growth and acceptance, while erecting barriers to competition.

6.2.2 Duplication of labs in U.S. and overseas created English/ Metric standards, data, and new applications.

6.2.3 As field salespeople were all problem solvers, a new application was rapidly multiplied around the world in user acceptance and new sales. Tri-Wall created an applications newsletter with international circulation.

6.2.4 Two new product areas that were developed in the U.S. rapidly were delivered into the international marketplace through the joint ventures.

6.3 Glitches

6.3.1 One partner had low productivity, which affected product cost and quality. When asked to fix it, they were unable to for fear of their union's reaction.

Tri-Wall asked permission to help and achieved a substantial increase to the Joint Venture's productivity, thereby enabling the partner to become more profitable.

6.3.2 One partner made a box product using equipment specifically and solely designated for the Joint Venture product. It was outside the realm of the Tri-Wall patents, and was slightly competitive to the Joint Venture product line (stronger than normal corrugated, equal to Tri-Wall's lowest grade—but not manufactured by the Joint Venture because Tri-Wall believed it had little competitive advantage).

Tri-Wall objected, but had no legal grounds,—the partner was not displacing Tri-Wall's product—and was not competing with Tri-Wall's major competitor in the region, who had latched on to some of Tri-Wall's ideas.

Tri-Wall's distributor screamed that he was being "gored." The partner offered to stop production on the designated machinery if he could maker lower-grade triple wall. Tri-Wall said no, and ws gratified to find six months later that the partner's accountants found no margin in the "new" product that had been "pirated," because the competitor was pricing their product ruinously.

6.3.3 Eventually Tri-Wall's Japanese, UK, and Dutch partners were bought by multinationals, one of whom was a direct competitor of Tri-Wall's in the U.S. The multinationals did not know what they had, and no major problems occurred. In retrospect, Tri-Wall should have had an option either to buy out or withdraw from the Joint Venture if their partner was acquired by an unwanted suitor.

7.0 CORPORATE PERFORMANCE RESULTS

7.1 Markets

7.1.1 In 1961 Tri-Wall was a small regional firm in the Northeast of the U.S.

7.1.2 By 1967, Tri-Wall had become a multinational corporation with plants in U.S., UK, Holland, Israel, Japan, and Australia.

7.2 Financial

7.2.1 Tri-Wall went public in 1969, was sold to a conglomerate in 1974, who was then bought by the largest private firm in the world in 1976, and was sold again to Weyerhauser in 1989. The joint ventures still exist.

7.2.2 Sales grew exponentially, from $3 million to $25 million in ten years.

7.2.3 Profit after taxes grew from 1% to 10% in ten years.

7.2.4 Return on Investment grew to 45% (in 1990 dollars and currency translations, would be $100 million in 10 years).

7.2.5 Gross Profit Margin for standard corrugated boxes was 20–25%, but for Tri-Wall's specialty product, GPM's were 40–45%!

Index